Deep Reinforcement Learning

Mohit Sewak

Deep Reinforcement Learning

Frontiers of Artificial Intelligence

Springer

Mohit Sewak
Pune, Maharashtra, India

ISBN 978-981-13-8284-0 ISBN 978-981-13-8285-7 (eBook)
https://doi.org/10.1007/978-981-13-8285-7

This Springer imprint is published by the registered company Springer Nature Singapore Pte Ltd.
The registered company address is: 152 Beach Road, #21-01/04 Gateway East, Singapore 189721, Singapore

Preface

Reinforcement Learning has evolved a long way with the enhancements from deep learning. Recent research efforts into combining deep learning with Reinforcement Learning have led to the development of some very powerful *deep Reinforcement Learning* systems, algorithms, and agents which have already achieved some extraordinary accomplishment. Not only have such systems surpassed the capabilities of most of the classical and non-deep-learning-based Reinforcement Learning agents, but have also started outperforming the best of human intelligence at tasks which were believed to require extreme human intelligence, creativity, and planning skills. Some of the DQN-based agents consistently beating the best of human players at the complex game of AlphaGo are very good examples of this.

This book starts with the basics of Reinforcement Learning and explains each concept using very intuitive and easy to understand examples and applications. Continuing with similar examples, this book then builds upon to introduce some cutting-edge researches and advancements that make Reinforcement Learning outperform many of the other (artificial) intelligent systems. This book aims to not only equip the readers with just the mathematical understanding of multiple cutting-edge Reinforcement Learning algorithms, but also prepares them to implement these and similar advanced *Deep Reinforcement Learning* agents and system hands-on in their own domain and application area.

This book starts from the basic building blocks of Reinforcement Learning, then covers the popular classical DP and classical RL approaches like value and policy iteration, and then covers some popular traditional Reinforcement Learning algorithms like the TD learning, SARSA, and the Q-Learning. After building this foundation, this book introduces deep learning and implementation aids for modern Reinforcement Learning environments and agents. After this, the book starts diving deeper into the concepts of *Deep Reinforcement Learning* and covers algorithms like the deep Q networks, double DQN, dueling DQN, (deep) synchronous actor-critic, (deep) asynchronous advantage actor-critic, and the deep deterministic policy gradient. Each of the theoretical/mathematical chapters on these concepts is followed by a chapter on practical coding and implementation of these agents' grounds-up connecting the concepts to the code.

Pune, India Mohit Sewak

Who This Book Is For?

This book will equally appeal to readers with prior experience in deep learning, who want to learn new skills in Reinforcement Learning, and to readers who have been the practitioner of Reinforcement Learning or other automation systems and who want to scale their knowledge and skills to *Deep Reinforcement Learning*. By combining the concepts from deep learning and Reinforcement Learning, we could come closer to realizing the true potential of 'general artificial intelligence'.

Besides presenting the mathematical concepts and contemporary research in the field of *Deep Reinforcement Learning*, this book also covers algorithms, codes, and practical implementation aids for both Reinforcement Learning environments and agents. This book is intended to be a guide and an aid for both the types of readers, for the ones who are interested in the academic understanding and being abreast with some of the latest advancements in *Deep Reinforcement Learning* and also for the ones who want to implement these advanced agents and systems into their own fields.

Ranging from application in autonomous vehicles to dynamic scheduling and management of production process, to intelligent maintenance of critical machineries, to driving efficiency in utility management, to making automated systems for health care, to intelligent financial trading and transaction monitoring, to aiding intelligent customer engagement, and to mitigating high-throughput cyber threats, the concepts learnt in this book could be applied to multiple fields of interest.

The code in the book is in Python 3x. The deep learning part of the code uses the TensorFlow library. Some code also uses the Keras wrapper to TensorFlow. *Deep Reinforcement Learning* wrappers like Keras-RL are also demonstrated. This book expects basic familiarization in Python with object-oriented programming concepts to enable implementation of distributed and scalable systems.

What This Book Covers?

Chapter 1—*Introduction to Reinforcement Learning*—covers the basic design of Reinforcement Learning and explains in detail the concepts like the environment, actor, state, and rewards, and the challenges in each.

Chapter 2—*Mathematical and Algorithmic Understanding of Reinforcement Learning*—builds upon a strong mathematical and algorithmic foundation to understand the internal functioning in different types of agents.

Chapter 3—*Coding the Environment and MDP Solution*—illustrates how to build a custom Reinforcement Learning environment in code over which different reinforcement agents can train and also implements the value iteration and policy iteration algorithms over a custom environment.

Chapter 4—*Temporal Difference Learning, SARSA, and Q-Learning*—covers the TD learning estimation process and the on-policy SARSA and off-policy Q-Learning algorithms along with different types of exploration mechanism.

Chapter 5—*Q-Learning in Code*—implements the Q-Learning algorithm in Python via the tabular approach using the epsilon-greedy algorithm for behavior policy.

Chapter 6—*Introduction to Deep Learning*—introduces the concepts of deep learning like layer architecture, activation, loss functions, and optimizers for the MLP-DNN and CNN algorithms.

Chapter 7—*Implementation Resources*—covers the different types of resources available to implement, test, and compare cutting-edge deep Reinforcement Learning models and environments.

Chapter 8—*Deep Q Network (DQN), Double DQN, and Dueling DQN*—covers the deep Q networks and its variants the double DQN and the dueling DQN and how these models surpassed the best of human adversaries' performance at the game of AlphaGo.

Chapter 9—*Double DQN in Code*—covers implementation of a double DQN with an online active Q network coupled with another offline target Q network with both networks having customizable deep learning architecture, built using Keras on TensorFlow.

Chapter 10—*Policy-Based Reinforcement Learning Approaches*—covers the basic understanding of policy-based Reinforcement Learning approaches and explains the policy-gradient mechanism with the reinforce algorithm.

Chapter 11—*Actor-Critic Models and the A3C*—covers stochastic policy-gradient-based actor-critic algorithm with its different variants like the one using 'advantage' as a baseline and those that could be implemented in 'synchronous' and 'asynchronous' distributed parallel architectures.

Chapter 12—*A3C in Code*—covers the implementation of the asynchronous variant of the distributed parallel actor-critic mechanism with multiple agents working simultaneously to update the master's gradient. The agent algorithm is implemented using the TensorFlow library, using the libraries' 'eager execution' and model's 'sub-classing' features.

Chapter 13—*Deterministic Policy Gradient and the DDPG*—covers the deterministic policy-gradient theorem and the algorithm and also explains the enhancements made to enable the deep learning variant of deep deterministic policy gradient (DDPG).

Chapter 14—*DDPG in Code*—covers the implementation of the DDPG algorithm to enable the Reinforcement Learning tasks requiring continuous-action control and implements it in a very few lines of code using the Keras-RL wrapper library.

Contents

About the Author

Mohit Sewak is a Ph.D. scholar in CS&IS (Artificial Intelligence and Cyber Security) with BITS Pilani - Goa, India, and is also a lecturer on subjects like Artificial Intelligence, Machine Learning, Deep Learning and NLP for the post-graduate technical degree program. He holds several patents (USPTO & Worldwide) and publications in the field of Artificial Intelligence and Machine Learning.

Besides his academic linkages, Mohit is also actively engaged with the industry and has many accomplishments while leading the research and development initiatives of many international AI products. Mohit has been leading the Reinforcement Learning practice at QiO Technologies, the youngest player in Gartner's magic quadrant for Industry 4.0.

In his previous roles, Mohit had led the IBM Watson Commerce in India's innovation initiative in cognitive line of feature as Sr. Cognitive Data Scientist. Mohit had also been the Principal Data Scientist for IBM's global IoT products like IBM Predictive Maintenance & Quality. He had also been the advanced analytics architect for IBM's SPSS suite in India.

Mohit has over 14 years of very rich experience in researching, architecting and solutioning with technologies like TensorFlow, Torch, Caffe, Theano, Keras, Open AI, OpenCV, SpaCy, Gensim, Spark, Kafka, ES, Kubernetes, and Tinkerpop.

Chapter 1
Introduction to Reinforcement Learning

The Intelligence Behind the AI Agent

Abstract In this chapter, we will discuss what is Reinforcement Learning and its relationship with Artificial Intelligence. We would then try to go deeper to understand the basic building blocks of Reinforcement Learning like state, actor, environment, and the reward, and will try to understand the challenges in each of the aspect as revealed by using multiple examples so that the intuition is well established, and we build a solid foundation before going ahead into some advanced topics. We would also discuss how the agent learns to take the best action and the policy for learning the same. We will also learn the difference between the On-Policy and the Off-Policy methods.

1.1 What Is Artificial Intelligence and How Does Reinforcement Learning Relate to It?

Artificial Intelligence from a marketing perspective of different organizations may mean a lot of things encompassing systems ranging from conventional analytics, to more contemporary deep learning and chatbots. But technically the use of Artificial Intelligence (AI) terminology is restricted to the study and design of "**Rational**" agents, which could act "**Humanly**". Of the many definitions given by different researchers and authors of Artificial Intelligence, the criteria for calling an agent an AI agent is that it should possess ability to demonstrate "*thought-process* and *reasoning*", "*intelligent-behavior*", "*success* in terms of human performance", and "*rationality*". This identification should be our guiding factor to identify the marketing jargons from real Artificial Intelligence systems and applications from the marketing hype.

Among the different Artificial Intelligence agents, Reinforcement Learning agents are considered to be among the most advanced and very capable of demonstrating high level of intelligence and rational behavior. A reinforcement learning agent interacts with its environment. The environment itself could

M. Sewak, *Deep Reinforcement Learning*,
https://doi.org/10.1007/978-981-13-8285-7_1

demonstrate multiple states. The agent acts upon the environment to change the environment's state, thereby also receiving a reward or penalty as determined by the achieved state and the objective of the agent. This definition may look naïve, but the concepts empowering it led to the development of a many advanced AI agents to perform very complex tasks, sometimes even challenging human performance at specific tasks.

1.2 Understanding the Basic Design of Reinforcement Learning

The diagram as in Fig 1.1 represents a very basic design of Reinforcement Learning system with its "learning" and "action" loops. Here an agent as described in the above introductory definition interacts with its environment to learn to take the best possible action (a_t in the above figure) under the given state (S_t) that the environment is in at step t. The action of the agent in turn changes the state of the environment from S_t to S_{t+1} (as shown in the figure) and generates a reward r_t for the agent. Then the agent takes the best possible action for this new state (S_{t+1}), thereby invoking a reward r_{t+1} and so on. Over a period of iterations (which are referred to as experiments during the training process of the agent) the agent tries to improve upon its decision of which is the "best action" that could be taken in a given state of the environment using the rewards that it receives during the training process.

The role of the environment here is thus to present the agent with different possible/probable states that could exist in the problem that the agent may need to react to, or a representative subset of the same. To assist the learning process of the agent, the environment also gives the reward or penalty (a negative reward) corresponding to the action decisions taken by the agent in a given state. Thus, the reward is a function of both the action and the state, and not of the action alone. Which means that the same action could (and ideally should) receive a different reward under different states.

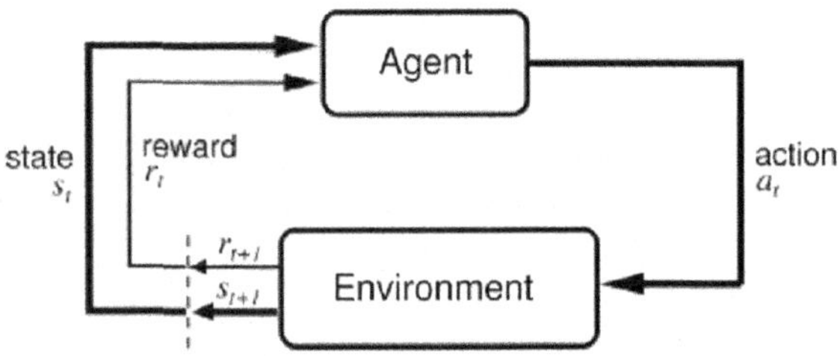

Fig. 1.1 Design for a Reinforcement Learning system

1.3 The Reward and the Challenges in Determining a Good Reward Function for Reinforcement Learning

The role of the agent, as should be obvious from the above discussion, is to take the action that pays the maximum reward in a given state. But this is not so trivial, as we will determine in this section.

1.3.1 Future Rewards

The actual reward for a right action taken in a particular state may not be realized immediately. Imagine a real-life scenario, where you have an option to go out and play now or to sit and study for your upcoming exams now and play later after the exams. Playing now may give a small adrenaline rush immediately, which in the terms of reinforcement learning could be treated as a reward if we consider it a positive outcome. Whereas studying now may seem boring in the short run (this could theoretically be also treated as a small penalty depending upon the objective) but probable may pay off very well in the long run, which may be considered as a bigger reward (for the actions decision to be taken now) but the reward is realized only in the future. Figure 1.2 shows an illustration between such present and future sense of rewards.

There are quite some well-established solutions to this problem like using a *discounting-factor* to discount the future rewards to present time (like in finance we discount the future returns/cash flows from different projects to present time to compare between projects of varying lengths and different time periods of realization of the cash flows) for comparison. We will discuss the solutions using this

Fig. 1.2 Instantaneous versus future rewards

technique later in this book, but for now our objective is to highlight the challenges pertaining to achieving the parity across rewards of varying quantum coming from different time/step spans in the future which could be attributed to the action taken in the present time/step.

1.3.2 Probabilistic/Uncertain Rewards

Another complexity in reinforcement learning is the probabilistic nature of the rewards or uncertainty in the rewards. Let us take the same example of studying now for a reward (good marks) later. Suppose we have 10 chapters in the course and we know that the questions are going to come only from six of these chapters, but we do not know from which specific six chapters the questions are going to come, and how much weightage will each of the chosen six chapters will have in the exams. Let us also assume that in a slot of 3 h that our protagonist could spend in playing an outdoor game, she could study only any one of the 10 chapters.

So even if we assume that the perceived value of the future reward is worth studying for instead of playing, we are not sure if we would be spending the present time studying a particular chapter from which there could be no questions at all. Even if we consider that the chosen chapter is an important one, we do not know the specific weightage of the marks of the questions that would come from this chapter. So the rewards from studying now would not only be realized in the future but could also be probabilistic or uncertain.

1.3.3 Attribution of Rewards to Different Actions Taken in the Past

Another important consideration is the attribution of the rewards to the specific action/s taken in the past. Continuing with the above example, suppose out of the 10 chapters or corresponding 10 slots-to-play, we decide that the protagonist/agent would randomly pick six instances where she/it would study any one of the 10 chapters (assume chosen randomly) and would play in the remaining four slots. We make specific choices with the objective being to maximize the sum total of all the rewards comprising of the small but immediate reward and larger but futuristic and probabilistic rewards.

Assume that with the choices made the protagonist/agent finally end up scoring 50% in its exam. Further assume that of the six chapters we chose to study for, the questions came from only four of them with weightages of marks as 5%, 8%, 12%, and 15%, respectively, and the remaining 50% questions came from the four chapters that we could not prepare as we decided to go to play instead (yes we were sort of unlucky). Assume that of the questions that the agent answered (worth maximum of 50 marks) it received 40 marks (i.e., a total of 40% of the maximum achievable 100 marks in the exam).

Now, one solution for attribution of this reward (40% marks) could be that we divide this reward equally across each of the six slots where the agent decided to studying instead of playing.

Yet another solution could be that we give as much reward to each specific slot as the weightage of question that came from the chapter the agent decided to study for in that slot.

If the agent had not scored universally well across each of the chapters that came, then yet another solution could have been to reward each slot with the amount of marks that the agent scored (irrespective of the weightage of the questions) from what it studied in that particular slot. So this essentially takes into account both the weightage of marks coming from the chapter that the agent decided to study in that slot and its demonstrated performance for questions from that chapter in the exam as well.

Yet another solution could be to treat the reward for the agent as a function of the percentage of marks that we scored of the questions that came from the chapter we prepared in that slot. That is, the reward is a function of only our performance on what we decided to study. Since which chapters are going to come in the exams and what will be the weightage of each of the chapters that will appear in the exam is not in the agent's control so this method could rightly reward the protagonist with what is in her control. The reward in this approach is completely a function of the agent's performance in choosing the subjects that it can deliver the best results if it devotes the given 3 h in studying it, completely ignoring the total marks achieved in the exams.

But one problem in all these approaches is that we assume that we do not know the distribution of question weights from different chapters, and we do not want the agent to mistakenly learn the weightages just from this single example/experiment as we understand that these could be random across different experiments.

So should we actually equally divide this reward (40% marks) across all the slots in which we decided to study instead of going to play? If so, how do we reward the choice of choosing specific subjects to study where we could have performed better had we studied them as compared to some other subjects where 3 h of study might not have added that much incremental value? Another observation could be that whether there are any specific slots where studying could have been more productive than playing, for example, if we alternate across studying and playing, would a healthy body before each studying slot positively affect our performance in studies as well?

Any of the above solutions could be correct, and all of them could be suboptimal solutions could be wrong depending upon the purpose of our training. For example, if the overall purpose of the training is to score maximum marks in exams, then the last option which seems to be righteous makes no sense, and instead we should try to train an agent which scores decently well irrespective of the uncertainty in chapter/weightage selection. On the contrary, if the purpose is to select the right chapters pertaining to the strength of the protagonist then the later approach could be better than some of the former approaches. Yet the simplest approach could be the first one to have an equal attribution to remove bias from training.

So deciding reward attribution is both an art and a science and would determine the decisions that the agent finally learns to take in different scenarios. Hence, the attribution criteria and function should be devised considering the intended behavior and objective of the agent.

1.3.4 Determining a Good Reward Function

By now you would have understood that the problem of attribution of reward is not trivial. Not only it is challenging to decide the right attribution from a domain perspective, but even a slight change in the reward function may force a distinctive behavior for the agent and the agent may decide to take different actions based on how we decide to formulate our rewards.

Compare the two examples in the previous section where we use absolute scores and percentage scores as the reward functions, respectively. The attribution with respect to which action (slot/chapter selection) receives the reward is unchanged in these two cases. What differs is the magnitude of reward given or the reward function formulation. By changing the magnitude of reward, we may differ the behavior of the agent as well as it is evident from the above example.

1.3.5 Dealing with Different Types of Reward

Beyond the attribution and reward function for the specific scenario we discussed, there is yet another challenge that we have not observed or discussed so far. How do we equate two different types of rewards?

We have only one numerical value that we could give as a reward (or penalty—i.e., a negative value for the reward). Assume even if we were to correctly standardize/normalize and apply all relevant transformations to correctly fix the reward formulation and attribution problem, how do we account for the rewards from our decisions to go to play instead of spending that time studying a particular chapter in that slot?

Playing could have a different type of reward altogether. If we were to represent it mathematically, then the rewards could have a different unit and scale. In the chosen example, may be playing instead of studying helps (pays reward to) to keep us healthy, may help us attain a good position for our team in the tournaments, etc. So how do we compare our better health, to the marks we obtained (or for that matter missed) in our exams? For the sake of simplicity, let us not get into the details of attributions of the specific hours we played to the improvement of our overall health in that week/month to answer this question for now, that is, could be a topic for another research altogether.

One solution to this problem could be that we device a conversion function between the health improvements and marks obtained. That is going to challenging! Not only it may be difficult to arrive at a single conversion system that may be generic enough to fit the needs of different instances and individuals for whom we want to train this agent for. Thus, defeating the very purpose of training such a reinforcement learning system. Also, because such a conversion function could be mathematically very complex in a real-life scenario and could make the optimization or convergence of the loss function very difficult during training.

Therefore, such challenges of equating different types of rewards fall mainly on experimentation and domain-focused research with domain expertise and experience coming into play.

1.3.6 Domain Aspects and Solutions to the Reward Problem

Although the design blueprint as given in Fig. 1.1 looks simple, but from the discussion in this section, it must be clear that the problem of converting a real-life problem to a reinforcement learning one itself is very challenging.

As we discussed in the concluding notes of each of these challenges, it must be clear that the above-stated challenges are more domain-focused challenges than technology focussed and a better solution to these are likely to come from the respective researches happening in various domains.

Though in some of the coding problems and examples that we will be visiting, the readers will get a fair idea of how to get to a descent reward function and account for different types of rewards, but this book is more focussed toward understanding the technical/mathematical problems with respect to Reinforcement Learning, formulating a good environment/states and training the agents; knowledge and techniques that are useful in formulating a reinforcement learning system irrespective of the chosen application domain.

If these technical, mathematical, and algorithmic challenges look less daunting, the next section should dispel some doubts. We would just touch the surface of the remaining challenges in this chapter and would go into greater details of each in some of the later chapters where we cover specific solutions and techniques to answer these challenges.

1.4 The State in Reinforcement Learning

The state during training of a Reinforcement Learning represents a context that the environment presents to the agent to take actions for and then generates a reward for the action taken in that state context. Such a state at best is a simplified representation of the real-world scenario that the agent would be facing in production/deployment when dealing with real-life uncertainties.

For a Reinforcement Learning agent deployed and subjected to real-life scenario, the state is represented by all the aspects that the agent could perceive in any form. Anything that may affect the outcome of the scenario (state achieved and the reward received upon taking an action in a given state) and could be measured should be ideally included in the state. Though there could be many other factors that affect the outcome of the process, but some of these could not be measured or even could not be known in advance. Until we are not able to either know these factors or measure them with a certain degree of accuracy we would refer to all these factors and occurrences as noise henceforth.

When transitioning from a training environment to a test/validation or other preproduction environments (scenario where the agent still face the real-world environment, but its actions are sandboxed and not used to change the state in the real world, for example, a self-driving reinforcement learning agent operating under controlled environment as opposed to autonomously driving in real-world traffic) the data would be gathered to continually train the agent and prepare it for any production deployment. At times when there is too much divergence between training and pre-production environments, the training states may need to be reconfigured and some over-simplified assumptions reconsidered so that the states during training may better represent the real-life conditions. The agents subsequently are made to relearn with the new state sequences and rewards from the training environment before validation reoccurs.

Sometimes the state may be comprised of a stacked matrix of readings from all the sensors and other inputs that the agent/environment has access to in real time. But often these manifestations of the state might not be optimal for training an agent as we will discover later, and then we need to also consider how do we manifest the state from all the real-time and historic data we have from the inputs, observations, and previous actions taken.

Let us take some examples to understand the formulation of some states and thereby also understanding the challenges in these formulations. We would take examples from some popular games here so that all the readers irrespective of their domain could relate with the examples and understand the underlying principles. Next, we take examples from popular games to understand the challenges in state/observation formation to train the respective agents.

1.4.1 Let Us Score a Triplet in Tic-Tac-Toe

Taking the example of a simple game like tic-tac-toe (Fig. 1.3), our state may be comprised of a simple matrix of [n, 9] (or [n, 3, 3] for that matter) where n represents the sequence of events or the experiments. For a given event in the sequence, the event space would be an array or length [9] or alternatively a matrix of [1, 9] (or a [3, 3] matrix) where each cell of the array/matrix denotes one cell in the real-life tic-tac-toe problem, and value of the cell could be a 0 if it is vacant, 1 if there is a "x" in it, and 2 if there is a "o" in it. This simple representation should suffice for the agent to learn the strategies corresponding to the side ("x" or "o") that we want to train it for with adequate number of sample experiments (episodes) in hand.

It does not matter if the state (event space) is [1, 9] or a [3, 3] matrix till each cell uniquely represents the value in a real-life tic-tac-toe, and the previous sequence of the events also does not makes any difference. All that matters is the values (0, 1, or 2) in each of the nine cells of our matrix, and our agent should be able to learn the best strategy given the reward for different actions from this state. The output from such an agent would be the action corresponding to location of the cell which it wants to play in (if it is vacant). The action from the agent will determine and lead to the next state which is similar to the previous one, except for that one vacant cell (value 0) being now taken over by our agent. If the agent wins, it receives the reward, else the subsequent state is presented to the human or the adversary agent to play. On the human's/adversary's valid turn the resulting state is served back to our agent again for action and the process continues till there is a winner or no remaining vacant cells to play.

We took this simple example just to get the readers started in conceptualizing how we will be converting a real-life scenario and observations into mathematical notation and computer science data structures which would make sense to our agent and the agent could be trained well provided the data is exhaustive and represents adequate coverage of all important scenarios in real life through our chosen formulation of the state. Next, we will take slightly more advanced examples to uncover some challenges in the state formulation.

Fig. 1.3 The tic-tac-toe game

1.4.2 Let Us Balance a Pole on a Cart (The CartPole Problem)

This is a typical beginner's problem in Reinforcement Learning, and in this problem we have a straight pole fixed to a cart. We need to balance the pole such that it does not fall. We could achieve this by moving the cart forward (say indicated by an output of +1) or backward (output of −1), or remaining stationary (a 0 output). There could be implementations where you could either move the cart by only a specific amount in either direction (± a constant say 1) in a single turn, while in other implementations we could also adjust the speed (a number from a continuous range of +v to −v in each unit time step) making it slightly more complex.

Though these changes relates more to the agent's action, but this will also influence how you should formulate your state such that the agent could take a well-informed action. Some implementations in the discrete variety could also give an option to stay there (−1 to go back, 0 to stay, and +1 to go forward), while others would have a binary action (0 to go back and 1 to go forward) such that a static equilibrium is not allowed. Figure 1.4 illustrates a typical cart-pole example where the pole appears balanced on a cart, which could move horizontally on a line.

Though prima facie this may look to be a complex problem mainly because as humans we are not so good in cognitively determining the angles and speeds that may result in balancing the pole, for the agent these might not be as difficult if we get the state formulation correct.

Also, it may appear that the balancing of the pole may require a lot of understanding of physics, gravity, momentum, and angular velocities that need to be fed into the system, but these details are what we will leave on the agent to learn on its own (directly or indirectly), and here we will just code the state as we observe it and feed into the environment. What we observe is just the angle of the pole from the cart which lies between −90° (pole fell flat in anticlockwise direction) and +90° (pole fell flat in clockwise direction), where 0° represents a perfectly centered pole.

Fig. 1.4 The CartPole problem

1.4.2.1 State Enhancements for a Continuous-Action Agent for the CartPole Balancing Problem

The information above should be sufficient for training a discrete-action agent where some hunting is acceptable. But for a continuous-action agent or where an objective is also to minimize hunting more information to account for angular velocity could be required. In most of the cases, the system may not have a direct input for angular velocity, but as we stated that we would leave the math and physics for our agent to learn, and we could use a simple representation of some form with which the agent could learn these details.

The simplest representation in this example to include the information on angular velocity could be the position (in angles as described earlier) of the pole a unit time prior to the current time step (a millisecond or whatever unit makes sense from a responsiveness-hunting balance perspective). If this unit time is also the time between turns that we allow agent to react to (generate the speed direction recommendations as actions) then this additional input is exactly our previous state itself. Remember that the only state we were giving as input in the previous example was the angular position of pole in this previous time step (or previous state if the step difference is the same as state difference). So essentially we simplified the problem of including the angular velocity (besides angular position) and other related complexities to just sending two consecutive states (instead of just the current state/angular position) to train a continuous-action agent (as opposed to a discrete-action agent).

As we discovered in this example, to make things simple yet effective, we may use some representations of the real world that are easier to capture and use to formulate the state for our Reinforcement Learning agent; and the agent, with the right models/algorithms and sufficient training experiments might be better placed to learn the complex interacting mechanisms to indirectly learn the right physics that affects the outcome. Under these conditions, the state might not be a direct conversion of the real-time observations that we observe/receive (unlike as we did in the tic-tac-toe example), but may require some ingenuity to make the problem simple, yet effective. This approach may have a great effect on the accuracies and efficiencies for the agent as well.

Now let us take the complexity of the state formulation a bit higher so that we could better understand the challenges in this area.

1.4.3 Let Us Help Mario Win the Princess

1.4.3.1 A Quick Intro to the Vision-Related Reinforcement Learning Problems

Until now, we have discussed examples in which the data was structured (numeric), and either directly obtained or perceived through a digital sensor. But if we were to employ the Reinforcement Learning agent into jobs that human do, it is quintessential that the agent could consume all the form of inputs that we humans do. One major and very complex source of data acquisition for humans is our vision. Imagine the challenges that a self-driving or autonomous cars need to undertake. If we want our agents to overcome these challenges, and yet drive safely for both their own passengers and other people/cars on the road, the digital (numeric) sensor based inputs may not be sufficient and we may also require multitude of optical sensors (cameras) and high processing power systems to process the images coming from these optical sensors in real time for our agents to process and take action. The agents themselves need very high computational power and efficient models to make sense of these sources of data.

1.4.3.2 About the Mario Game

Since we want to keep this section domain neutral, we would continue with our theme of taking popular games as example domains for this discussion. We would in this section take the example of the popular game Mario, where our hero needs to rescue (and win) the princess while crossing many obstacles, tunneling and jumping around his way, while evading or killing many creatures, and fighting with the dragon; may be optionally also collecting some coins for their wedding celebrations. All these activities are rewarded in the game, and though the primary reward is crossing as many levels as possible within three lives (could be augmented through gathering 1-ups or crossing certain score thresholds in the game), the secondary reward is the total score being accumulated across these activities. Since the game already has a weighing scheme to convert the different activities (like smashing or evading creatures, completing a round within a given time, etc.) into scores/points, we are not bothered with this specific challenge here (Fig. 1.5).

1.4.3.3 The Vision Challenge While Playing Graphical Games

Assuming that we do not have an API hook to abstract the information in this game such as where the coins are, what creature is in front of us and at how much distance it is, what are the topological assets (like walls to jump over) or barriers (ditches) we have everywhere, we may have to create an external computer vision system that would extract and abstract these information for us from the visual frames in the games and then we feed this abstracted numerical information into our system. But this approach would lead us to manually selecting and training a system to identify (classify) and position the required objects/information that we want to extract and then convert the extracted information into structured data (like position coordinates) and then train algorithms to first identify (called object detection in computer vision) them from the real-time feed of images (all games and videos could be conceived as a continuous feed of images frames of a given resolution at a particular frame-per-second/feed-rate), then count and identify each of their

Fig. 1.5 The “Mario” video game

instances (called instance segmentation) from these image frames and then abstract the required objects to some structured format into the state formulation.

This not only seems to be an aeneous but also has an assumption that we have the best knowledge of all what is important for the agent to learn. Also, in this methodology, the major work of making such systems for this complex computer-vision-related tasks and subsequent simplification is outside of the agent and the agent’s performance is highly dependent on these external decisions and systems. This approach is also suboptimal as we discussed earlier that we would like the complex work to be done by the agent and we would like to serve it with the information that is simple for us to acquire and manipulate. In the next section, we will discuss a better approach to achieve these goals.

1.4.3.4 Example of State Formulation for Graphical Games

The previous approach of an external intelligently designed and comprehensive computer vision system that extracts and abstracts all the objects of importance for the state/agent is definitively possible but is not the best possible for two major reasons.

First, we need a lot of human, technical, and game SME involvement to do this. Second, as we identified in the last two sub-sections, there are many complex tasks that we may easily delegate to the agent’s intelligence (underlying models of the agent) and let the agent decipher the most important information to extract and the best way to abstract it on its own (for example, refer to the CartPole example where instead of computing the angular velocities to feed to the agent we just served it a state which comprised of two subsequent angular positions of the pole separated by a fixed unit of time). We just need to ensure that the state formulation is in sync with the models that the agent such that the agent's model could make sense from the data of the state and automatically identify and extract important information from the way the state is structured.

One solution to achieve this is that we directly embed the complete image data of each frame as the state. Assuming the response rate of the agent is in sync with the frame rate of the game, the agents action could be synced with the game activities. The agent could learn from each game frame (image frame served as state) which action to take from one of the nine possible actions, namely, walk-ahead, run-ahead, walk-back, jump-in-place, jump-ahead, jump-back, duck, duck-and-jump, stay-there, using a model that ends in some classifier (with nine output classes representing these nine actions) to classify/select the best action. But we have already seen in the previous sub-section of cart pole that in some cases sequence is important. Knowing the sequence of events and having the knowledge of previous frames could be of good use here as well.

So should we collect a sequence of some frames (say 10 frames) and have the agent take actions on that? That is doable but imagine the size of the state (which will be of the dimension 10 $\times$ frame-width $\times$ frame-height $\times$ color-channels-of-frames) and computational load that would be required just to process the state. We have not even started to understand complexity of the agent and its model till now, and once we do so we will understand the complexity of the processing that will be required by the agent to give it the intelligence required to do take action on such complex state. So this solution is technically possible, but not computationally efficient and may be not even possible to implement with the systems available in general use today.

A better solution may encompass the technological and academic advancements made in the field of deep learning for vision and sequence data. The details of some similar systems we will be covering later in this book. For the purpose of this section, we could say that our state would comprise features of convolutional tensors for one or more frames of the game. Such sequence of convolutional maps in turn could be abstracted into some form of recurrent deep learning architectures. The agent in turn would be equipped with the necessary transformations and algorithms to understand and draw intelligence from this formulation of the state. The agent would recommend the best action that action would be fed to the game controller procedure, and the resulting frames again extracted and fed to the agent (via the environment) for the next action's recommendation.

1.5 The Agent in Reinforcement Learning

The agent is by far the most important piece of the Reinforcement Learning as it contains the intelligence to take decisions and recommend the optimal action in any given situation. It is for the sole purpose of training the agent's underlying intelligence that we created the representations of a similar environment that it will be facing and formulated a way to abstract the environment and the context for our agent in the form of a suitable state.

Since agent is so important, a lot of research has gone into its learning architecture and associated models. So there are a lot of things we need to discuss with respect to the agent and we will take it one by one distributed across several chapters. Here we would try to give the insights of the objective of the agent in general at a high level and also discuss some differences that led to the development of different types of agents.

1.5.1 The Value Function

The agent needs to decide which is the best action it can take when facing a specific state. There are essentially two ways the agent could reach to that decision. The first focuses on identifying which is the next best state to be in (reachable from the current state) as determined from the history of present and future rewards that the agent has received when it was in this particular state earlier. We could extend this logic to similar state, and that is where a lot of learning to convert a state into a representative function will come. But essentially in all these techniques, we are trying to predict the "Value" (or utility) of any state (or state–action combination), even the unseen ones, based on the ones that we have seen. This value could be a function of all present and (discounted) future rewards that could be attributed to being in this state.

The "(State) Value Function" is denoted by $V_{(s)}$, where the subscript s (for state) denotes that this V (value) is a function of the state. Such a value function encapsulates the different problems we had discussed like that of dealing with future/delayed and probabilistic/uncertain rewards by converting the different rewards into one homogenous function tied to a state that the agent will try to learn. The agent's recommendation in turn will be influenced by its identification of the most lucrative/profitable state to be in from the different states that are possible to reach from its given state by taking that particular action (the action that it will recommend). Then the agent recommends an action that will transition it to the identified most lucrative state from where it will have to decide again on the next most lucrative state reachable from this new state and so on. The underlying training of the agent tries to learn this very important "Value Function" that could represent the most accurate possible "Value" of each state using the training data/ experiments.

1.5.2 The Action–Value/Q-Function

In the last sub-section, we discussed the "Value Function", and how using it the agent decides the best state to be in and then on the basis of that decision it takes an appropriate action to maximize its chances of attaining that state. But this is a very indirect way to decide the best action. We could as well take such a decision directly by determining the best action possible while in a given (present) state. This is where the "Action–Value Function", denoted by $Q_{(s,\ a)}$, helps. Because of the Q-symbol used for its notation, and also to avoid confusion because of the reference to value function, the action–value function is also referred to as the "***Q-Function***". Note that where the "Value Function" is just a function of (denoted by subscript in parenthesis) state—s, the "Q-Function" is a function of both the state—s and the action—a.

1.5.3 Explore Versus Exploit Dilemma

We discussed the "Action/Value Function" in the previous sections. To train an optimal value for these functions, we can start with a function with randomly initialized values or some fixed/heuristic initialization as default. The values of this "Action/Value Function" are improved from the defaults by conducting a lot of experiments over the training data/scenarios/episodes.

If the agent gets predisposed to any default value or any intermediary "Action/Value Function" it can definitely take decisions on the basis of the so evolved "Action/Value Function" or in other words "Exploit" the already learned information, but it will not be able to improve this function further by "Exploring" new information. So we need to create a mechanism that the agent could use to choose the decision criterion. There are essentially two approaches in which this could be done, namely, the On-Policy and Off-Policy approaches which we will explain in the next section.

1.5.4 The Policy and the On-Policy and Off-Policy Approaches

The strategy that the learning mechanism uses to determine the next best action that should be taken based on the current state is called the "**Policy**" and is denoted by the symbol "π". The "Policy" is stated as a function of the state "$\pi_{(s)}$" and determines the best action to be taken in a given state. This "Policy" remains valid for the entire learning/training phase. But during the actual deployment, we may consider a different and often a simpler strategy, mainly to favor exploitation over balancing between exploration and exploitation.

Now let us take an approach to learn the "Q-Function" in a way that we will compute the probability of goodness of each action and then scale all to sum up to one and pick the one action stochastically based on the respective scaled probabilities of different actions. Under this policy, the action with the highest probability of reward also has the highest probability of being selected and the others have less probability of being selected in similar order. So the "Policy" we chose has the probabilistic nature of exploration and exploitation already built it in this approach. If we use such an approach for learning then it is called an **"On-Policy" learning**.

On the other hand, we may come up with a learning mechanism in which with some probability, say $\varepsilon = 0.2$ (the symbol ε is pronounced epsilon), we would "Explore" (the outcomes of) new actions/decisions instead of going by the current best action estimated/predicted to be taken in the current state. During the "Explore" phase for the sake of simplicity let us assume that we just select action/decision randomly for now (with equal probability for all probable actions in the current state). But keep in mind that there are many different and even better ways (and hence policies) to conduct similar "exploration".

On the remaining occasions when we are not exploring (i.e., with a probability of $(1 - \varepsilon) = 0.8$), we would "Exploit" or take a "Greedy" decision so as to take the action which has the best "Q-Value". This "Q-Value" in turn is being learnt using different mechanisms/algorithms. Thus, we use a different policy for "Estimation" or update of our "Q-Function" and different policy for the "Behavior" of the agent. These approaches where exploitation is not in-built in the "Estimation" policy, and hence a separate "Behavior" or policy is required for the same, is called the "**Off-Policy**" learning approach.

1.6 Summary

In this chapter, we started with giving a more formal definition of Artificial Intelligence and identified where Reinforcement Learning fits with respect to this definition. We then discussed the basic design of Reinforcement Learning. In Reinforcement Learning, the actor interacts with the environment to change it and in the process receives a reward/penalty. Having an understanding of what rewards are received in various combinations of state and actions, the goal of the Reinforcement Learning agent is to maximize the total rewards.

We then discussed why this task of maximizing the total rewards is not as trivial. We discussed the concept of future rewards attributed to current action. We also discussed how rewards themselves could be uncertain, or difficult to attribute correctly to different actions in sequence. It may be difficult to arrive at a reward function that quantify all rewards on a common numerical scale and any changes in the reward function has a potential to significantly alter the agent's behavior.

Next, we discussed the state or to be more precise an observable state or simply observation which is how we represent the state of the agent's environment at any step in the form of a data structure using which as input the agent could be trained. We discussed how even very complex scenario involving intensive interaction of the domain behavior and physics laws could be represented as simple data structures from which the agent might be better place to implicitly learn these interactions instead of us coding them into the observation feed. We also took the example of situations where we would input the whole series of images/video-feed as a human would see environment into the agent to make sense of it.

We discussed the working of the agent. The agent's objective is to maximize the rewards that it receives by taking the different actions corresponding to the states that it receives. The concept of total rewards with all the complexities of dealing with the rewards is converted into a uniform scale of value. This value could either be just a function of the state (V—the Value function) or of a combination of an action taken in a particular state (Q—the Action–Value function). To learn this function, the agent goes through explore and exploit mechanisms to visit new states/actions or update the value of the existing ones, respectively.

Chapter 2
Mathematical and Algorithmic Understanding of Reinforcement Learning

The Markov Decision Process and Solution Approaches

Abstract In this chapter, we will discuss the Bellman Equation and the Markov Decision Process (MDP), which are the basis for almost all the approaches that we will be discussing further. We will thereafter discuss some of the non-model-based approaches for Reinforcement Learning like Dynamic Programming. It is imperative to understand these concepts before going forward to discussing some advanced topics ahead. Finally, we will cover the algorithms like value iteration and policy iteration for solving the MDP.

2.1 The Markov Decision Process (MDP)

Markov Decision Process (MDP) is the underlying basis of any Reinforcement Learning Process, and all that we discussed in the previous chapter in short could be summed up as an MDP. MDP is formed of two terms, namely, "Markov" and the "Decision Process".

The "Markov" term refers to the "**Markov Property**" which is the underlying principle of the "**Markov Chain**" phenomena of which MDP is a form. Markov Property is also called the "memoryless" property for stochastic (or probabilistic/uncertain in simpler words) processes. For a process that has gone through several states, and is in a specific given state now, if this process follows the Markov Property, then the conditional probability distribution of the probable next state would depend only on the present state, irrespective of the sequence of states the process has gone through to reach this specific current state. Therefore, even if there are several ways (sequences) to reach a particular state, no matter which particular way (sequence) the current the process adopt to reach a specific state, the conditional probability distribution of next states from this specific state remains the same.

M. Sewak, *Deep Reinforcement Learning*,
https://doi.org/10.1007/978-981-13-8285-7_2

Markov Chain applies the Markov Property to a sequence of stochastic events. It refers to a ***stochastic model*** which comprises a sequence of events such that the probability of next event is based solely on the state achieved in the previous event. The sequence of events in a Markov Chain could occur either in discrete or continuous time but are comprised of countable state spaces. From the description in the last chapter, it should be clear that the states we described were either following a similar pattern (data structure) from the onset or we otherwise converted it into a uniform pattern. Remember the examples of continuous cart pole where some lengths of sequence were required to training our agent. For this example, we had the relevant number of previous positions accumulated in a single state such that our sequence of states by themselves does not depend on any other previous state except the present/current state.

The Markov Decision Process (MDP) is defined as a discrete time stochastic control process. MDP applies the Markov Chain property to a given Decision Process. The decision process in context of Reinforcement Learning implies to the "Policy" $\pi_{(s)}$ which helps the agent determine the best action to take or transition to make when it is in a specific current state. The Markov Decision Process provides a mathematical basis for modeling the decision process where the outcomes are partly in our control (affected by the decision of action we took) and are partly random (corresponding to the challenges of estimating and uncertainties we discovered in the previous chapter).

2.1.1 MDP Notations in Tuple Format

The Markov Decision Process (MDP) defines the state transition probability function, i.e., the probabilities of transitioning from the current state—s, to any of the next possible state—s′, by taking an action—a. The state transition probability function is conditioned on the action that is taken. Such probability function is denoted as $\mathbf{P_a}$ **(s, s′)**.

Following the Markov Property, the given state transition probability function is conditionally independent of any of the previous states or actions except the current ones. Similarly, $\mathbf{R_a}$ **(s, s′)** defines the reward function for the rewards received on attaining (transitioning to) state—s′ from the current state—s, conditioned on the action—a taken. The probability of attaining the new state—s′ from the previous state—s on taking an action—a under $\mathbf{P_a}$**(s, s′)** is given by $\mathbf{P_a}$**(s, a s′)**; and the instantaneous reward achieved on attaining the new state—s′ from the previous state —s on taking an action—a could be computed from the reward function $\mathbf{R_a}$**(s, s′)** as $\mathbf{R_a}$**(s, a, s′)**.

The Markov Decision Process or the MDP, hence, could also defined as a set of five tuples comprising of (S, A, P_a, R_a, γ), where S is the present/current state, A is the action taken, P_a and R_a are abbreviations for $\mathbf{P_a}$**(s, a, s′)** the next state probability, and $\mathbf{R_a}$**(s, a, s′)** the reward achieved on transitioning from the current to the new state. In the last chapter, we discussed the future rewards and hinted at discounting the future rewards to the present time so that it could be fairly compared with the present rewards; the discounting factor γ (a real number between 0 and 1) is the discounting factor that does exactly this. In terms of the discounting rate r, the discounting factor γ is given by $\gamma = 1/(1 + r)$. To discount a reward attained n steps ahead to the present step, the future reward is discounted by a factor of γ^n to account for it to the present time step.

2.1.2 MDP—Mathematical Objective

The objective of the MDP or a Reinforcement Learning agent under MDP is to maximize the sum total of all discounted rewards. Maximizing the sum total of all discounted rewards may in turn require to find a policy that may do so. The MDP therefore needs to be coupled with a particular policy. The following process of taking actions as per the (optimized) policy in each subsequent state gets reduced to a Markov Chain.

The subsequent action—a_t (at any time t) taken in any state—s is given by the policy which is denoted by $\pi_{(s)}$. Using the notations discussed earlier, under this policy we have the discounted reward at time t is given as

$$\gamma^t R_{a_t}(s_t, s_{t+1}) \tag{2.1a}$$

Accumulating the rewards at all time steps, the total reward under this policy is given by

$$\sum_{t=0}^{\infty} \gamma^t R_{a_t}(s_t, s_{t+1}) \tag{2.1b}$$

The policy $\boldsymbol{\pi}_{(s)}$ that maximizes these cumulative rewards (objective function) is the solution to our MDP problem.

2.2 The Bellman Equation

The Bellman Equation (named after its researcher Richard Bellman, an American mathematician) gives a recursive solution to the MDP problem as given in the previous section. This recursive form of the MDP is used to solve the MDP using iterative computer science algorithms like dynamic programming and linear programming and is the basis for many other variations which forms the mathematical basis for other algorithms meant to train the Reinforcement Learning agent. The Bellman equation gives mathematical solution to estimate both the value function and the action–value/Q-function.

2.2.1 Bellman Equation for Estimating the Value Function

The MDP objective function as derived in the earlier section is given as below:

$$\sum_{t=0}^{\infty} \gamma^t R_{a_t}(s_t, s_{t+1}) \tag{2.2}$$

The value function is the expected value, which includes both the present and discounted future rewards that could be attributed to being in a state that could be mathematically framed as

$$V_\pi(s) = \mathbb{E}_\pi\left[R_t|_{s_t=s}\right] \tag{2.3}$$

The "$\mathbb{E}$" symbol denotes the expectancy of a stochastic function, and "|" is the conditioning operator. So, the value function under a given policy "π" for a given state "s" is given by the expectancy of all Rewards at time $t(R_t)$ given that (conditioned on) the state at time $t(s_t) = s$.

From the discussion in the MDP section about $P_a(s, s')$ and R_a (s, s′), these could also be represented in stochastic notations as below:

$$\mathcal{P}_{a(ss')} = \mathbb{P}(s_{t+1} = s|_{s_t=s, a_t=a}) \tag{2.4}$$

$$\mathcal{R}_{a(ss')} = \mathbb{E}[r_{t+1}|_{s_t=s, s_{t+1}=s', a_t=a}] \tag{2.5}$$

which states the same similar ideas as we discussed earlier, i.e., the state transition probability $P_a(s, s')$ is the probability of reaching the state—s′ (at time t + 1) from state—s (from the previous time step t) on taking an action "a" at time t.

Similarly, $R_a(s, s')$ is the expectancy of the reward r received at time t + 1, when transitioning from state—s at time step t to state—s′ at time step t + 1 by taking an action a at time step t to enable this transition.

Combining (2.2) and (2.3) and using the expressions for P_a and R_a from (2.4), and (2.5), we have

$$V_\pi(s) = \mathbb{E}_\pi\left[\sum_{i=0}^{\infty} \gamma^i R_{a_{(t+i)}} \mathbb{P}_{(s_{t+i}, s_{t+i+1})}\right] \tag{2.6}$$

Instead of summing up from $i = [0, \infty]$, we could do the same thing recursively such that we just take the present rewards and add to it the discounted (discounted by a single time step) "Value" (and not just rewards) of the next state. This expression will be equivalent to the discounted rewards from all subsequent time steps to infinity as per the Markov Property. Equation (2.6) could be rewritten in the recursive form as

$$V_\pi(s) = \mathbb{E}_\pi\left[R_{t+1} + \gamma \sum_{i=0}^{\infty} R_{a_{t+i+1}} \mathbb{P}_{(s_{t+i+1}, s_{t+i+2})}\right] \tag{2.7}$$

$$V_\pi(s) = \mathbb{E}_\pi[R_{t+1} + \gamma V_\pi(s')] \tag{2.8}$$

As we would have noticed by observing the subnotations in these expressions, all these equations are valid under a given policy. The role of the policy here is to give us the probability distribution of taking different possible actions which may lead to different possible states. So, we can include this probability of reaching different states under this policy as weights and multiple it by the outcomes from those state to further simplify this equation as a weighted sum of the different possibilities we have

$$V_\pi(s) = \sum_a \pi_{(s,a)} \sum_{s'} \mathbb{P}_{sas'}(R_{sas'} + \gamma V_{\pi(s')}) \tag{2.9}$$

2.2.2 *Bellman Equation for estimating the Action–Value/ Q-function*

For the purpose of action–value (Q-function) estimation, we would first like to estimate the value of any given action when the agent is in a particular state. Unlike what we did value function estimation in Eq. (2.9), i.e., to sum across all the actions and weigh them with their respective probabilities, here we would like to sum across all the states that could be reached by taking a particular action. Since the Q-function is parameterized over a particular action, so in this the action is also fixed besides the present state that the agent is in.

We need to also consider that by taking a particular action we may stochastically reach different states and such transitions may be accompanied by different cumulative rewards (values) associated with them. So, we will change Eqs. (2.8) and (2.9) for value function slightly to adapt it for the action–value/Q-function as below (note the changes in subscripts as well):

$$Q_\pi(s,a) = \sum_{s'} \pi_{(s,s')}\left[R_{sas'} + \gamma \mathbb{E}_\pi\left[\sum_{i=0}^{\infty} \gamma^i r_{t+k+2}|_{s_{t+1}=s'}\right]\right] \tag{2.10}$$

This equation simply says that the action–value/Q-value of a given action when the agent is in a particular state is the sum of the expectancy of discounted rewards of each state that could be reached by taking this particular action when the agent is in the given current state, weighed by the probability of reaching that new state from the given current state by taking the specified action in consideration.

2.3 Dynamic Programming and the Bellman Equation

2.3.1 About Dynamic Programming

Like Linear Programming, Dynamic Programming is a way to solve a complex problem by breaking it down into smaller subproblems. But unlike Linear Programming, Dynamic Programming is a bottom-up approach, i.e., it aims to solve the smallest or the simplest problem first and then iterative use the solution of the smaller problems to solve the larger problems till the sub-solutions recursively combine and leads to the solution of the initial complex/problem as a whole.

If the “approach” to the solution of a smaller subproblem is also a good “approach” for a larger subproblem, then we can say that the way the problem has been broken down constitutes an “**Optimal Substructure**” (a given problem could be broken down into smaller problems which could be solved recursively), and have “**Overlapping Subproblems**” (the solution approach of smaller subproblem works for the larger subproblem as well, and so on) which are the *two pre-requisite for the feasibility of application of dynamic programming* on a given problem.

Let us try to understand this with an example. Suppose we are trying to make an application similar to “Google Maps”, in which we would like to find the best/shortest paths between the entered source, and destination locations/coordinates. This is a complex problem as there could be many paths between source and destinations. But imagine if we could break this problem down to two similar subproblems, first of which is of finding the best/shortest path between the source location/coordinate and some intermediary location/coordinate, and the second is to find the best/shortest path between the destination location/coordinate and the chosen intermediary location/coordinate. In this case, we would be left with solving two “similar” subproblems (Optimal Substructure property) which is finding the best path between the source and that intermediary and finding the best path between the destination and the intermediary, and then combining the solutions to these two subproblems to obtain the solution for our original complex problem.

These two subproblems could further be broken down in a similar manner, i.e., for each of the subproblem, we would again end up finding intermediaries within each, till the so-obtained subproblems cannot be further broken down (i.e., when we are left with just a straight path between two locations without a possible intermediary location between them; in that case, the solution for the best path between these two locations will be the only direct path between them), the solution to which is simple, which is a direct path. So, if we solve the lower most/smallest/simplest problem, the higher level problems get solved simply by combining the solution to these subproblems, which indicates that the problem has an “Overlapping Subproblems.”

2.3.2 *Optimality for Application of Dynamic Programming to Solve Bellman Equation*

The Bellman Equation brings the Markov Decision Process (MDP) into a suitable structure such that it fulfills the pre-requisites for the application of Dynamic Programming (i.e., it fulfills the conditions of Optimal Substructure and Overlapping Subproblem) to solve the MDP.

Equation (2.9) needs to be optimized in order to find the best/optimal value function, i.e., we need to find the most optimal actions when the agent is in a given state to maximize that state's value (or the utility of being in that state). This problem is broken down into a format that the state's value does not depend on any future reward directly except that of the current reward (which is easy to know as is received instantaneously and hence is also definite), and the value of the next state that is estimated/computed as of the current optimization step. The value of the next state could similarly be found, by knowing the value of the state next to it and so on recursively.

So, Eq. (2.9) gives the "Optimal Substructure" and since all these problems are similar and have overlapping solutions, the "Overlapping Subproblem" property is also satisfied. Hence, MDP using the Bellman Equation formation is a good candidate to be solved using Dynamic Programming.

2.4 Value Iteration and Policy Iteration Methods

There are two broad approaches that could be used to solve the MDP using Bellman Equation, namely, the value iteration and policy iteration methods. Both of these methods are iterative in nature and theoretically could be implemented using dynamic programming. But due to high computational load and some other drawbacks in using dynamic programming as we will discuss later, it might not be practical to convert all the problems using these methods to be solved using dynamic programming.

Before discussing both of these briefly, we would cover two more variations coming from the Bellman equations, which are called the "Bellman Equation for Optimal Value Function" and the "Bellman Equation for Optimal Policy" which gives the mathematical basis for these methods.

2.4.1 *Bellman Equation for Optimal Value Function and Optimal Policy*

The Bellman Equation for "Optimal Value Function" is given by Eq. (2.11) and that for "Optimal Value" is given by Eq. (2.12) below:

$$V_\pi(s) = R_s + \max_a \gamma \sum_{s'} \mathbb{P}_{sas'} V_{\pi(s')} \tag{2.11}$$

$$\pi(s) = \underset{a}{\operatorname{argmax}} \sum_{s'} \mathbb{P}_{sas'} V_{\pi(s')} \tag{2.12}$$

It could be observed easily that Eq. (2.11) is derived from Eq. (2.9) and is iterative in nature such that in each step we update the value function, to update any changes in value function till it converges (difference between successive updates are below a specified threshold). The updated value of a state in each iteration is sum of the current reward and the maximum discounted value of any of the next states weighed by the probability of attaining that state in the next step.

Equation (2.12) is a further extension of Eq. (2.11) for the policy optimization. It says that the optimal policy is the one which recommends an action when the agent is in a current state such that it leads to a state that maximizes the value of the current state by taking that action. This is because as per Eq. (2.11) the value of a state is dependent on the maximum value of the next state that is possible from a given state.

The argmax argument in Eq. (2.12) selects the action that maximizes the underlying function, which in this case is the value of the next state that could be reached by this action, weighed by the probability of reaching that state by taking this action.

2.4.2 Value Iteration and Synchronous and Asynchronous Update modes

The "**Value Iteration**" method is used for the discrete state–action space and is not suitable for continuous action space. Even within discrete state–action space, if the action space is large, this approach is not recommended to be used because of computational inefficiencies.

In the "Value Iteration" method, we first initialize the value function with some default values, these default values could be all 0s or any other value to start with. Then using the "Bellman equation for value function," i.e., Eq. (2.11), we update the value function with each iteration/experiment. There are two modes to update the value function, namely, the synchronous mode and the asynchronous mode.

In **Synchronous mode**, the updates are made only at the end of the iteration and then the values for all the states are updated simultaneously, whereas in **Asynchronous mode**, the values of individual states are updated as and when a change is observed.

After the value function converges (changes in value function are below a particular threshold), the optimal policy is estimated using the Bellman optimality Eq. (2.12).

2.4.3 Policy Iteration and Policy Evaluation

In the "**Policy Iteration**" method, as the name suggests, we iterate over a policy function in steps instead of the value function as in the value iteration method. We first initialize our policy (assign probability of taking any action for a discrete action space) randomly or with suitable default values.

After initializing the policy, we iterate across the following steps till the given policy is converged (changes in probabilities across each iteration is below a particular threshold). The first step in each iteration is that of the "**Policy Evaluation**", in which we estimate the value function using the Bellman equation for value function (Eq. 2.11), and then we iterate the policy using the Bellman equation for optimal policy (Eq. 2.12).

The Policy Evaluation step is computationally very expensive, and as the state space grows, so does the complexity (remember in the case of value iteration the complexity was more dependent on action space). So, the Policy Iteration method is used mostly for MDPs with a small and mostly discrete state space. But since the agent is actually trying to work on a policy, and since value iteration proves to be an indirect way to improve policy, so sometimes policy iteration may offer a faster or better guaranteed convergence than value iteration.

2.5 Summary

This chapter covers the very important mathematical background of Reinforcement Learning. We discussed the Markov Decision Process, which is the underlying basis of any Reinforcement Learning process, and then converted the Reinforcement Learning objective into a mathematical optimization equation. Owing to the underlying complexity of the system, we required a better to optimize this objective function. This is where we introduce the Dynamic Programming and illustrated how the Bellman's equation is ideally suited to be solved by Dynamic Programming.

We then discussed the two formulations of the Bellman's equation, namely, the "Bellman Equation for Policy Iteration" and "Bellman Equation for Value iteration" to solve the MDP using any of the two approaches depending upon which is better suited for specific scenarios.

Chapter 3
Coding the Environment and MDP Solution

Coding the Environment, Value Iteration, and Policy Iteration Algorithms

Abstract In this chapter, we will learn one of the most critical skills of coding our environment for any Reinforcement Learning agent to train against. We will create an environment for the grid-world problem such that it is compatible with OpenAI Gym's environment such that most out-of-box agents could also work on our environment. Next, we will implement the value iteration and the policy iteration algorithm in code and make them work with our environment.

3.1 The Grid-World Problem Example

In the chapter, we intend to solve an MDP problem hands-on using Dynamic Programming. We will take the easy-to-understand Grid-World problem to illustrate the problem and code its solution. In this section, we will describe the problem briefly.

3.1.1 Understanding the Grid-World

The objective of this game/MDP is to accumulate the maximum possible points while navigating the Grid-World as shown in Fig. 3.1 above. We get a reward of (say) +100 on reaching the terminal state (state numbered 64 in the grid world in Fig. 3.1), whereas we get a reward of (say) −1 (penalties are denoted as negative rewards) for every turn.

Without this penalty, the agent may never reach the terminal state or may reach the terminal state very late as in that case the total reward will remain across the nonterminal states, which may even lead to the agent getting "stuck" hunting across/between some intermittent states till infinity.

M. Sewak, *Deep Reinforcement Learning*,
https://doi.org/10.1007/978-981-13-8285-7_3

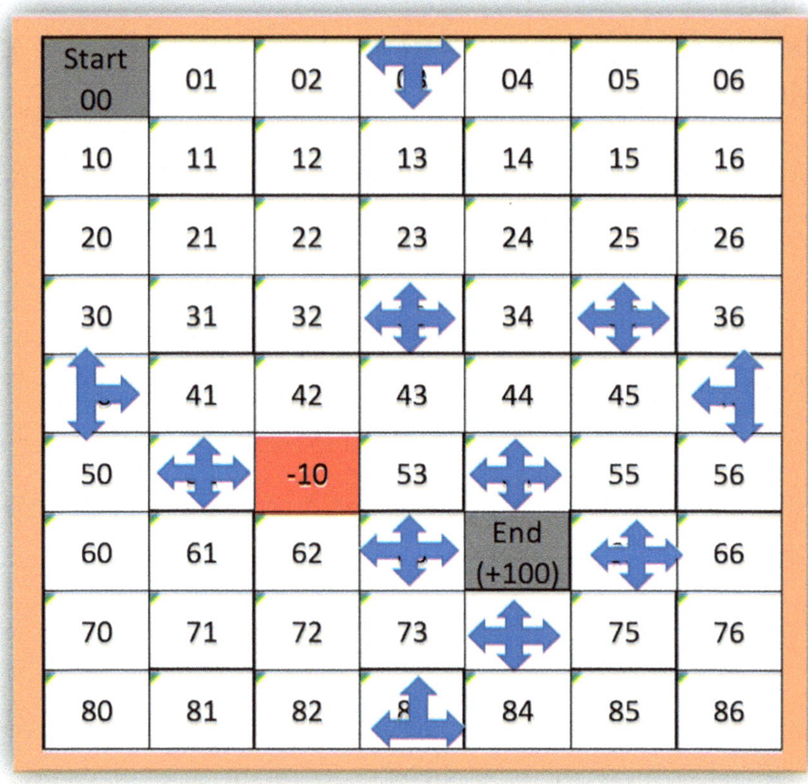

Fig. 3.1 Grid-world example illustration

Another way to force convergence is to limit the total number of turns allowed. For this illustration, we will use the earlier method and use the penalty of −1 for each turn taken by the agent.

Additionally, to make the problem more interesting, we have introduced some ditches in the grid. If the agent happens to get to a grid with a ditch, a penalty/ negative reward of −10 will be accrued.

3.1.2 Permissible State Transitions in Grid-World

In the previous chapters in multiple contexts, we used the disclaimer about transitions mentioning "of the states/action possible from a given state." This is because not all the states are possible to be visited directly from a given state. In the mathematical form, this could be represented as nonzero state transition probabilities for all the states that could be visited from a given state. In this example, we will take a different approach to accomplish this.

In the example of grid world, the agent from a given state/cell could move only to the adjacent, non-diagonal cells within the grid from a particular cell in a given turn. From a given state, the agent can move in either of the four directions, UP (U), DOWN (D), LEFT (L), or RIGHT (R). If there exists a valid state on taking these actions, the state is transitioned to that valid state, else it remains the same. For example, if the agent is on state 53 and it takes an action to move LEFT/(L), then it will reach state 52 and get a penalty of -10 for reaching a ditch and another -1 for a turn used. Whereas if the agent is in state 50 and decides to move LEFT (L), then that is considered as an invalid state (as it goes out of the grid), so the agent's new state is the same as the previous state, i.e., 50, and the receives a penalty of -1 for a turn used.

3.2 Constructing the Environment

The environment serves the purpose of presenting the state and providing the relevant responses to the agent to train it. There are many projects that offer an environment class that we could inherit to start with. Alternatively, we could choose to build our own environment class either from scratch or by extending some of the popular environment classes from different libraries.

There also exists readymade environment for some use cases that we could use. "OpenAI's Gym" is a very popular platform that offers a lot of different types of environments to use to build agents. These environments, besides having specialized features and methods, expose some standardized methods (as we will discuss in details later in this chapter) which are compatible with many agents. If the environment is compatible with the agent, then we can simply create an object from the environment class and pass it to the agent class object as a parameter.

We can test our agents against these environments and generate reference scores against them. Since these are standardized environments, the results that the agents scored (cumulative rewards) while using these environments could also be compared against the communities' (of researchers/developers) similar work/agents.

3.2.1 Inheriting an Environment Class or Building a Custom Environment Class

Often the purpose of building a Reinforcement Learning agent is to deploy it in real life to take actions in a real-life scenario/environment, and that is a skill that this book focuses to inculcate in its readers. With this motivation, we would not like to rely only on using the default environments provided by "OpenAI Gym" or other similar projects.

"Keras-RL" another popular project for training Reinforcement Learning agents also offers similar environments and its environments are also compatible with the OpenAI Gym's environment class.

In the later chapters when we focus on building Deep Reinforcement Agents, we would require a standardized environment to test our agents and compare its performance against some of the community works, and that is when we may leverage these existing environments. In this chapter, however, we would like to enable our users with the know-how of creating their own environment classes so that they could comfortably build a unique environment that closely mimics the real scenarios of their respective domain and could pose realistic challenges for the Reinforcement Learning agent so that the trained agent's performance in their respective domains is closer to expectations.

Having said so, there are two options that we could use to build a custom environment. The first is, of-course, building a custom environment from scratch, that is, building a python class that just inherits the object class for python 2, and no class for python 3 (in Python 2 all base classes inherit the object class).

The second option is that we inherit one of the standard base environment classes from some of the projects that offer it and then customize it to implement the required functionalities. This option is not only easier to implement than the former option but also has some inherent advantages. When implementing a real-life project, often we would like to utilize a base agent from a given library/project and customize it further for our specific advanced need. Most of the default agents from common Reinforcement Learning libraries are compatible with specific standardized environment class from some specific libraries in addition to some other custom environment class that inherits the supported environment class. For example, Keras-RL environment class extends the OpenAI Gym's environment class, so the Reinforcement Learning agents in the Keras-RL library are compatible with both the Keras-RL environment class objects and the OpenAI Gym environment class objects. So, it could be a good idea to follow this easier route of extending a standardized environment class with the required features and enhancements to implement a custom environment.

But for the purpose of this chapter, instead of taking the latter easier approach, we want to focus on enabling the readers to understand the environment class in detail and would use the former option. Next, we will discuss some essential recipes (common patterns) that will help users understand some important decision criteria, before discussing the actual code.

3.2.2 Recipes to Build Our Own Custom Environment Class

Whether we are inheriting a base environment class, or building one from scratch, there are some recipes (patterns) that if we follow, it would become easier to build the agents that can work seamlessly with our environments. Also, often we may be able to use some of the default agents provided by other libraries/packages to work with our environment or alternatively will have significantly less to code to build a custom agent from scratch.

The essential pre-requisites for building a custom environment compatible with many standard libraries are fairly short and simple. There are just two functions that we need to implement (at a bare minimum), with the specified required input and output formats.

These two functions are the "step" and "reset" methods/functions which are explained below. Class functions are also called methods, and this is the terminology we would follow to refer to the environment class' functions to avoid confusing reference to any stand-alone functions. Besides these two methods, we are free to and often recommended to code as many additional functions to increase the versatility and applicability of our environment for different agents and for different purposes that we may want to use it for. Here, in the example that we would be illustrating in this chapter later, we have separated the contents of the "step" function into separate discrete public functions that are also being used to train our agent. This is also done deliberately to illustrate some advanced concepts. Additionally, we have other methods/functions in our implementation to enhance the versatility of the agent and to enhance understandability and ease-of-debugging of our code.

The Step () Method

To train a Reinforcement Learning agent, we need a mechanism to present to it a state; the agent then takes the best possible action possible for that state (as per its current learning); subsequently, we need a mechanism to give the agent a reward/penalty corresponding to that action, and to change the state that occurs because of the action. This new state is again served to the agent for taking the next action and so on.

The essential responses in this sequence that the environment delivers are the new states and reward by taking a given action (in the current state). For this, the environment requires a method that accepts the action (as suggested by the agent against the current state). In case the current state was generated by some other method or otherwise could be altered outside of this method such that this method may lack the complete information of the current state, then the current state may also be required by a custom implementation of this method.

The step method on receiving the above inputs processes them to returns a tuple in the format (***observation***, ***reward***, ***done***, ***info***). A brief description of the elements of this tuple is as follows. The element names are followed by the element's data type in brackets.

Observation (object)

This variable constitutes the (new/next) state that is returned from the environment on taking the particular action by the agent (as sent in the step method's input). This state could have observations in the way best represented in the environment. Some examples of these states are provided in Chap. 1. The python data type for the observation class inherits the object class.

Reward (float)

This is the instantaneous reward received by the agent for reaching the particular new state on taking the action (input). The data type for reward is float. This is only the instantaneous reward; in case an accumulated reward is of interest, that needs to be maintained outside this method/environment object separately.

Done (boolean)

This is a Boolean flag and is of importance in environments, which deals with episodes. An episode is a series of experiments/turns that has a beginning and an end. For example, in our Grid World example, when we reach a terminal state, the game "Ends" and on reaching such a state, the returned value for the element "done" will be "True". The "done" element's value will again be reset to "False" when the next episode starts. The start of a new episode is triggered when the environment is "reset" as we will discuss in the next subsection on the reset () method. The "done" element's value will remain "False" until the episode is not complete. If the environment is in done state (i.e., done == True), the step function will not work, until the environment is not reset, as a next step is not feasible in a completed episode.

Info (dict)

This is an optional parameter and is used to share the information required for debugging but could optionally be used for other purposes as well in a custom implementation. This is a dictionary (python dict) and must contain the key, value pairs of the information that is sent. We can also send the state probabilities, for example, to indicate why the particular state was chodes, or some hints on the reward computation. Often in the agent code it might not be required, and hence instead is received in an _ variable, which means that its values are not stored in any callable variable.

The Reset () Method

Whenever the environment is instantiated for the first time, or whenever a new episode starts, the state of the environment needs to be reset.

The reset function takes no argument and returns an observation/state corresponding to the start of a fresh episode. Depending upon specific environments, other internal variables that need to be reset/instantiated for a fresh episode's start are also reset in this function.

3.3 Platform Requirements and Project Structure for the Code

We are using Python 3.x (3.6.5 to be precise) for this code example and have written the classes in Python 3.x format. In this book, whenever we refer to Python, we would mean the CPython variant of Python (which uses the C compiler). Besides CPython, there are many other variants of Python like Jython, PyPython,

IronPython, etc., but we would use the most commonly used CPython throughout. The only Python library that we would be using in this chapter is “numpy”. Besides “numpy”, there is no other dependency that this code has on any other Python or external library. In case if the readers are using a distribution of Python like Anaconda (or miniconda), the “numpy” dependency would come bundled in the distribution, else this could be installed by using the terminal/shell/cmd command “pip install numpy” in their system (requires internet connectivity).

In some of the later projects where we would be also using other third-party libraries, there would be some additional dependencies that we need to download/install. But for the purpose of this chapter since we intend to write everything from scratch, we do not have any other dependency. If the readers are more comfortable with Python 2.X, they are welcome and encouraged to adapt the code for Python 2.X distribution.

As a good coding practice, we will be using separate python package for the environment. A package could be imported in any other python project (assuming no dependency incompatibilities/collisions), so using this approach we could use this environment in many other projects as well. The package we are using to build this environment is called “envs” and is in a subfolder in our python project.

There is a blank python file, named “__init__.py”, in the folder named “envs”. The “__init__.py” is created in a folder to tell python that this is a sub-module root folder. Whenever the interpreter encounters an import statement that tries to import anything from the “envs” (name of the sub-module is the same as the name of the folder) module, then it will be known that it should look into this folder for the subsequent items in the import statements in sequence. The project structure is as shown in Fig. 3.2 below.

We would strive to have all the different environments in the project in their dedicated Python class, and we would preferably have them in their dedicated “.py” file. The agent is in the base project folder and is implemented in its own class in a dedicated “.py” file. Each class file has a “if __name__ == ‘__main__’ section” which has the code for debugging/testing the respective classes and is invoked only when that particular “.py” file is run as the main file. So, for example, if the solver’s “.py” file imports the environment from the env’s “.py” file and uses its contents, the test code written below the “if __name__…” section of the env’s “.py” file is not invoked.

Next, we will be listing the code for the environment, which is common for both the solution implementations. After that, we will present the two approaches, i.e., the value iteration and policy iteration, that will use this environment to solve the Grid World.

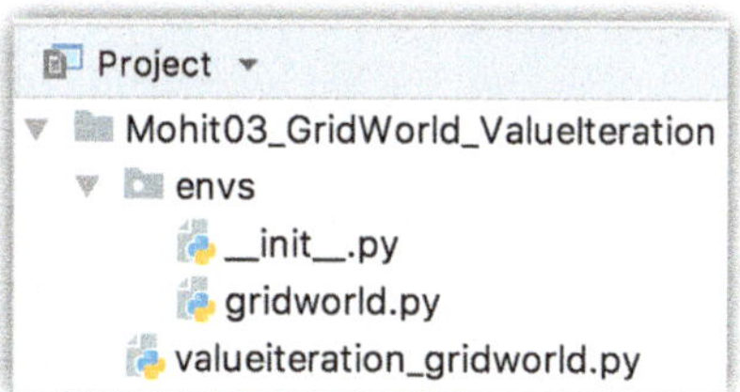

Fig. 3.2 Project folder structure

Readers are encouraged to browse through the code and the structure of the classes, and try to reason-out the purpose of each instance variable and method on their own, before going through the explanation. It would also be a good exercise to think about the sequence of calls as per the explanation for the value iteration and policy iteration approaches as given in the last chapter before seeing the actual invocation sequence.

3.4 Code for Creating the Grid-World Environment

This code is in a file called "gridworld.py" under the folder (/sub-module) "envs" in the main project folder.

```
"""Grid World Environment
Custom Environment for the GridWorld Problem as in the book Deep Reinforce-
ment Learning, Chapter 2.

Runtime: Python 3.6.5
Dependencies: None
DocStrings: NumpyStyle

Author : Mohit Sewak (p20150023@goa-bits-pilani.ac.in)
"""


class GridWorldEnv():
    """Grid-World Environment Class
    """

    def __init__(self, gridsize=7, startState='00', terminalStates=['64'], ditches=['52'],
                 ditchPenalty = -10, turnPenalty = -1, winReward= 100,
                 mode = 'prod'):
        """Initialize an instance of Grid-World environment

        Parameters
        -----------
        gridsize : int
            The size of the (square) grid n x n.
        startState : str
            The entry point for the game in terms of coordinates as string.
        terminalStates : str
            The goal/ terminal state for the game in terms of coordinates as string.
        ditches : list(str)
            A list of ditches/ penalty-spots. Each element coded as str of coordinates.
        ditchPenalty : int
            A Negative Reward for arriving at any of the ditch cell as in ditches
parameter.
        turnPenalty : int
            A Negative Reward for every turn to ensure that agent completes the epi-
sode in minimum number of turns.
        winReward : int
            A Negative Reward for reaching the goal/ terminal state.
        mode : str
            Mode (prod/debug) indicating the run mode. Effects the information/ ver-
bosity of messages.
```

```
        Examples
        --------
        env = GridWorldEnv(mode='debug')

        """
        self.mode = mode
        self.gridsize = min(gridsize,9)
        self.create_statespace()
        self.actionspace = [0,1,2,3]
        self.actionDict = {0:'UP', 1:'DOWN', 2:'LEFT', 3:'RIGHT'}
        self.startState = startState
        self.terminalStates = terminalStates
        self.ditches = ditches
        self.winReward = winReward
        self.ditchPenalty = ditchPenalty
        self.turnPenalty = turnPenalty
        self.stateCount = self.get_statespace_len()
        self.actionCount = self.get_actionspace_len()
        self.stateDict = {k:v for k,v in zip(self.statespace,range(self.stateCount))}
        self.currentState = self.startState

        if self.mode == 'debug':
            print("State Space", self.statespace)
            print("State Dict", self.stateDict)
            print("Action Space", self.actionspace)
            print("Action Dict", self.actionDict)
            print("Start State",self.startState)
            print("Termninal States",self.terminalStates)
            print("Ditches", self.ditches)
            print("WinReward:{}, TurnPenalty:{}, DitchPenalty:{}"
                  .format(self.winReward,self.turnPenalty,self.ditchPenalty))

    def create_statespace(self):
        """Create Statespace

        Makes the grid worl space with as many grid-cells as requested during in-
stantiation gridsize parameter.

        """
        self.statespace = []
        for row in range(self.gridsize):
            for col in range(self.gridsize):
                self.statespace.append(str(row)+str(col))

    def set_mode(self,mode):
        self.mode = mode

    def get_statespace(self):
        return self.statespace

    def get_actionspace(self):
```

```
        return self.actionspace

    def get_actiondict(self):
        return self.actionDict

    def get_statespace_len(self):
        return len(self.statespace)

    def get_actionspace_len(self):
        return len(self.actionspace)

    def next_state(self, current_state, action):
        """Next State

            Determines the next state, given the current state and action as per the
game rule.

        Parameters
        ----------
        current_state : (int, int)
            A tuple of current state coordinate
        action : int
            Action index

        Returns
        -------
        str
            New state coded as str of coordinates

        """
        s_row = int(current_state[0])
        s_col = int(current_state[1])
        next_row = s_row
        next_col = s_col
        if action == 0: next_row = max(0,s_row - 1)
        if action == 1: next_row = min (self.gridsize-1, s_row+1)
        if action == 2: next_col = max(0,s_col - 1)
        if action == 3: next_col = min(self.gridsize - 1, s_col+1)

        new_state = str(next_row)+str(next_col)
        if new_state in self.statespace:
            if new_state in self.terminalStates: self.isGameEnd = True
            if self.mode=='debug':
                print("CurrentState:{}, Action:{}, NextState:{}"
                    .format(current_state,action,new_state))
            return new_state
        else:
            return current_state

    def compute_reward(self, state):
        """Compute Reward
```

```
        Computes the reward for arriving at a given state based on ditches, and
goals as requested during instatiations.

        Parameters
        ----------
        state : str
            Current state in coordinates coded as single str

        Returns
        -------
        float
            reward corresponding to the entered state

        """
        reward = 0
        reward += self.turnPenalty
        if state in self.ditches: reward += self.ditchPenalty
        if state in self.terminalStates: reward += self.winReward
        return reward

    def reset(self):
        """reset

            Resets the environment. Required in gym standard format.

        Returns
        -------
        str
            A string representing the reset state, i.e. the entry point for the agent at
start of game.

        Examples
        --------
        env.reset()

        """
        self.isGameEnd = False
        self.totalAccumulatedReward = 0
        self.totalTurns = 0
        self.currentState = self.startState
        return self.currentState

    def step(self,action):
        """step

            Takes a step corresponding to the action suggested. Required in gym
standard format.

        Parameters
        ----------
```

```
        action : int
            Index of the action taken

        Returns
        -------
        tuple
            A tuple of (next_state, instantaneous_reward, done_flag, info)

        Examples
        --------
        observation_tuple = env.step(1)
        next_state, reward, done, _ = env.step(2)

        """
        if self.isGameEnd:
            raise ('Game is Over Exception')
        if action not in self.actionspace:
            raise ('Invalid Action Exception')
        self.currentState = self.next_state(self.currentState, action)
        obs = self.currentState
        reward = self.compute_reward(obs)
        done = self.isGameEnd
        self.totalTurns += 1
        if self.mode == 'debug':
            print("Obs:{}, Reward:{}, Done:{}, TotalTurns:{}"
                  .format(obs, reward, done, self.totalTurns))
        return obs, reward, done, self.totalTurns


if __name__ == '__main__':
    """Main function
        Main function to test the code and show an example.
    """
    env = GridWorldEnv(mode='debug')
    print("Reseting Env...")
    env.reset()
    print("Go DOWN...")
    env.step(1)
    print("Go RIGHT...")
    env.step(3)
    print("Go LEFT...")
    env.step(2)
    print("Go UP...")
    env.step(0)
    print("Invalid ACTION...")
    # env.step(4)
```

3.5 Code for the Value Iteration Approach of Solving the Grid-World

This code is in a file named "valueiteration_gridworld.py" under the main project folder.

```
"""Value Iteration Algorithm
Code to demonstrate the Value Iteration method for solving Grid World

Runtime: Python 3.6.5
Dependencies: numpy
DocStrings: NumpyStyle

Author : Mohit Sewak (p20150023@goa-bits-pilani.ac.in)
"""

from envs.gridworld import GridWorldEnv
import numpy as np


class ValueIteration:
    """The Value Iteration Algorithm
    """

    def __init__(self, env = GridWorldEnv(), discountingFactor = 0.9,
                 convergenceThreshold = 1e-4, iterationThreshold = 1000,
                 mode='prod'):
        """Initialize the ValueIteration Class

        Parameters
        ----------
        env : (object)
            An instance of environment type
        discountingFactor : float
            The discounting factor for future rewards
        convergenceThreshold : float
            Threshold value for determining convergence
        iterationThreshold : int
            The maximum number of iteration to check for convergence
        mode : str
            Mode (prod/debug) indicating the run mode. Effects the information/ ver-
bosity of messages.

        Examples
        --------
        valueIteration = ValueIteration(env = GridWorldEnv(),mode='debug')

        """
```

```
        self.env = env
        self.gamma = discountingFactor
        self.th = convergenceThreshold
        self.maxIter = iterationThreshold
        self.stateCount = self.env.get_statespace_len()
        self.actionCount = self.env.get_actionspace_len()
        self.uniformActionProbability = 1.0/self.actionCount
        self.stateDict = self.env.stateDict
        self.actionDict = self.env.actionDict
        self.mode = mode
        self.stateCount = self.env.get_statespace_len()
        self.V = np.zeros(self.stateCount)
        self.Q = [np.zeros(self.actionCount) for s in range(self.stateCount)]
        self.Policy = np.zeros(self.stateCount)
        self.totalReward = 0
        self.totalSteps = 0

    def reset_episode(self):
        """Resets the episode
        """
        self.totalReward = 0
        self.totalSteps = 0

    def iterate_value(self):
        """Iterates value and check for convergence
        """
        self.V = np.zeros(self.stateCount)
        for i in range(self.maxIter):
            last_V = np.copy(self.V)
            for state_index in range(self.stateCount):
                current_state = self.env.statespace[state_index]
                for action in self.env.actionspace:
                    next_state = self.env.next_state(current_state,action)
                    reward = self.env.compute_reward(next_state)
                    next_state_index = self.env.stateDict[next_state]
                    self.Q[state_index][action] = reward +
self.gamma*last_V[next_state_index]
                if self.mode == 'debug':
                    print("Q(s={}):{}".format(current_state,self.Q[state_index]))
                self.V[state_index] = max(self.Q[state_index])
            if np.sum(np.fabs(last_V - self.V)) <= self.th:
                print ("Convergene Achieved in {}th iteration. "
                       "Breaking V_Iteration loop!".format(i))
                break

    def extract_optimal_policy(self):
        """Determines the best action(Policy) for any state-action
        """
        self.Policy = np.argmax(self.Q, axis=1)
        if self.mode == 'debug':
            print("Optimal Policy:",self.Policy)
```

```
def run_episode(self):
    """Starts and runs a new episode

    Returns
    -------
    float:
        Total episode reward
    """
    self.reset_episode()
    obs = self.env.reset()
    while True:
        action = self.Policy[self.env.stateDict[obs]]
        new_obs, reward, done, _ = self.env.step(action)
        if self.mode=='debug':
            print("PrevObs:{}, Action:{}, Obs:{}, Reward:{}, Done:{}"
                          .format(obs, action, new_obs,reward,done))
        self.totalReward += reward
        self.totalSteps += 1
        if done:
            break
        else:
            obs = new_obs
    return self.totalReward

def evaluate_policy(self, n_episodes = 100):
    """Evaluates the goodness(mean score across different episodes) as per a
policy

    Returns
    -------
    float:
        Policy score

    """
    episode_scores = []
    if self.mode=='debug':print("Running {} episodes!".format(n_episodes))
    for e,episode in enumerate(range(n_episodes)):
        score = self.run_episode()
        episode_scores.append(score)
        if self.mode == 'debug': print("Score in {} episode = {}".format(e,score))
    return np.mean(episode_scores)

def solve_mdp(self, n_episode=100):
    """Solves an MDP (a reinforcement learning environment)

    Returns
    -------
    float:
        The best/ converged policy score
    """
```

```
        if self.mode == 'debug':
            print("Iterating Values...")
        self.iterate_value()
        if self.mode == 'debug':
            print("Extracting Optimal Policy...")
            self.extract_optimal_policy()
        if self.mode == 'debug':
            print("Scoring Policy...")
        return self.evaluate_policy(n_episode)


if __name__ == '__main__':
    """Main function
        Main function to test the code and show an example.
    """
    print("Initializing variables and setting environment...")
    valueIteration = ValueIteration(env = GridWorldEnv(),mode='debug')
    print('Policy Evaluation Score = ', valueIteration.solve_mdp())
```

3.6 Code for the Policy Iteration Approach of Solving the Grid-World

This code is in a file named "policyiteration_gridworld.py" under the main project folder. We have used dedicated projects for value iteration and policy iteration examples, but you could also have these files in the same project.

```
"""Policy Iteration Algorithm
Code to demonstrate the Policy Iteration method for solving Grid World

Runtime: Python 3.6.5
Dependencies: numpy
DocStrings: NumpyStyle

Author : Mohit Sewak (p20150023@goa-bits-pilani.ac.in)
"""

from envs.gridworld import GridWorldEnv
import numpy as np


class PolicyIteration:
    """Policy Iteration Algorithm
    """
    def __init__(self, env = GridWorldEnv(), discountingFactor = 0.9,
                 convergenceThreshold = 1e-4,
                 iterationThresholdValue = 1000,
                 iterationThresholdPolicy = 100,
                 mode='prod'):
        """Initialize the PolicyIteration Class

        Parameters
        ----------
        env : (object)
            An instance of environment type
        discountingFactor : float
            The discounting factor for future rewards
        convergenceThreshold : float
            Threshold value for determining convergence
        iterationThresholdValue : int
            The maximum number of iteration to check for convergence of value
        iterationThresholdPolicy:
            The maximum number of iteration to check for convergence of policy
        mode : str
            Mode (prod/debug) indicating the run mode. Effects the information/ ver-
bosity of messages.
```

```
        Examples
        --------
        policyIteration = PolicyIteration(env = GridWorldEnv(),mode='debug')

        """
        self.env = env
        self.gamma = discountingFactor
        self.th = convergenceThreshold
        self.maxIterValue = iterationThresholdValue
        self.maxIterPolicy = iterationThresholdPolicy
        self.stateCount = self.env.get_statespace_len()
        self.actionCount = self.env.get_actionspace_len()
        self.uniformActionProbability = 1.0/self.actionCount
        self.stateDict = env.stateDict
        self.actionDict = env.actionDict
        self.mode = mode
        self.stateCount = self.env.get_statespace_len()
        self.V = np.zeros(self.stateCount)
        self.Q = [np.zeros(self.actionCount) for s in range(self.stateCount)]
        self.Policy = np.zeros(self.stateCount)
        self.totalReward = 0
        self.totalSteps = 0

    def reset_episode(self):
        """Resets the episode
        """
        self.totalReward = 0
        self.totalSteps = 0

    def compute_value_under_policy(self):
        self.V = np.zeros(self.stateCount)
        for i in range(self.maxIterValue):
            last_V = np.copy(self.V)
            for state_index in range(self.stateCount):
                current_state = self.env.statespace[state_index]
                for action in self.env.actionspace:
                    next_state = self.env.next_state(current_state,action)
                    reward = self.env.compute_reward(next_state)
                    next_state_index = self.env.stateDict[next_state]
                    self.Q[state_index][action] = reward +
self.gamma*last_V[next_state_index]
                if self.mode == 'debug':
                    print("Q(s={}):{}".format(current_state,self.Q[state_index]))
                self.V[state_index] = max(self.Q[state_index])
            if np.sum(np.fabs(last_V - self.V)) <= self.th:
                print ("Convergene Achieved in {}th iteration. "
                       "Breaking V_Iteration loop!".format(i))
                break

    def iterate_policy(self):
        """Iterates over different (updated) policies
```

```
        Returns
        -------
        list
            A list of int with each element representing the action index in that state
        """
        self.Policy = [np.random.choice(self.actionCount) for s in
range(self.stateCount)]
        for i in range(self.maxIterPolicy):
            self.compute_value_under_policy()
            old_policy = self.Policy
            self.improve_policy()
            new_policy = self.Policy
            if np.all(old_policy == new_policy):
                print('Policy Convergence achieved in step ',i)
                break
            self.Policy = new_policy
        return self.Policy

    def improve_policy(self):
        """Improves a policy
        Improves a policy by setting action for any state that gives the best Q value in
that state
        """
        self.Policy = np.argmax(self.Q, axis=1)
        if self.mode == 'debug':
            print("Optimal Policy:",self.Policy)

    def run_episode(self):
        """Starts and runs a new episode

        Returns
        -------
        float:
            Total episode reward
        """
        self.reset_episode()
        obs = self.env.reset()
        while True:
            action = self.Policy[self.env.stateDict[obs]]
            new_obs, reward, done, _ = self.env.step(action)
            if self.mode=='debug':
                print("PrevObs:{}, Action:{}, Obs:{}, Reward:{}, Done:{}"
                        .format(obs, action, new_obs,reward,done))
            self.totalReward += reward
            self.totalSteps += 1
            if done:
                break
            else:
                obs = new_obs
        return self.totalReward
```

```
    def evaluate_policy(self, n_episodes = 100):
        """evaluate a policy

        Parameters
        ----------
        n_episodes : int
            Max episodes to evaluate policy

        Returns
        -------
        float
            The policy score

        """
        episode_scores = []
        if self.mode == 'debug': print("Running {} episodes!".format(n_episodes))
        for e,episode in enumerate(range(n_episodes)):
            score = self.run_episode()
            episode_scores.append(score)
            if self.mode == 'debug': print("Score in {} episode = {}".format(e,score))
        return np.mean(episode_scores)

    def solve_mdp(self, n_episode=10):
        """Solves an MDP (a reinforcement learning environment)

        Returns
        -------
        float:
            The best/ converged policy score
        """
        if self.mode == 'debug':
            print("Initializing variables and setting environment...")
        self.iterate_policy()

        if self.mode == 'debug':
            print("Scoring Policy...")
        return self.evaluate_policy(n_episode)


if __name__ == '__main__':
    """Main function
        Main function to test the code and show an example.
    """
    print("Initializing variables and setting environment...")
    policyIteration = PolicyIteration(env = GridWorldEnv(),mode='debug')
    print('Policy Evaluation Score = ', policyIteration.solve_mdp())
```

3.7 Summary

This book aims to enable users to implement (Deep) Reinforcement Learning in their respective domains. The logical step to do this is to first understand the theory and mathematics behind the Reinforcement Learning and then to learn to code them effectively. Before we discuss the theory on Deep Learning and some Deep Learning Reinforcement Learning agents, we introduced this chapter so that the readers could start putting to practice what they have already learnt. We did not introduce the deep part of the Deep Reinforcement Learning to code as of now, but otherwise we implemented most of the pieces we would require to implement a Reinforcement Learning agent.

Besides coding the “Value Iteration” and “Policy Iteration”-based agents for Reinforcement Learning, the most important aspect we covered in this chapter is understanding the Reinforcement Learning environment and coding it in from scratch in such a manner that it could be used by our custom agent and standard Reinforcement Learning agents available from different popular Reinforcement Learning libraries alike. We took this important decision to code a custom environment instead of just extending an existing environment because not only it uncovers the building blocks of the Reinforcement Learning’s environment but also enables us with the required capability to code the environment for our respective domains.

Chapter 4
Temporal Difference Learning, SARSA, and Q-Learning

Some Popular Value Approximation Based Reinforcement Learning Approaches

Abstract In this chapter, we will discuss the very important Q-Learning algorithm which is the basis of Deep Q Networks (DQN) that we will discuss in later chapters. Q-Learning serves to provide solutions for the control side of the problem in Reinforcement Learning and leaves the estimation side of the problem to the Temporal Difference Learning algorithm. Q-Learning provides the control solution in an off-policy approach. The counterpart SARSA algorithm also uses TD Learning for estimation but provides the solution to the control problem in an on-policy manner. In this chapter, we cover the important concepts of the TD Learning, SARSA, and Q-Learning. Also, since Q-Learning is an off-policy algorithm, so it uses different mechanisms for the behavior as opposed to the estimation policy. So, we will also cover the epsilon-greedy and some other similar algorithms that can help us explore the different actions in an off-policy approach.

4.1 Challenges with Classical DP

Until now, approaches like value iteration and policy-iteration that we studied to solve the MDP are typically called the "**Classical Dynamic Programming**" or "**Classical DP**", and are not exactly considered as modern Reinforcement Learning based solutions. Though Classical DP is very important to understand theoretically as we highlighted earlier, there are some drawbacks with. Some drawbacks are as we highlighted in the respective sections of value-iteration and Policy-Iterations sections are that they are computationally very expensive, and could work with limited discrete actions, or limited state size, etc.

Besides the computational complexity, what makes it challenging to implement these approaches in practical application is that of their underlying assumption of a "**model**". The use of the term "model" in Reinforcement Learning has a special reference. Generally, we refer to the term "model" to refer to the machine-learning or supervised-learning models like neural-networks, decision-trees, SVMs,

M. Sewak, *Deep Reinforcement Learning*,
https://doi.org/10.1007/978-981-13-8285-7_4

deep-learning models, etc. But the term "model" in Reinforcement Learning has a different meaning as we will understand in the next section.

The machine-learning or supervised-learning models (like SVM, neural-networksfunction-approximators, ANN, DNN, CNN, MLP, etc.), are instead referred to in Reinforcement Learning as "**function-approximators**". But to make the discussion clearer, beyond this chapter, we will continue to use the "model" terminology even for the supervised-learning models and refer to the statistical-model as for the purpose of "modeling the MDP" as "**MDP model**". The "MDP model" terminology is not standard as per the literature on reinforcement learning, but to avoid any confusion between machine-learning models (which we will refer to as model beyond this chapter), we will use this terminology in this book.

For Classical DP to work well and to solve the MDP effectively, it requires to perfectly "model" the environment of the MDP to compute optimal policies. As we discovered earlier, the value-iteration and Policy-Iteration had to understand the environment completely by exploring all the possible actions in all the possible states. Then these algorithm computes the value of each of the possible combination to solve the MDP. But in real life, especially with sizable states and actions combinations, it will be next to impossible to know all these combinations and compute the value of each of these combinations to train the agent. Therefore, in this chapter, we will go beyond the classical DP approaches and learn some more modern and Classical Reinforcement Learning (note the difference in terminology shifting from Classical Dynamic Programming to Classical Reinforcement Learning for non-Dynamic Programming based approaches) algorithms as well.

Since our focus is to move quickly to Deep Reinforcement Learning approaches, we would not be able to cover an exhaustive list of "**Classical Reinforcement Learning**", or "**Classical RL**" or non-deep-learning based Reinforcement Learning approaches; but nevertheless, we would cover the important ones, the understanding of which would also be required to understand the Deep-Learning based Reinforcement Learning approaches.

4.2 Model-Based and Model-Free Approaches

As we discussed in the last section, the term "model" in Reinforcement Learning is used to mean the "model" of the MDP. That is understanding the MDP so as to have/generate a "model" of the state-transition probabilities (probability of going from state—s to a new state—s' on taking an action a) and action probabilities for the given MDP. Any approach that relies on making/understanding the "model" of the MDP to work is called a "**model-based**" approach. On the contrary, the approaches that do not use or require to know this "model" (of the MDP) to work are called "**model-free**" approaches.

"Model-based" approaches require a prior understanding of the "model" to suggest the optimal policy, and to understand this "model" they need the availability of exhaustive data (assuming the learning is happening from data samples) to "model" the MDP effectively. Hence such approaches are generally not used in an online manner where the agent learns and recommend actions in real-time or on mini-batch feeds of data. There are some hybrid approaches also possible. In such hybrid approaches, the "model" is learned from the existing data samples, and then the so trained "model" in "offline" mode is used in an "online" approach, probably with some incremental improvement/learning loops as well.

Model-based approaches are not just limited to Classical Dynamic Programming. In Classical Reinforcement Learning as well there are some very popular model-based approaches. One of the very popular, and important to understand model-based Reinforcement Learning approach is the **Temporal Difference (TD) Learning**, which is also sometime called **Temporal Difference Model (TDM)** due to the "model-based" approach that it follows.

In this chapter, we will cover Temporal Difference (TD) Learning, which is a "model-based" approach, and two model-free approaches, namely the "Q-Learning" and the "SARSA". With reference to our discussion on "On-Policy" and "Off-Policy" approaches in Chap. 2, it is worth noting that of the two model-free approaches that we will be covering, Q-Learning is an "Off-Policy", "model-free" approach and SARSA in an "On-Policy", "model-free" approach.

4.3 Temporal Difference (TD) Learning

While discussing the disadvantage of Dynamic Programming based methods we discussed that such methods need a perfect knowledge of the "model" (MDP-model) to work and cannot use "experience" to compensate for any lack of prior knowledge of the "model" (or lack of data). There is yet another technique in non-Reinforcement-Learning (non-RL) methods called the "**Monte Carlo Simulation**", which is at the exact opposite end of the spectrum and it uses mostly experience and could not use "knowledge" (or prior data) directly (though it uses historical data to abstract distributions from it which could serve as experience) to solve the MDP. MC (for Monte Carlo) Simulation, tries to understand the underlying distribution of the data (of each variable and their covariance with other variables), and then it could create new data by generating samples from the abstracted distributions. This is similar to the role of "experience" in humans. We use the memories/experience of the past, to make informed assumptions of what the future could likely be.

Though Monte Carlo Simulation based approach looks good theoretically, it has a disadvantage of having to wait for the completion of all (or a large number of) the episodes to gather the underlying distributions/experiences for it to work. TD (for

Temporal Difference) Learning does a good balance between the Dynamic Programming based approaches of requiring "no-experience" and Monte Carlo based approaches of using "only-experience". TD (0) a variant of the TD learning approach is a fully "**online**" (here online refers to the ability of incrementally updating the learning in real-time) "**bootstrapping**" (in statistics bootstrapping refers to the technique of picking samples from a data with "*replacement*" to update statics of the population) technique and can continuously update the values even during an episode.

In case if the reader failed to understand the significance of the above-stated advantages in real-life applications, let us for a moment step back to walk through some of the great benefits of alleviating the bottlenecks of offline learning (or requiring to wait for the episode to end to update the learning). If we do not have to wait for the episode to end to update the values, then that implies that this technique could also be employed into scenarios with very long episodes. Imagine a self-driving car for inter-state services!

Another extension of this bottleneck is that for "*continuous-tasks*" which are essentially "*non-episodic*" tasks (or tasks where a single episode runs into infinite steps). In the paradigm of episodes, "continuous-tasks" are equivalent to a single episode that does not ever end. Imagine a continuous running robotic assemble-line!

There are other variants of TD Learning as well, like the TD (1), and the more generalist TD (λ) (pronounced TD Lambda). But in this section, we will cover the TD (0) variant only. But before that we will briefly discuss about the role of TD, SARSA and Q-Learning in terms of Reinforcement Learning problems.

4.3.1 Estimation and Control Problems of Reinforcement Learning

For an agent that acts on the basis of value functions optimization/maximization, the problem could be broken down into two sub-problems. The first is the "**Estimation**" sub-problem which is "estimating" (as opposed to "computing" that what we did in the case of Classical Dynamic Programming exercise) the value function (given a "policy"), and subsequently the second is the "**Control**" sub-problem, which is acting or taking or recommending actions corresponding to a given current state. The "control" problem may use the outcomes of the "estimation" problem as inputs along with other mechanisms/algorithms to determine/recommend the best possible next action.

TD (0) essentially gives a good approach for the "estimation" part of the problem. For the "control" we can use either the SARSA or Q-Learning methods that we will be covering next.

4.3.2 TD (0)

TD (0) is the simplest Temporal Difference Learning algorithm that "estimates" the "value function" of a finite (MDP) under a given "policy" $\pi_{(s)}$. In Chap. 2, Eqs. (2.2)–(2.3), we discussed one variant of Bellman Equation for value-function which was based on expectancy of total rewards, as given below:

$$V_{\pi}(s) = \mathbb{E}_{\pi}\left[R_t|_{s_t=s}\right] \tag{4.1}$$

This was further shown to be expanded to include the future discounted rewards as:

$$V_{\pi}(s) = \mathbb{E}_{\pi}\left[\sum_{i=0}^{\infty} \gamma^i R_{a_{(t+i)}}\left(s_{(t+i)}, s_{(t+i+1)}\right)\right] \tag{4.2}$$

Another way the above equation could be represented in the form of just two consecutive steps is as follows:

$$V_{\pi}(s) = \mathbb{E}_{\pi}\left[r_0 + \gamma V_{\pi}(s_1)|_{s_0=s}\right] \tag{4.3}$$

In this Eq. (4.3), $r_0 + \gamma V_{\pi}(s_1)$ is the unbiased estimate of $V_{\pi}(s)$. These could be updated, and all subsequent estimates revised in a tabular format. Owing to this capability of being updated directly in a tabular format TD (0) is also known to be a tabular approach. The initial value-function-table (as in table used in the tabular approach) could be initialized arbitrarily and later revised with each step (not just each episode). The "policy" under which this value-function-table is "estimated" or updated is "evaluated" (In policy-iteration we discussed the two required repetitive steps, i.e., of policy-evaluation and policy-improvement, we use only the policy "evaluation" step here). During "evaluation", we may get new rewards (*r*), and with every step the value-function/table is updated as per the below equation:

$$V_{(s)} = V_{(s)} + \alpha(r + \gamma V_{(s')} - V_{(s)}) \tag{4.4}$$

where the symbol "α" (alpha) here is the learning rate, s is the previous state before the action and s' is the new state after the cation.

The Eq. (4.4) essentially suggests that the value of a particular state (s) in the value-function, could be updated in each step such that it is equal to the previous value of that state plus the learning rate times any difference between the new "***TD target***" for the state (that is the term r + γV(s′) and the previous value of the same state. The new "***TD target***" for the current state V(s) is the instantaneous reward received in this step plus the discounted value of the immediate *next* step. At times the "TD target" of a state during such updated may vary significantly from the previous value of that state. This may even be because of noise in the data. Such large divergence between the "TD target" and present value of the current state in a single iteration may affect convergence and may warrant smoothening. The addition of learning rate in the equation provides this required smoothening effect and also prevents few noisy data instances from adversely affecting the learning largely.

4.3.3 TD (λ) and Eligibility Trace

Temporal Difference Lambda or TD (λ) is a popular variant of the Temporal Difference (TD) Learning. So, we will cover this briefly here for the purpose of intuition without going into great details of the same. In TD (0) we saw that the value in any given value-update iteration is equal to the instantaneous reward in that step plus the discounted value of only the state in the very next step. By including only, the very next step in the value computation we assumed that the difference in value targets for any state in a given step is only a function of the last step's state in the sequence that the agent visited. For episodes or scenarios where sequence is of importance, this may not be a very good assumption. The TD (λ) algorithm alleviates this assumption of TD (0).

In TD (λ) we can distribute the attribution of reward to different previous states that the agent visited in sequence and hence the states in these steps were assumingly responsible for this reward that the agent received in the current step in the current value-update iteration. The proportion of credit attribution of rewards/value to different previous states and actions is controlled by the parameter λ, where λ lies between 0, and 1 ($1 \geq \lambda \geq 0$). When λ is set to 0, it behaves similar to a TD (0) algorithm where we just take the instantaneous reward for the last step only, whereas when λ is set to 1 it gives an equal attribution of credit for rewards/value to all previous states visited and actions taken. With $\lambda = 1$, the algorithm behave similar to how a Monte Carlo Simulation would work in an episode, i.e., by averaging the reward across all states visited in that episode.

For any intermediary value of λ, the attribution is weighted by λ^n, where n denotes the number of steps prior to the last step that a state was visited by taking the chosen action in the previous state. This approach is quite similar in intuition to an approach in which one would wait for some number of steps (say i) before making an update to see what all states the agent has visited. Under such condition though we have decided that any reward attribution should happen only until i previous states, but with TD (λ) we could achieve this without exactly waiting for the updates. Thus TD (λ) could work under similar assumptions as Monte Carlo Simulation even in a purely online scenario.

Such an approach to distribute the attribution of reward/penalty to different states visited in previous steps is referred to as "***Eligibility Traces***". That is to mean that we would like to trace the eligibility of the attribution of rewards to previous occurrences in the previous steps in the sequence of events. The λ based approach for implementing and managing (the proportion of attribution to different steps in the past) "Eligibility Traces" is known as the "***forward view***", whereas the other approach mentioned in the example above, in which one would wait for certain steps and then roll the attributions to previous steps after seeing the ***reward*** is known as the "***backward view***" for implementing "Eligibility Traces".

4.4 SARSA

The acronym SARSA stands for State-Action-Reward-State-Action, or to be more precise in terms of steps, it stands for $State_{(t)}$-$Action_{(t)}$-$Reward_{(t)}$-$State_{(t+1)}$-$Action_{(t+1)}$. It uses the same principal for value function (/ table) updates as what we discussed in for the Temporal Difference learning and applies it to the action-value function (also known as Q Function) updates. SARSA works on "control" side of the problem. Given that the action-value function $Q_{(s,\ a)}$ works on a pair of state and action, i.e., (s, a) or action when the agent is in a given state, the SARSA acronym could be grouped as [(s, a), r, (s′, a′)], or further augmented by the correct action-value notation Q as [$Q_{(s,\ a)}$, r, $Q_{(s',\ a')}$].

From the above Q format depiction, it should be clear how SARSA updates the Q function. SARSA updates the Q value of a given (s, a) combination, using the instantaneous rewards that the agent receives in any step and the Q value of the resulting state-action pair, i.e., (s′, a′). As in the case of TD (0), this iterative update could be represented in the form of an equation as follows. The symbols α, γ, s, s′, etc. all have same meaning as we discussed in TD (0) section; that is α is the learning rate, γ is the discounting factor, s is the current state and s′ is the subsequent state when the agent takes an action—a in the state—s.

$$Q_{(s,a)} = Q_{(s,a)} + \alpha(r + \gamma Q_{(s',a')} - Q_{(s,a)}) \tag{4.5}$$

Or

$$Q_{(s,a)} = (1 - \alpha)Q_{(s,a)} + \alpha(r + \gamma Q_{(s',a')}) \tag{4.6}$$

If the readers would have noticed carefully, Eq. (4.5) is exactly the same as Eq. (4.4) in TD (0), except we have replaced the term V(s) with the term Q(s, a), i.e., instead of updating the value function in an online manner, here we are updating the action-value function or the Q Function.

As we mentioned in an earlier section with reference to the "on-policy", and "off-policy" differences the algorithms could be classified into one of these depending upon whether the algorithm uses the same mechanism (policy) for taking an action (behavior) and updating (estimating)/exploring the functions on the basis of which the best action is determined or different mechanisms for both. SARSA follows the same policy to take the actions that it uses to update the action-value function. As we discussed in Chap. 2, such approaches which use the same policy for both their behavior and estimation are said to be "on-policy" learning algorithm. Therefore, SARSA is an "on-policy" learning algorithm.

Unlike some of the other algorithms that we discussed earlier in which we could have initialized the function being estimated (value function or Q function) randomly while initiating the training, this is not done so in the case of SARSA. SARSA being an "on-policy" learning algorithm, in it the actions are dependent on the existing Q values. Therefore, a randomly assigned set of values could mean that some Q (s, a) sequences have a relatively high initial values, and if the agent use that as a criteria to decide its next action, then it may always keep following that particular sequence of actions, not giving an opportunity to visit (explore) other state-action (s, a) pairs, and hence will not be able to update their respective Q values. In other words, the agent would end up mostly exploiting the randomly assigned sub-optimal Q function values instead of exploring all/most of the state-action combinations and rightly estimating the values of each state-action (s, a) to correctly update the Q function. Therefore, in SARSA, the initial Q value space is initialized with a very low initial value, also known as "***optimistic-initial-condition***".

4.5 Q-Learning

Like SARSA, Q-Learning also use Temporal Difference Learning (TD Learning) for the estimation side of the problem. Also, like SARSA, Q-Learning provides solution for the "control" part of the problem and tries to estimate the action-value/ Q Function to take the best possible action (this is called the "control"). So, the estimation part for Q-Learning is similar to that of SARSA and it also updates the Q Function iteratively in every step. Albeit, there is a slight change in the equations of SARSA and Q-Learning as we will discuss later in this section. Q-Learning use the (state-action-reward-state) tuples as experience to estimate the Q Function.

But unlike SARSA, Q-Learning is an "Off-Policy" approach and does not use the Q Function to decide the behavior (or the policy to determine the next action). Therefore, unlike SARSA, the initialization of the Q-Table/Variable could be done using all zeros. This is because Q-Learning use another policy for behavior and a zero initialization of Q-Table or the initial action-value function variables will not create the convergence problem for the agent as we discussed in the earlier section on SARSA. In fact an "Off-Policy" learner is said to be capable of learning a good policy irrespective of the effectiveness of the estimation function because the built-in exploration effect works in isolation from the estimation function.

So, Q-Learning in addition to the temporal difference learning's action-value (Q Function) estimation, will also require another policy to balance between the "Explore" and "Exploit" trade-offs. In Chap. 1, we have discussed about the "Explore vs Exploit dilemma", and mentioned that the process of choosing an action as recommended (as indicated by action corresponding to the argmax of the value/action-value functions) by the Estimation Function is known as the "Exploit" decision. Whereas using some other/additional mechanism to take similar decision is known as the "Explore" decision. In "explore" phase the agents would like to further explore the environment and probably also visit states or take actions or estimate state action combinations that it otherwise could not have visited or taken or explored because as per the estimated function going these would not have made sense or does not have provided an optimal/argmax value that would have warranted such behavior.

To understand Q-Learning in details first we will discuss the way the decision is made in the "Exploit" as this is a dependent directly on the Estimated function (here Q Function). It is because we have already been doing something similar in SARSA and hence it could be easy to understand. But as we discussed in this section earlier, the equation for the estimation/update of Q function is slightly different. This is because now since we have a different mechanism for "exploration", we want to focus the Q function updates completely for the "exploit" part. So, instead take the **max** of all the next Q (s′, a′) combinations possible from the next state—s′. That is also the reason why instead of 5-element tuple combination (state, action, reward-next-state, next action) as in SARSA, we would only require a 4-element tuple (state, action, reward, next-state) as Q-Learning's experience instance. The equation for Q-Learning's action-value function's estimation/update is as follows:

$$Q_{(s,a)} = (1-\alpha)Q_{(s,a)} + \alpha(r + \gamma \max_{a'} Q_{(s',a')}) \tag{4.7}$$

Note that the only difference between Eq. (4.7) used for Q-Learning, and the Eq. (4.6) used for SARSA is that instead of taking the difference from the next action-value, i.e., Q (s′, a′) value (where next a′ is known and is explicit) as in SARSA, in Q-Learning all the possible Q (s′, a′) combinations for a given (nest) state—s′ are evaluated and the max action-value out of these is considered. This in turn means reflects the maximum value possible of the next state possible from any action possible in that state. Hence this value is parametrized only as a function of the state and not state-action combination. Thus, the last part of the tuple in Q-Learning's experience instance has only the state in it, unlike SARSA's experience instance's tuple which requires state-action combination.

Next, we will discuss the "Explore" phase in Q-Learning. In "explore" phase mostly an action is chosen from the available action space for the given state based on some chosen probability function. The decision between "Explore" and "Exploit" happens stochastically and there are different algorithms to determine the probability of being in "explore" vs. "exploit" phase. In the next section, we will cover some of these algorithms. These class of algorithms sometimes are also referred to as "***Bandit Algorithms***" inspired by the famous "Multi-Bandit Algorithm" as used in "A/B Testing" scenarios.

4.6 Algorithms for Deciding Between the "Explore" and "Exploit" Probabilities (Bandit Algorithms)

4.6.1 Epsilon-Greedy (ε-Greedy)

Epsilon-Greedy is the most popular and the simplest algorithm to strike the trade-off between the "exploration" and "exploitation" phases. A ***constant "epsilon" (ε)***, which represents the probability with which the agent decides to "explore" in every turn. So, for example, if the value of $\varepsilon = 0.1$, then there is 10% probability in any given turn that the agent will take a ***random action*** (explore), and 90% probability that it will "exploit" the existing Q function estimates that ***greedily*** chooses the action as per the best value estimates from the Q function as updated until that iteration. Hence the name ***epsilon-greedy***.

Note the emphasis on the adjectives "constant" for the epsilon, and "random" for action choice during "exploration". The choice of these two properties is what changes across most of the algorithms in these class of algorithms that we will discuss next. In "epsilon-greedy" as stated, the value of "epsilon" once chosen remains constant for the behavior policy. The larger the "epsilon", the greater the number of times the agent is likely to "explore" random actions, and the smaller the "epsilon" the greater the number of times the agent is likely to greedily "exploit" the estimated value/Q function. So, the choice of "epsilon" should be based on the "***deterministic-ness***" of the underlying Markov Decision Process (MDP). The more "deterministic" the MDP is, the less it needs to be explored, and hence correspondingly warranting a smaller value for the "epsilon". Conversely, the more "***stochastic***" the MDP is, the more it needs to be explored, and hence correspondingly warranting a larger value for the "epsilon". Hence, the required balance between exploration vs exploitation requirements is the guiding principle to determine the value of "epsilon" as shown in Fig. 4.1.

4.6.2 Time Adaptive "epsilon" Algorithms (e.g., Annealing ε)

As we discussed in the earlier section of basic epsilon-greedy, the value of epsilon remains constant throughout the training process. We also discussed some heuristic on how to choose a good value for epsilon based on the "deterministic-ness" of the "stochastic" problem in hand (the underlying MDP). This heuristic is good while comparing one Markov Decision Process to another. But while working upon a given stochastic problem or MDP, the process will be less known in the beginning and as we start exploring it will keep becoming more and more of charted territory. Hence if the heuristic indicates a higher value of epsilon for a relatively less known process and a lower value of epsilon for a relatively known process then intuitively even the algorithm for a single MDP should have a higher epsilon (more

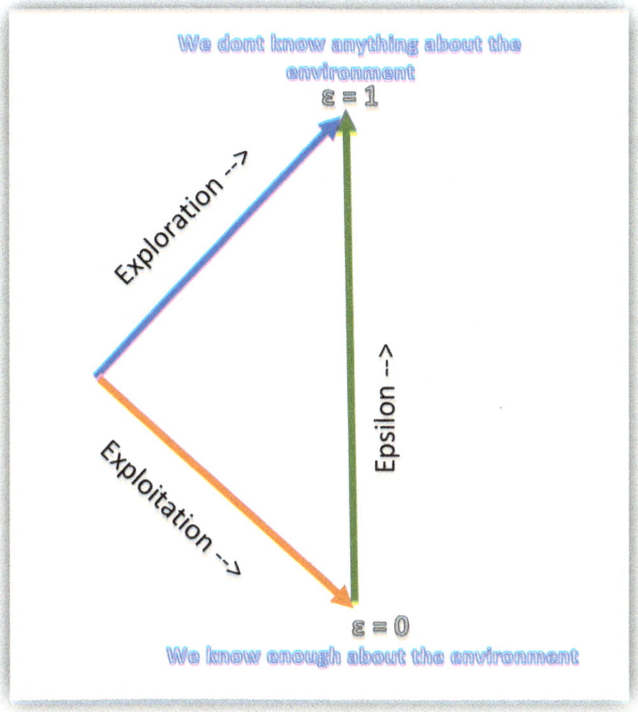

Fig. 4.1 Choosing the ideal epsilon for the problem

"exploration" opportunities) in the beginning, and a progressively lower epsilon (enabling it to "exploit" more "greedy" options) as we keep gaining more information about the environment.

Annealing Epsilon, ***Epsilon First***, and ***Decreasing Epsilon*** are some of the algorithms that decreases the epsilon as the training process with an intention to reduce the convergence time and rely on more informed predictions as opposed to random selections as we learn more about the process. We will not go into the details of each of these algorithms individually, but just for the purpose of illustrating on how these algorithms work we will take the example of the "Annealing Epsilon" algorithm.

Annealing Epsilon algorithm varies the epsilon (ε) with respect to time/steps as:

$$\varepsilon = \frac{1}{\log(\text{time} + c)} \tag{4.8}$$

where, c is small constant of the order of 1e−7 to avoid divide by zero error (as log 1 = 0).

4.6.3 Action Adaptive Epsilon Algorithms (e.g., Epsilon Soft)

Another way to further balance between the probability of the "explore" and "exploit" opportunities apart from the choice of epsilon is on the basis of the number of actions available (that is the cardinality of the action space). Intuitively the more the number of actions available in a domain/process, the more exploration is warranted of that process, and vice versa. Epsilon soft does exactly that and even for a chosen epsilon, varies the "explore" probability in a given state on the basis of actions available for that state as:

$$\mathbb{P}_{\text{explore}} = \frac{\varepsilon}{|A_s|} \tag{4.9}$$

4.6.4 Value Adaptive Epsilon Algorithms (e.g., VDBE Based ε-Greedy)

Depending upon the stochastics of the underlying Markov Decision Process environment and the effectiveness of the policy, the estimation of different value functions may take varying times to converge, and hence instead of varying the epsilon with respect to time, it may be more intuitive to vary the epsilon with respect to the error in the estimation function (like the Q function in case of Q-Learning). The greater the delta change during the update of the estimation function from one iteration to another, the larger should be the "explore" opportunity in the subsequent iterations and hence the larger should be the value of "epsilon".

"VDBE" or "***Value Difference Based Exploration*" *adaptive ε-greedy*** algorithm achieves exactly that the above state objective and varies the value of epsilon (ε) on the basis of the change in estimated values in each step such as:

$$\varepsilon_{(t+1)}(s) = \delta f(s_t, a_t, \sigma) + (1 - \delta)\varepsilon_{(t)}(s) \tag{4.10}$$

where δ is the parameter that determines the influence of the selected action on the exploration rate and is selected similar to Eq. (4.9) above as in the case of action adaptive method, and σ is a positive constant called "inverse sensitivity".

4.6.5 Which Bandit Algorithm Should We Use?

There are many advantages over the basic epsilon-greedy algorithm that the other variants as discussed earlier offers. Any of the above algorithm (or different variants under the variant types) could be chosen to answer the specific challenges that the underlying the domain, or the training of the model or its subsequent usage poses. But the disadvantage with the subsequently discussed variants is that these are slightly more complex, requires optimization of a much larger number of parameters as compared to epsilon alone in the case of the basic epsilon-greedy variant, and at times the specific algorithm variant may even call for storing the values during the estimation process to work well. All these factors increase the complexity of the behavior policy even further.

In most of the scenarios, it is observed that by carefully hand tuning the value of a single parameter "epsilon" in the case of the basic epsilon-greedy algorithm, optimal results could be achieved. So, in the examples in this book, we will use the basic epsilon-greedy algorithm alone with specific choice of the epsilon parameter.

4.7 Summary

Moving beyond the classical approaches of computation of value function(s), in this chapter, we discussed the more practical approach of estimating the value function (s) and entered the modern Reinforcement Learning paradigm. Unlike the computational paradigm where everything was known and hence the behavior could be modeled accordingly, in the more practical paradigm, we divided the Reinforcement Learning problem into that of the estimation and the control problems.

The temporal difference algorithm provides an online mechanism for the estimation problem. temporal difference could be adaptive to be used in an approach which is either similar to dynamic programming or the Monte Carlo simulation or anything in between. Also, since it is a forward-looking mechanism, these variations could provide a similar result as in the case of dynamic programming or Monte Carlo simulation even in a true online environment and for non-episodic MDPs.

SARSA and the Q-Learning provides the solution for the control side of the problem in non-classical Reinforcement Learning. SARSA is an on-policy approaches and uses the same policy for behavior and for estimation and requires careful selection of initialization values to avoid possible drawbacks, Q-Learning, on the other hand, is an off-policy algorithm and uses another policy to determine the explore vs exploit decision balance for it. Epsilon-greedy and many other advanced algorithms exist to help here. The advanced variants could dynamically vary the explore-exploit balance for more optimal results but may require correspondingly higher overheads to implement.

Chapter 5
Q-Learning in Code

Coding the Off-Policy Q-Learning Agent and Behavior Policy

Abstract In this chapter, we would put what we have learnt on Q-Learning in the last chapter in code. We would implement a Q-Table-based Off-Policy Q-Learning agent class, and to complement with a behavior policy, we would implement another class on Behavior Policy with an implementation of the epsilon-greedy algorithm.

5.1 Project Structure and Dependencies

For Q-Learning as well, we will use the "Grid World" Environment we created for the Value/Policy Iteration code as in Chap. 2 earlier. So, we will import the environment from the gridworld.py under the "envs" folder.

Besides we will use a virtual environment, which we are calling DRL and is based on Python 3.6.5 runtime. We have used "miniconda" to create this environment. This could be created by the shell/cmd command "conda create -n DRL python=3.6", and then activated as "source activate DRL" (for Windows, the command is only "activate DRL"). The project structure and the requirements.txt (dependencies) are shown in Figs. 5.1 and 5.2 respectively.

The requireents.txt contains the external library dependencies, which is "numpy" and "matplotlib" (optional for plotting). This could be installed from pip package using command "pip install <dependency>". Alternatively, an IDE like pycharm will prompt to automatically install the libraries scanning the requirements.txt. To activate the DRL virtual environment in pycharm, goto settings->project_ interpreter->add new, and then select the Python file from the bin folder of your virtual environment. In case of miniconda/anaconda the envs folder's default location is <user_dir>/miniconda/envs/<env_name=DRL>/bin.

M. Sewak, *Deep Reinforcement Learning*,
https://doi.org/10.1007/978-981-13-8285-7_5

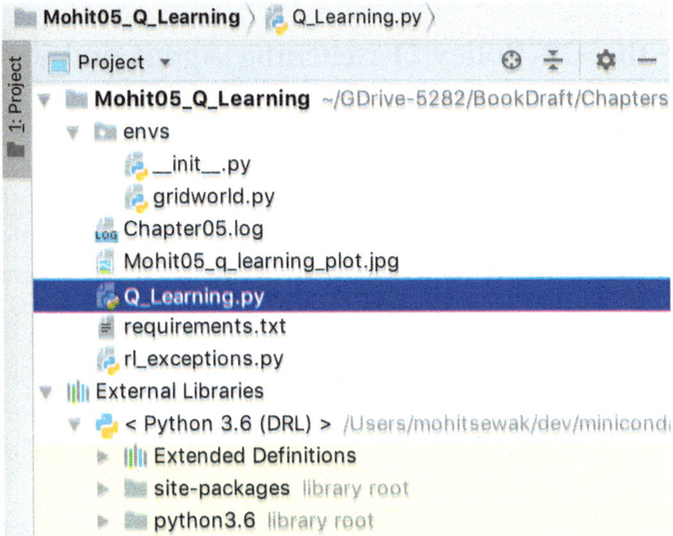

Fig. 5.1 Code project structure

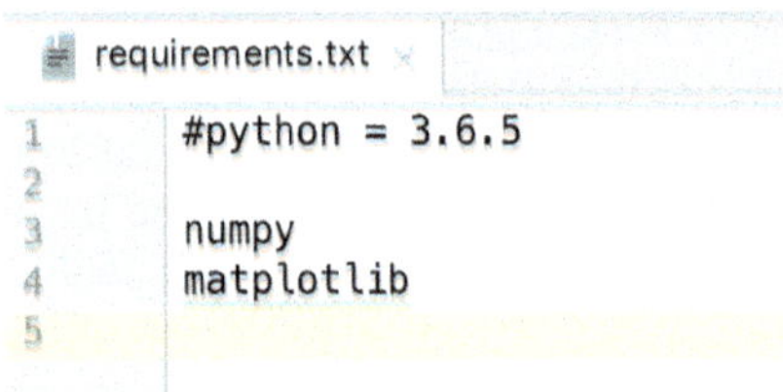

Fig. 5.2 Requirements.txt contents

5.2 Code

```
""" Q Learning in Code

Q Learning Code (on custom environment as created in Chapter 2) as in the book
Deep Reinforcement Learning, Chapter 5.

Runtime: Python 3.6.5
Dependencies: numpy, matplotlib (optional for plotting, else the plotting function
can be commented)
DocStrings: GoogleStyle

Author : Mohit Sewak (p20150023@goa-bits-pilani.ac.in)

"""
```

5.2.1 Imports and Logging (file Q_Lerning.py)

```
#including necessary imports
import logging
import numpy as np
from itertools import count
import matplotlib.pyplot as plt
# import custom exceptions that we coded to receive for more meaningful messag-
es
from rl_exceptions import PolicyDoesNotExistException
# Import the custom environment we built in Chapter 02. We will use the same en-
vironment here.
from envs.gridworld import GridWorldEnv

# Configure logging for the project
# Create file logger, to be used for deployment
# logging.basicConfig(filename="Chapter05.log", format='%(asctime)s %(mes-
sage)s', filemode='w')
logging.basicConfig()
# Creating a stream logger for receiving inline logs
logger = logging.getLogger()
# Setting the logging threshold of logger to DEBUG
logger.setLevel(logging.DEBUG)
```

5.2.2 Code for the Behavior Policy Class

```
class BehaviorPolicy:
    """Behavior Policy Class
    Class for different behavior policies for use with an Off-Policy Reinforcement
Learning agent.

    Args:
        n_actions (int): the cardinality of the action space
        policy_type (str): type of behavior policy to be implemented.

        policy_parameters (dict) : A dict of relevant policy parameters for the request-
ed policy.
            The epsilon-greedy policy as implemented requires only the value of the
"epsilon" as float.


        None

    """

    def __init__(self, n_actions, policy_type = "epsilon_greedy", policy_parameters
= {"epsilon":0.1}):
        self.policy = policy_type
        self.n_actions = n_actions
        self.policy_type = policy_type
        self.policy_parameters = policy_parameters

    def getPolicy(self):
        """Get the requested behavior policy

        This function returns a function corresponding to the requested behavior poli-
cy

        Args:
            None

        Returns:
            function: A function of the requested behavior policy type.

        Raises:
            PolicyDoesNotExistException: When a policy corresponding to the parame-
ter policy_type is not implemented.
        """
        if self.policy_type == "epsilon_greedy":
            self.epsilon = self.policy_parameters["epsilon"]
            return self.return_epsilon_greedy_policy()
        else:
            raise PolicyDoesNotExistException("The selected policy does not
```

```
exists! The implemented policies are "
                                    "epsilon-greedy.")

    def return_epsilon_greedy_policy(self):
        """Epsilon-Greedy Policy Implementation

        This is the implementation of the Epsilon-Greedy policy as returned by the
getPolicy method when "epsilon-greedy"
        policy type is selected.

        Args:
            None

        Returns:
            function: a function that could be directly called for selecting the recom-
mended action as per e-greedy.

        """
        def choose_action_by_epsilon_greedy(values_of_all_possible_actions):
            """Action-Selection by epsilon-Greedy

            This function chooses the action as the epsilon greedy policy

            Args:
                values_of_all_possible_actions (list): A list of values of all actions in the
current state

            Returns:
                int: the index of the action recommended by the policy

            """
            logger.debug("Taking e-greedy action for action val-
ues"+str(values_of_all_possible_actions))
            prob_taking_best_action_only = 1 - self.epsilon
            prob_taking_any_random_action = self.epsilon / self.n_actions
            action_probability_vector = [prob_taking_any_random_action] *
self.n_actions
            exploitation_action_index = np.argmax(values_of_all_possible_actions)
            action_probability_vector[exploitation_action_index] +=
prob_taking_best_action_only
            chosen_action = np.random.choice(np.arange(self.n_actions),
p=action_probability_vector)
            return chosen_action
        return choose_action_by_epsilon_greedy
```

5.2.3 Code for the Q-Learning Agent's Class

```
class QLearning:
    """Q Learning Agent

    Class for training a Q Learning agent on any custom environment.

    Args:
        env (Object): An object instantiation of a custom env class like the GridWorld()
environment
        number_episodes (int): The maximum number of episodes to be executed for
training the agent
        discounting_factor (float): The discounting factor (gamma) used to discount
the future rewards to current step
        behavior_policy (str): The behavior policy chosen (as q learning is off policy).
Example "epsilon-greedy"
        epsilon (float): The value of epsilon, a parameters that defines the probability
of taking a random action
        learning_rate (float): The learning rate (alpha) used to update the q values in
each step

    Examples:
        q_agent = QLearning()

    """

    def __init__(self, env=GridWorldEnv(), number_episodes=500, discount-
ing_factor=0.9,
                behavior_policy="epsilon_greedy", epsilon=0.1, learning_rate=0.5):
        self.env = env
        self.n_states = env.get_statespace_len()
        self.n_actions = env.get_actionspace_len()
        self.stateDict = self.env.stateDict
        self.n_episodes = number_episodes
        self.gamma = discounting_factor
        self.alpha = learning_rate
        self.policy = BehaviorPolicy(n_actions=self.n_actions, poli-
cy_type=behavior_policy).getPolicy()
        self.policyParameter = epsilon
        self.episodes_completed = 0
        self.trainingStats_steps_in_each_episode = []
        self.trainingStats_rewards_in_each_episode = []
        self.q_table = np.zeros((self.n_states,self.n_actions),dtype = float)

    def train_agent(self):
        """Train the Q Learning Agent

        This is the main function to be called to start the training of the Q Learning
```

```
agent in the given environment
        and with the given parameters.

        Args:
            None

        Returns:
            list: list (int) of steps used in each training episode
            list: list (float) of rewards received in each training episode

        Examples:
            training_statistics = q_agent.train_agent()

        """
        logger.debug("Number of States: {}".format(str(self.n_states)))
        logger.debug("Number of Actions: {}".format(str(self.n_actions)))
        logger.debug("Initial Q Table: {}".format(str(self.q_table)))
        for episode in range(self.n_episodes):
            logger.debug("Starting episode {}".format(episode))
            self.start_new_episode()
        return self.trainingStats_steps_in_each_episode,
self.trainingStats_rewards_in_each_episode

    def start_new_episode(self):
        """Starts New Episode

        Function to Starts New Episode for training the agent. It also resets the envi-
ronment.

        Args:
            None

        Returns:
            None

        """
        current_state = self.env.reset()
        logger.debug("Env reset, state received: {}".format(current_state))
        cumulative_this_episode_reward = 0
        for iteration in count():
            current_state_index = self.stateDict.get(current_state)
            policy_defined_action = self.policy(self.q_table[current_state_index])
            next_state, reward, done, _ = self.env.step(policy_defined_action)
            next_state_index = self.stateDict.get(next_state)
            logger.debug("Action Taken in Episode {}, Iteration {}: next_state={},
reward={}, done={}".
                         format(self.episodes_completed, iteration, next_state, reward,
done))
            if done:

self.trainingStats_rewards_in_each_episode.append(cumulative_this_episode_rew
```

```
ard)
            self.trainingStats_steps_in_each_episode.append(iteration)
            self.episodes_completed += 1
            break
        cumulative_this_episode_reward += reward
        self.update_q_table(current_state_index, policy_defined_action, reward,
next_state_index)
        current_state = next_state

  def update_q_table(self, current_state_index, action, reward, next_state_index):
      """Update Q Table

      Function to update the value of the q table

      Args:
        current_state_index (int): Index of the current state
        action (int): Index of the action taken in the current state
        reward (float): The instantaneous reward received by the agent by taking
the action
        next_state_index (int): The index of the next state reached by taking the ac-
tion

      Returns:
        None

      """
      target_q = reward + self.gamma * np.max(self.q_table[next_state_index])
      current_q = self.q_table[current_state_index, action]
      q_difference = target_q - current_q
      q_update = self.alpha * q_difference
      self.q_table[current_state_index,action] += q_update

  def plot_statistics(self):
      """Plot Training Statistics

      Function to plot training statistics of the Q Learning agent's training. This func-
tion plots the dual axis plot,
      with the episode count on the x axis and the steps and rewards in each epi-
sode on the y axis.

      Args:
        None

      Returns:
        None

      Examples:
        q_agent.plot_statistics()

      """
```

```
        trainingStats_episodes = np.arange(len(self.train
ingStats_steps_in_each_episode))
        fig, ax1 = plt.subplots()
        ax1.set_xlabel('Episodes (e)')
        ax1.set_ylabel('Steps To Episode Completion', color="red")
        ax1.plot(trainingStats_episodes, self.trainingStats_steps_in_each_episode,
color="red")
        ax2 = ax1.twinx()
        ax2.set_ylabel('Reward in each Episode', color="blue")
        ax2.plot(trainingStats_episodes, self.trainingStats_rewards_in_each_episode,
color="blue")
        fig.tight_layout()
        plt.show()
```

5.2.4 Code for Testing the Agent Implementation (Main Function)

```
if __name__ =="__main__":
    """Main function

    A sample implementation of the above classes (BehaviorPolicy and
QLearning) for testing purpose.
    This function is executed when this file is run from the command propt di-
rectly or by selection.

    """

    logger.info("Q Learning - Creating the agent")
    q_agent = QLearning()
    logger.info("Q Learning - Training the agent")
    training_statistics = q_agent.train_agent()
    logger.info("Q Learning - Plotting training statistics")
    q_agent.plot_statistics()
```

5.2.5 Code for Custom Exceptions (File rl_exceptions.py)

```
class PolicyDoesNotExistException(Exception):
    pass
```

5.3 Training Statistics Plot

See Fig. 5.3.

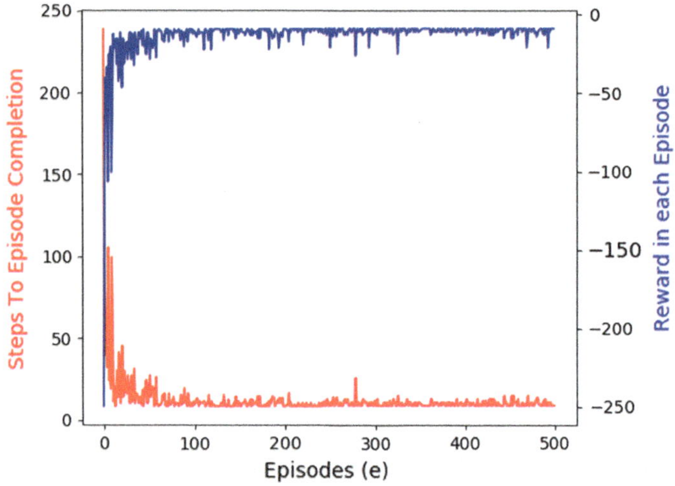

Fig. 5.3 Steps and cumulative rewards in each subsequent episode

Chapter 6
Introduction to Deep Learning

Enter the World of Modern Machine Learning

Abstract In this chapter we will cover the essentials of Deep Learning to the point required in this book. We will be discussing the basic architecture of deep learning network like an MLP-DNN and its internal working. Since many of the Reinforcement Learning algorithm work on game feeds have image/video as input states, we will also cover CNN, the deep learning networks for vision in this chapter.

6.1 Artificial Neurons—The Building Blocks of Deep Learning

A neural network is made up of many artificial neurons. Originally the artificial neuron is modeled on the working and constitution of a real biological neuron (Fig. 6.1). A biological neuron is connected to multiple other neurons and parts of the brains, from which it receives signals and based on these inputs and its internal processing of these inputs generates an output which may be used to trigger other neurons or travel through a nerve to activate some muscles.

Now, we will try to understand how an artificial neuron is modeled mathematically (Fig. 6.2). The input values $x_1, x_2, \ldots, x_n$ are provided to the neuron. We will represent this input as an input vector X, such that $X = \{x_1, x_2, \ldots, x_n\}$. These inputs could directly represent the raw data but should be properly scaled for effective working. At times normalization of the input features across a batch may be required (transforming into unit mean and unit variance) if the neuron is part of a large network having activation that may saturate the nonlinearities of the output in a deep network. The inputs are weighed with the weight vector. The weight vector has elements from $w_1, w_2, \ldots, w_n$. We would denote the weight vector as W, such that $W = \{w_1, w_2, \ldots, w_n\}$. It is this weight vector W that we need to train or in other words find the optimal values of the weight elements so as to obtain the best output. Here the best output is the one which produces the least error/loss between the actual and the predicted values across different samples in the data set. We call the actual output as y and the predicted output from the neuron as

M. Sewak, *Deep Reinforcement Learning*,
https://doi.org/10.1007/978-981-13-8285-7_6

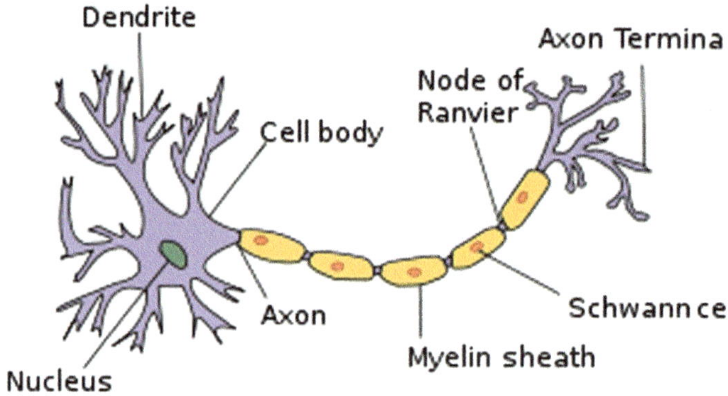

Fig. 6.1 A biological neuron (*Source* Wikipedia)

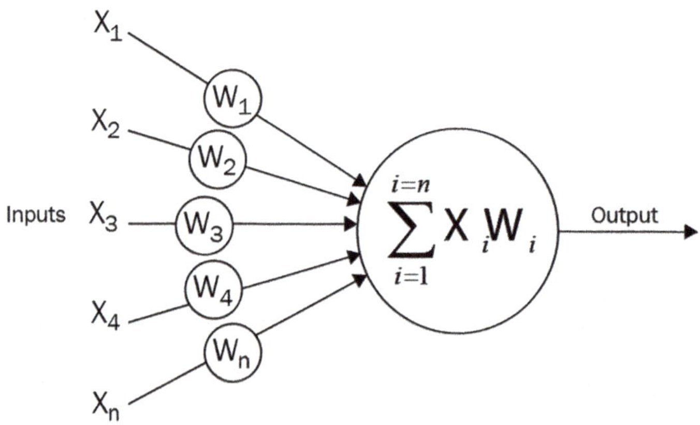

Fig. 6.2 Functioning of an artificial neuron (*Source* Sewak et al. Practical CNN)

$\hat{y}$. In addition to the weights, the neuron could have a bias (say b), which is a real number.

The processing inside the neuron is done using a function called the "Activation Function". The input to the activation function is called Z, which is equal to $w_1x_1 + w_2x_2 + \cdots + w_nx_n + b(W^TX + b)$. The output of the neuron could be represented as $\hat{y}$ = Activation (Z). A suitable activation function needs to be chosen for the purpose intended. The activation function also is influenced form the fact that whether the so trained predictions needs to be categorical (class probability) or continuous.

The above description corresponds to the forward pass on a single data element/row/tuple. We would require multiple data elements to train the weights of the network. During training, we try to minimize the losses over the complete training/

evaluation set of data. This loss is obtained by applying a loss function over the actual output (y) and the predicted output ($\hat{y}$). As in the case of activation function, there are multiple loss functions to choose from and one that best suits the application and input data could be chosen. Once training is complete, the neuron is ready for any prediction/estimation work.

6.2 Feed-Forward Deep Neural Networks (DNN)

An artificial neuron is seldom used alone. As in the case of brain, individual neuron in isolation are not very powerful, but still when millions of neurons combine, they empower the entire functioning of the brain. Similarly, instead of using an artificial neuron in isolation, these could be used to build an ***Artificial Neural Network (ANN)***. An artificial neural network, has three layers of neurons, first is called the input layer, next is called the hidden layer, and the last is called the output layer. The input layer has as many neurons as the elements in the input feature vector, thus providing a one-to-one mapping between the feature elements in the input and the neurons in the input layer. Similarly, the output layer has as many neurons as the number of outputs required. In case of a classification problem the number of outputs could be as many as the number of classes to be predicted from the network, whereas in the case of regression problem, the number of output could be one. The number of neurons in the hidden layer could be changed as per the application in hand, and it may also require some experience to arrive at the most optimal value for this number.

ANNs are known to be universal approximators. That means that given a proper activation function, they can approximate any continuous function on a compact subset of data with real numbered features. But despite these approximations, a function learnt in a single layer finds it challenging to model complex real-life data. That is where the ***Deep Neural Networks (DNN)*** come into play. These are also sometimes referred to as the ***Multilayer Perceptron (MLP)*** based deep neural network ***(MLP-DNN)***, where the term MLP indicates the type of underlying artificial neuron in these networks.

The Deep Neural Networks (DNNs) have more than one hidden layer of neurons (Fig. 6.3). Until sometime back, it was difficult to make a neural network very deep. This was due to a phenomenon called "***Vanishing Gradient***" in neural networks. In deep learning to train for the ideal weights for each layer, the error from the last layer onwards is propagated back layer-by-layer to update the weights of each layer starting from the last layer's weight. The weights of these layers are optimized/updated by taking the gradient of the loss function so that the weights could be updated in a direction such that the loss could be minimized. The losses could be minimized by moving to a minima in the loss function, and this minima could be reached by moving in the direction of the so computed gradients of the loss functions.

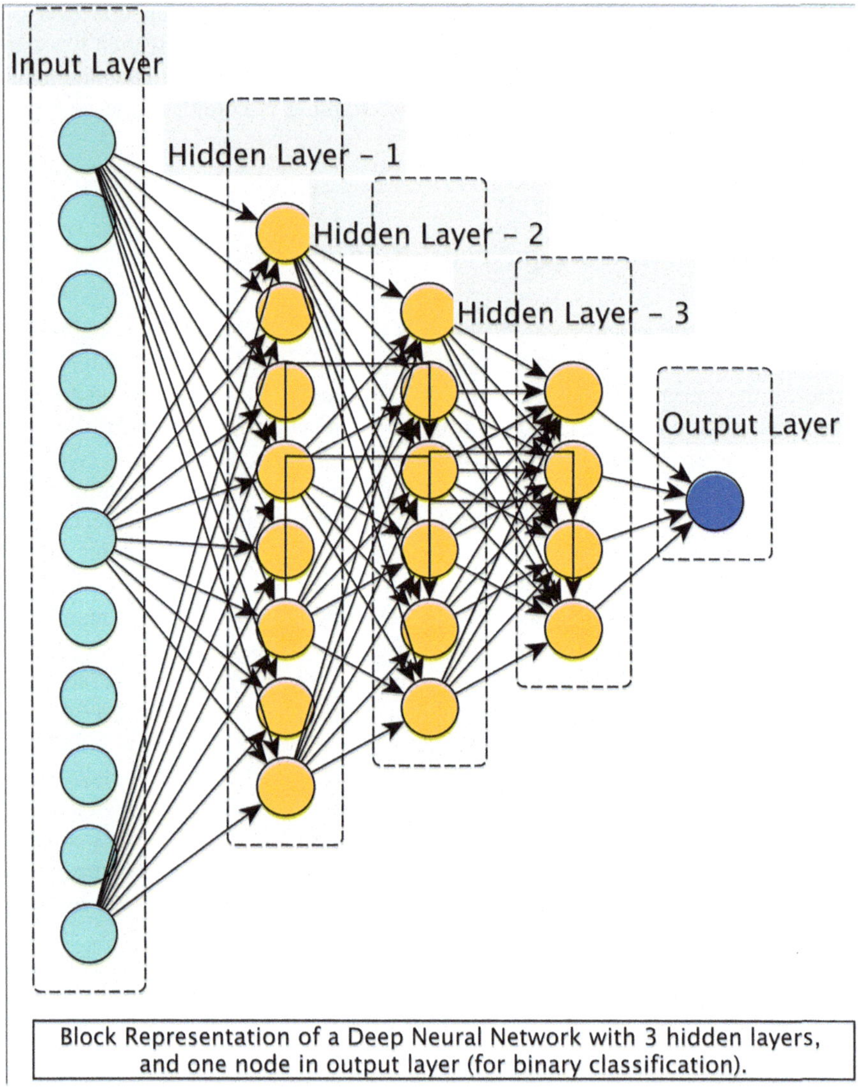

Fig. 6.3 A deep neural network (*Source* Sewak et al. Overview of deep learning architectures)

This method of training is called "***Backpropagation***". As the errors are propagated back in the network for finding the gradients and hence optimizing the network. The backpropagation is possible because of the chain rule of derivatives.

So the gradient between say layer $(n-2)$th and the last layer (nth layer) is the product of the gradient (partial differentiation) between the $(n-1)$th layer and the

(n)th layer and that between ($n - 2$)th layer and ($n - 1$)th layer. If the network is deep then to propagate the error to the starting layers requires long chain of gradient multiplications. The use of a suboptimal activation function like the ***Sigmoid*** and the ***Tanh*** (as was prevalent till sometime back), leads to a small absolute value ($\ll 1$) of the resulting gradient, which when continuously multiplied with a series of similarly small absolute values as in the chain rule leads to the gradient tending to zero. This is what is called as Vanishing Gradient effect.

Geoffrey Hinton, known as the father of Deep Learning proposed using a set of activation functions that overcame the vanishing gradient problem thus making it possible to make neural networks very deep. A deep neural networks could learn multiple functions in different layers, which when combined led to very powerful model, enabling capabilities to work with complex structured data and unstructured data like that representing vision and speech. Figure 6.3 here shows a similar Deep Neural Network with 3 hidden layers for predicting on structured data.

6.2.1 Feed-Forward Mechanism in Deep Neural Networks

In the earlier section on artificial neurons, we covered the activation of a single neuron. The activation in a ***Feed-Forward*** Deep Neural Network is similar. In a feed-forward network, the signal propagates only in the forward direction from neurons in one layer to the ones in subsequent layer. In a hidden layer of a DNN, all the neurons in a given layer have their inputs connected to all the neurons in the layer before (also known as the dense or fully connected layers), and their output connected to each of the neurons in the layer next. The neurons in the input are connected to the features in the input data with a one-one mapping (similar to flattening layer) and the output layer has either one node for regression or binary classification or as many numbers of nodes as the classes in data in case of multinomial classification. The output layer generally has a different activation function as compared to the input and the hidden layers.

Figure 6.4 illustrates the internal working of a single neuron in a hidden layer of a deep neural network during the forward pass. In a DNN all the neurons within a given layer could have different weights and hence all the weights of all the neurons in every layer need to be trained, thus making the training process very computationally involved. In a later section on Convolution Neural Network, we will learn about a mechanism in which the weights could be shared across neurons in a given layer, thus reducing the computational complexity of training for a network especially meant for working with spatially correlated input data like images.

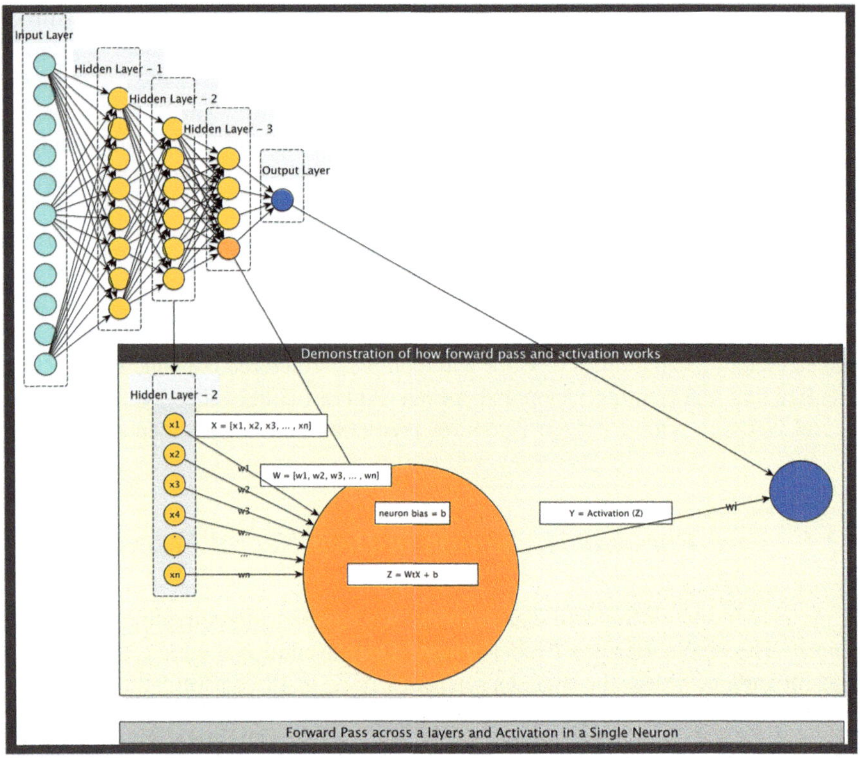

Fig. 6.4 Forward pass and activation of a neuron in a layer of DNN (*Source* Sewak et al. Overview of deep learning architectures)

6.3 Architectural Considerations in Deep Learning

The type and number of layers in a Deep Learning network depend upon the specific use of and type of Deep Learning network used. One of the types of layer, namely the convolutional layer is discussed in the next section. We will not discuss about the specifics of architecture requirements for convolutional or other special types of network here. In this section, we will discuss the common considerations shared across different types of deep learning networks.

6.3.1 Activation Functions in Deep Learning

As discussed earlier in the section on artificial neurons, the neurons require an activation function to convert the weighted input "Z" of the neuron to its output. Also, in the section on Deep Neural Network, we discussed how the change in the activation function led to the success of Deep Learning and helped neural networks to scale. Therefore, we will discuss about some of the popular activation functions used in deep learning briefly.

SoftMax Activation

In case of the output layer for a deep learning used for classification, the output layer needs to have as many numbers of neurons as the number of classes in the data. Except for binary classification which requires only one neuron and can use Sigmoid Activation, most of the multinomial classification based deep learning ends in output layer having SoftMax Activation. The SoftMax Activation layer provides the class probabilities for each class under consideration, scaled to the sum of all the class' class probability.

$$P(y = c|x) = \frac{e^{x^T w_j}}{\sum_{k=1}^{K} e^{x^T w_k}} \tag{6.1}$$

Linear and Identity Activation

Unlike classification problems, which requires class probabilities, the regression problems in the output layer may have just a single neuron and require as output from it a value that corresponding to the estimate of the variable in the output. Often this value is a scaled representation of the data in hand instead of an absolute representation of it. In the case of Reinforcement Learning, the estimation of Value functions is a very good example of where Linear activation should be used in the output layer. The identity activation is as given in Eq. (6.2). Addition of scaling and bias factor to Identity function gives the Linear activation function.

$$\text{Identity}(x) = \sum_i x_i w_i \tag{6.2}$$

Rectifier Linear Unit (ReLU) and Variants

The previous two activation functions were important for use in an output layer. Now we will discuss the activation functions for the input and hidden layers. We discussed about the vanishing gradient problem earlier in this chapter. The Rectifier Linear Unit or the ReLU as proposed by Geoffrey Hinton earlier is used to solve this problem. This function is as given in Eq. (6.3) below. Later on some of its variants like the Leaky ReLU, as in Eq. (6.4), Randomized Leaky ReLU and Parametrized Leaky ReLU were proposed by other researchers. Many of the applications, especially the CNNs that we will discuss next use some form of ReLU activation in the input/hidden layers.

$$ReLU(x) = \max(0, x) \tag{6.3}$$

$$\text{Leaky ReLU}(x) = \begin{cases} ax & \text{if } x < 0 \\ x & \text{if } x \geq 0 \end{cases} \tag{6.4}$$

Exponential Linear Unit (ELU)

Though the ReLU activation solves the vanishing gradient problem and some other problems related to inactive or dead neurons, it has one problem of its own, that is called the "***Mean Shift***". Since the activations in ReLU are predisposed to positive outputs, their mean is not zero centered, which cause a problem in Training the network. This problem could be solved by using "Batch Normalization" in between layers. We have discussed this enhancement of batch normalization in the context of DDPG later in this book. DDPG use CNNs which mostly use ReLU, and hence Batch Normalization is required. The other way of elevating the "mean shift" problem is by replacing the ReLU activation with the Exponential Linear Unit (ELU) activation in the input/hidden layers. ELU is given as Eq. (6.5) below.

$$ELU(x) = \begin{cases} x & \text{if } x > 0 \\ \alpha(\exp(x) - 1) & \text{if } x \leq 0 \end{cases} \tag{6.5}$$

6.3.2 *Loss Functions in Deep Learning*

While training a network we need to backpropagate the error to optimize the weights/hyperparameters in each layer. This loss/error is computed using a loss function, which takes the actual and predicted values as its input to output the loss. Loss functions generally fall in two categories namely the L2 loss (based on square of difference between the actual and predicted values), and the L1 loss (based on the absolute difference between the actual and predicted value). L2 based loss functions provide a continuously differentiable function and are easy to optimize mathematically, whereas the L1 loss is more robust and not effected much by some outliers.

Besides the difference related to absolute difference and squared difference between the actual predicted values (L1 and L2 losses), some other changes in the computation can help in different types of scenarios. A list of different types of loss functions along with their L1 and L2 variants (wherever applicable) are as given in the set of Eq. (6.6) below. The crossentropy loss for classification problems and L2 Mean Square Error—MSE for regression problems are very popular.

$$
\begin{aligned}
&\text{L2 loss: } \|y - o\|^2 \\
&\text{Expectation Loss: } \|y - p(o)\| \\
&\text{Regularized Expectation Loss: } \|y - \sigma(o)\|^2 \\
&\text{Hinge Loss: } \sum_j \max\left(0, \frac{1}{2} - \hat{y}_j o_j\right) \\
&\text{Squared Hinge Loss: } \sum_j \max\left(0, \frac{1}{2} - \hat{y}_j o_j\right)^2 \\
&\text{CrossEntropy Loss: } -\sum_j y_j \log \sigma(0)_j \\
&\text{Squared log Loss: } -\sum_j \left[y_j \log \sigma(0)_j\right]^2
\end{aligned}
\tag{6.6}
$$

6.3.3 Optimizers in Deep Learning

The role of the loss functions in deep learning is to select the ideal combination of different weights/hyperparameters that optimizes/minimizes the loss. This is theoretically done by finding the gradient of the loss function, and if the loss function is convex (have a curved minimum towards the origin) in nature then updating the weights towards the gradient of the loss function will take us to a minima (may even be local minima instead of a global minimum) of the loss function.

But practically this is not as simple in Deep Learning as compared to some of the machine learning problems. This is mainly because of the high cardinality of the parameter space (or the number of hyperparameters) and the complexity of the function that needs to be optimized. There are various issues encountered while training in the gradient hyperspace like getting stuck in a local minima, ravines and saddles that we can encounter during the optimization and a good optimizer, besides being efficient and fast need to be robust against these issues. Some of the popular optimizers used in deep learning are RMSProp, and ADAM (Adaptive Moment Estimation). We will not go through details of the internal working of these optimizers or cover other optimizers holistically in this book. Readers are encouraged to go through the papers in the references and related texts for a greater understanding of these.

6.4 Convolutional Neural Networks—Deep Learning for Vision

A Convolutional Neural Network (CNN) or ConvNet is a very special kind of multilayer deep neural network. CNN is designed to recognize visual patterns directly from images with minimal processing. A graphical representation of this network is shown in Fig. 6.5.

Unlike structured data which could be represented as a vector of features, image is usually represented is a 3-dimensional matrix of real number. These three dimensions represent the width, height, and color-channels (depth) in an image. The value in each of the cell of the input matrix across represents the intensity (or brightness) corresponding to the image-pixel at that position for the given color channel. So essentially an image is a function which converts a 2-dimensional pixel map of RGB intensity to a 3-dimensional image map with the individual color intensities expressed as the third dimension.

Images, especially with higher resolution, represents a complex data structure. If we try to use a feed-forward DNN similar to the one covered earlier in this book, to model and process such a high dimensional data, it would require a very large and very deep neural network, requiring training of billions of individual weights, making image processing a very erroneous and computationally complex task. Fortunately, images represent spatially correlated data. Which means that value of intensities of pixels which are co-located (in space) in an image are very similar (correlated) and the information across them changes gradually. This aspect could be used to reduce the processing load of a deep learning network for images. This is where a Convolutional Neural Network excels over its Multilayer Perceptron (MLP) based Deep Neural Network (MLP-DNN) counterpart.

The CNNs, like the MLP-DNNs, has an input layer. But this is not a single dimensional vector/tensor. Instead, the input mimics the dimensions of the image (with an additional dimension representing the sample index) so as to preserve the spatial integrity of the pixel data. Therefore, for a 3-dimensional image the CNN input is a 4-dimensional ***tensor*** (a multidimensional array), where the 3 dimensions of the tensor represents the 3 dimensions of the image and each dimension has the

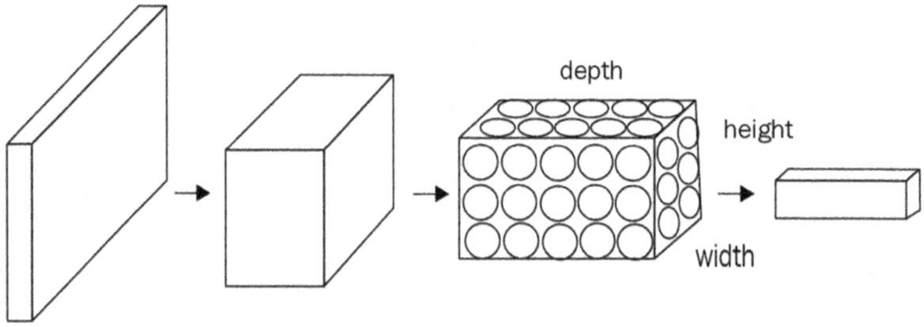

Fig. 6.5 Graphical representation of a CNN (*Source* Sewak et al. Practical CNN)

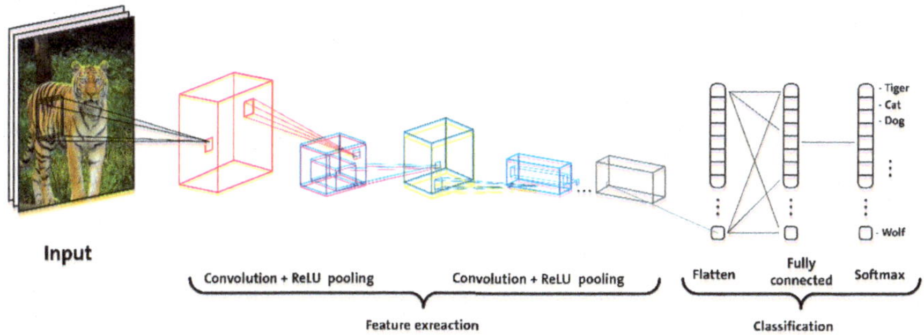

Fig. 6.6 An illustrative CNN architecture with convolutional, pooling and fully connected layers (*Source* Sewak et al. Practical CNN)

same cardinality as that of the image (width x height x color-channels), and the 4th dimension represents the image instance for training in mini-batch/batch environment. The images, especially the high resolution ones are often rescaled to reduce size and the color-channels adjusted (or reduced) for compatibility with the model.

Between the input layer and the output layer, there are 3 different types of hidden layers that make a convolution neural network. These are the convolutional layer, the pooling layer and the fully connected layer. A CNN network (Fig. 6.6) could have multiple instances of these types of layers arranged sequentially in a specific order such that the convolutional and pooling layers are mostly interleaved followed by all fully connected layers until the last fully connected layer connects to the output layer. A brief description of these layers is as follows.

6.4.1 Convolutional Layer

The term Convolutional in CNN refers to its usage of the Convolutional layer, which in turn is named after the convolution function in mathematics. In mathematics, convolution is a mathematical operation on two functions that produces a third function, that is the modified (convoluted) version of one of the original functions. The resulting function gives the integral of the pointwise multiplication of the two functions as a function of the magnitude that one of the original functions is translated. Convolutional layers actually use cross-correlations, which are very similar to this convolution operation.

The output from each convolution layer is a set of objects called feature maps, each map generated by a single kernel filter. Then the feature maps can be used to define a new input to the next layer. Each convolutional layer could have different number of kernel filters.

6.4.2 Pooling Layer

Since the images data is highly correlated, therefore for efficient computation these could be compressed in a way that retains the maximum information from it. This is also the case with each of the convolutional maps generated from each of the convolutional layer. Reducing the size of the input to any subsequent convolutional layer could reduce the computational load significantly, this is where the pooling layer helps.

The pooling layers are usually placed after the convolutional layers, for example, between two convolutional layers. A pooling layer extends into a m x n dimension subregion of the generated convolution map from the previous convolutional layer and then strides (using some stride value) across the width and depth of the convolutional map (the end landing can be adjusted using padding to ensure the m/n dimensions overlap the width/height dimension of the map) to cover the entire map. Then, a single representative value is selected from each stride, using either a max-pooling or an average pooling technique, thus reducing the output size to subsequently reduce the computational complexity of next convolutional layers. A pooling layer typically works on every input channel/convolutional-map independently. So, the output depth of the output from a pooling layer is the same as its input depth, and only the height and width of each convolutional map changes after pooling.

6.4.3 Flattened and Fully Connected Layers

Until now, as we discussed, the input layer and all the layers after that, though constituted of the same artificial neuron as that in the MLP-DNN, but differed widely in structure, composition and working from its MLP-DNN countered. This is because we required an efficient structure to generate good featured from spatially correlated data like that of an image. But after these special layers have done their work and we have converted the useful information in an image into a structured data format, similar to the input data of an MLP-DNN, we could convert them into a single dimension vector/tensor of data, similar to that of an input of a regular MLP-DNN. This work is done by the ***flattened layer***. The flattening/flattened layer has as many neurons as the total number of neurons in the multidimensional CNN/pooling layer just before it and provides a one-one mapping between the neurons in the previous layer to that of the flattened layer to change the structure of the data from a multidimensional one to a single dimensional one (except an additional dimension for the data sample index) as in the input layer of an MLP-DNN.

Connected to the flattening-layer, are a series of one or more ***fully connected layer (FC layer)***. These layers work exactly like the hidden layers of an MLP-DNN and have each of their neuron receiving input from every neuron in its previous layer. Also, each neuron's output in any FC layer is connected to all neuron's input in the layer next to it. This is the reason why it is called the Fully Connected layer. Finally, the last FC layer leads into the output layer, which in most cases could be a SoftMax activated classification layer with as many numbers of nodes as classes in the input image data. In the case of DQN and other Reinforcement Learning the last FC layer could be connected to a linearly activated single output node that predicts/estimates the value of a function (state-value, action-value, advantage).

At times when two different predictions are required as output but it is intended that they share all the underlying information of the input image (observation), then the FC connected layers after the flattening layer could start splitting into two different networks either just after the flattening layer or after some common FC layers after the flattening layer. Each of the two thus formed FC networks ends into their own individual output layer corresponding to the two different outputs that need to be predicted from this composite network. In the case of Reinforcement Leaning, the Dueling DQN network and some of the advanced Deep Learning based Actor-Critic models as we will subsequently study in a later chapter are a very good example of this type of architecture.

6.5 Summary

Deep Learning is a very important enhancement to Machine Learning. Deep Learning gives us the essential capability to develop human intelligence comparable systems for processing vision, speech and many other complex inputs. From empowering a modern object detector to enabling neural machine translations, Deep Learning is the way to go for modern machine learning. Deep Learning combined with Reinforcement Learning provides the essential ingredients to design Deep Reinforcement Learning Agents that takes us closer to the concept of general AI.

We discussed the working of a simple single artificial neuron like an MLP and how it converts its inputs to outputs using an activation function. We then discussed the networks of these neurons called the Artificial Neural Network having just a single hidden layer and also discussed the reasons why the ANNs could not become as popular then as what modern deep learning-based networks have become now.

We next discussed the solution to the vanishing gradient problem that has enabled the advancements in modern Deep Learning. We discussed how the deep learning networks especially the feed-forward types produce output in the forward pass and optimizes the loss function using a mechanism called the backpropagation. We also covered some important architectural considerations like the choices available for the activation function, loss function, and optimizers to design a powerful deep learning network.

Besides the MLP based DNN, we also covered CNNs in this chapter as many of the agents/algorithm covered in reinforcement learning literature works on game feeds and video data which requires processing of images using Deep Learning. We covered the essential differences between the architecture and structure of a CNN as compared to that of an MLP-DNN. We also covered the role of the convolutional layer, pooling layer (with mechanism for strides and padding), flattened layer and the FC layer in a CNN network. We also discussed how some advanced network could be designed to predict multiple functions (approximators) simultaneously as we will see have been implemented in the case of algorithms like the Dueling DQN and others that we will discuss later in this book.

Chapter 7
Implementation Resources

Training Environments and Agent Implementation Libraries

Abstract In this chapter, we will discuss some of the resources available for building one's own reinforcement learning agent easily, or implementing one with the least amount of code. We will also cover some standardized environment, platforms, and community boards against which one can evaluate their custom agent's performances on different types of reinforcement learning tasks and challenges.

7.1 You Are not Alone!

Often, the greatest predicament in starting a new journey, especially the one on a road less traveled by is a persistent apprehension that help might be difficult to get. Many enthusiasts even leave the journey midway after some struggle. But any journey could not just be completed by thinking about it, admiring the destination, or reading about the required skills. One has to take the physical steps to complete it. But often, the first step is the most difficult and also the most daunting. This book, besides covering sufficient theoretical and recent research developments in the area of Deep Reinforcement Learning, aspires to also be your aid in implementing these useful skills in your practical application. We want to assure the readers and let them know that they are not alone, and there is plenty of help and resources available to help them in their journey of implementing cutting-edge Deep Reinforcement Learning Algorithms hands-on.

Modern, Deep Reinforcement Learning is not a very old science, but it is maturing and gaining a lot of popularity recently. It may be very rewarding to hone a skill that many do not possess, but at the same time, it may be difficult to acquire decent level of proficiency in that skill, especially if there are not many standardized resources available to test your implementation, or to get fresh ideas from, or to reach out to a community when you have got stuck or need help. This chapter aims to cover some of the resources you may find helpful in both making your own agent based on a new idea, or experimenting with an already implemented agent on your custom environment, or testing the enhancements you made to an existing agent

M. Sewak, *Deep Reinforcement Learning*,
https://doi.org/10.1007/978-981-13-8285-7_7

against some standardized benchmarks. Since Reinforcement Learning is a very actively maturing practice, it is likely that these resources may get dated over time, and new ones arrive. Also, we may have missed out some good resources which others could have found useful. Therefore, the resources covered in this chapter are presented more from a reference perspective than from a comparison or endorsement perspective.

This chapter is divided into two subparts. The first covers some standardized reinforcement workbenches and environments that could be used to test our agents against, and the second deals in tools that we can use to code an agent easily. In this book, for most of the chapters, we will be code our own agents, mostly the hard way writing each line of code for enabling the agent. This is purposely done so as to make the readers comfortable with the idea of coding an agent even from scratch if they are required to. But if someone's primary purpose is just to focus on converting their application into a scenario where they could apply reinforcement learning, and not necessarily coding a new type of agent, then a lot of existing implementation of both reinforcement-specific mathematical libraries and complete implementation of the agents exists that could be utilized to quickly get started.

So ideally, there could be five different types of way that these resources could help the readers in their journey. First, is for the users who are just starting and want to get a feel of the state of the art in different types of implementations. For such users, there are available baseline agents for different standardized environments. Users can just download the code for the agent and the environment and test it. Second, is if someone would just like to enhance an existing model, may change the underlying deep learning model or apply some additional transformations, or optimizers, etc., and test how well their modifications perform, then there are community boards for some standardized environments which publish top scores, against which the user can run their custom agents and compare the scores. Third, is for the users who would like to implement a completely new agent and want some abstracted implementation of mathematical abstraction like automatic differentiation, etc., to ease their development. For these users, there are powerful and flexible libraries available that provide abstracted implementation of reinforcement-specific mathematics. Fourth, if the user has their own environment (or data) for their specific domain implementation, something like we have made in Chap. 3 earlier for the "Grid World" problem, and want a very fast and easy implementation of multiple types of standardized agents such that they can just run against their environment in not more than a few lines of codes, there are libraries available that provide such easy implementation of multiple standardized agents that could be tried. Fifth, if none of these standardized agents work on one's custom problem and someone want help and ideas from other researchers, who could develop new and advanced agents for one's specific problem, then it is also possible to submit a personal environment to the community which will not only help solve the problem with fresh ideas, but may even give rise to new stream of algorithms.

7.2 Standardized Training Environments and Platforms

In this section, we will discuss some of the initiatives, platforms, and environments available against which one can test their own agents, and provides a vibrant community of like-minded researchers to share ideas and implementations. Many of the new researches in the field of reinforcement learning have their genesis in making an agent that performs exceptionally well on one of these standardized problems as compared to the agents from an existing art on similar tasks/ environments. All the links for these resources are available in the "references" section.

7.2.1 OpenAI Universe and Retro

OpenAI Universe (deprecated giving way to Retro) and the related Gym initiatives are the most popular and interesting resources for any Reinforcement Learning researcher, professional, or enthusiast. OpenAI Universe is essentially a collection of custom environments that user can submit to the community OpenAI Gym being the interface to each of these submitted environments for training, similar to how a human would play a video game.

With Universe, even if one does not want to submit the actual code of the environment, the universe could spawn a docker container which captures the input controls and sends the video or other output to simulate a Reinforcement Learning environment.

OpenAI Universe is now deprecated in favor of Retro. Retro is a wrapper for video game emulator cores, and turn them into Gym environment using the Liberto API. It supports emulator for the popular video game systems like the Atari, Sega, Nintendo, and NEC.

7.2.2 OpenAI Gym

OpenAI Gym is by far the most popular toolkit for any Reinforcement Learning enthusiast and implementer. As discussed above, Gym offers an interface for different types of environments. These environment does not only include the video game environments the ones emulated using Universe or Retro but a wide variety of environments with different types of challenges and for different types of application domains.

Gym environments includes the environment groups like the ***Atari2600*** games for Atari video games, ***Box2D*** for six types of continuous control Box2D simulator games, ***Classic Control*** for five different types of environments on control discussed in classic reinforcement learning literature, ***MuJoCo*** for ten different types of continuous control tasks running in fast physics simulator, ***Robotics*** for eight different types of tasks simulator for a robotic hand, and ***ToyText*** for eight different types of simple text-based environments.

While discussing how to make one's custom environment, we have already discussed the specifications of a Gym standard environment and the important internal attributes and methods for a Gym environment. If your custom environment adheres to these guidelines, Gym also provides a "registry" mechanism so that you can register your environments inside the Gym library.

7.2.3 DeepMind Lab

Google's DeepMind Lab researches on two aspects of Reinforcement Learning. The first is on creating new agents, as we would have realized based on the so many recent literature that we have covered in this book itself. Another is on powerful environments for training agents. The DeepMind Lab provides an advanced 3D environment which could render scenes with advanced science fiction like rich visuals to train an agent. The different types of tasks in these environments aim to provide different challenges enabling training for General Artificial Intelligence.

7.2.4 DeepMind Control Suite

Like the OpenAI Gym, the DeepMind Control Suite provides the environment for training on continuous control environment of MuJoCo. This suite is written in Python and could be customized to include custom implementation of tasks based on MuJoCo physics engine.

7.2.5 Project Malmo by Microsoft

Malmo is a project by Microsoft to enable research in the field of Artificial Intelligence. It is based on Microsoft's popular video game Minecraft. It is written in Java, but the agents could be programmed in any popular language and run on multiple platforms including Windows, Linux, and Mac.

7.2.6 Garage

Sometime back "RLlab" used to be a very popular platform for reinforcement learning resources. It is now deprecated and no longer in active development.

Instead, it gave way to a project called Garage led by an alliance of researchers. Garage is based on Python 3.5 and offers both standardized agents and environments that are compatible with OpenAI. Garage also supports AWS EC2 cluster-based agent deployment.

7.3 Agent Development and Implementation Libraries

This section covers some of the libraries that could be helpful in either developing or implementing a Reinforcement Learning agent. Python is one of the most vibrant and popular programming platforms for Reinforcement Learning, so we would cover mostly Python-based libraries. But there are libraries in some others platforms also like the ones implemented in MATLAB (for example, Sutton's implementation) and Java (for example, BURLAP, and rl4j) that interested readers are encouraged to explore.

7.3.1 DeepMind's TRFL

In this book, we have directly worked on platforms like TensorFlow, or its wrappers like Keras for developing the code, but at times, the agents may become too involved mathematically and it may not be a good experience coding low-level mathematics directly. Under such scenario, a library that provides mathematical and other types of building blocks to aid the development of custom agents. TRFL (pronounced "Truffle") from DeepMind aims to do exactly that. TRFL is itself built over TensorFlow like some of the other libraries in this section.

7.3.2 OpenAI Baselines

OpenAI's Baselines project provides an implementation for some very good reinforcement learning agents for the research community for the purpose of not only providing an algorithmic baseline for many types of agent's implementation, but also to provide new implementation ideas.

7.3.3 Keras-RL

Built over Keras, which in turn is a high-level wrapper for TensorFlow and some other deep learning platforms, Keras-RL is a very popular and easy to use

Reinforcement Platform that provides a customizable instance of multiple types of agent and also an environment class that is compatible with OpenAI Gym's environment.

7.3.4 Coach (By Nervana Systems)

Coach aims to provide an exhaustive bundle of different types of reinforcement learning resources ranging from agents, environments, neural network architectures, policies, etc., which can be used, customized, and refined in isolation with others. Coach also provides capabilities to horizontally distribute the implementation of multiple agents, and also provides a dashboarding system to visualize the agent's performances.

7.3.5 RLlib

RLlib provides both the agent's implementations, as well as some primitives, to build one's own agents. It also provides preprocessors for both TensorFlow and Torch, as well as supports custom preprocessors. Besides distributed and multi-agents implementation like QMIX and IMPALA, it also offers distributed implementation of prioritized experience replay.

Chapter 8
Deep Q Network (DQN), Double DQN, and Dueling DQN

A Step Towards General Artificial Intelligence

Abstract In this chapter, we will take our first step towards Deep Learning based Reinforcement Learning. We will discuss the very popular Deep Q Networks and its very powerful variants like Double DQN and Dueling DQN. Extensive work has been done on these models and these models form the basis of some of the very popular applications like AlphaGo. We will also introduce the concept of General AI in this chapter and discuss how these models have been instrumental in inspiring hopes of achieving General AI through these Deep Reinforcement Learning model applications.

8.1 General Artificial Intelligence

Until now the Reinforcement Learning agents that we studied may be considered to be falling under the category of Artificial Intelligence agents. But is there something beyond Artificial Intelligence as well? In Chap. 1 while discussing what could be called as real "Intelligence", we stumbled upon the idea of "Human-Like" behavior as a benchmark for evaluating the degree of "Intelligence". Let's spend a moment discussing what a human's intelligence or human-like intelligence is capable of.

Taking our theme of games again for this discussion so that all the readers could relate. Ever since '80s many could have grown up playing video games like "Mario", then "Contra", and then could have explored some popular FPS (First

M. Sewak, *Deep Reinforcement Learning*,
https://doi.org/10.1007/978-981-13-8285-7_8

Person Shooter Categories) games like “Half-Life”, followed by “Arcade” genre games like “Counter-Strike”, and now addicted to the more popular “Battle-Royale” genre of games like “PUBG” and “Fortnite”. It may take someone a day or may be a week to gain a decent level of proficiency in any of these games, even while moving from one game to another, and at times even addicted to more than a single game simultaneously. As humans, even for the avid game enthusiasts, we do a lot of things besides playing games as well, and we could gain increasingly improved proficiency at all of them with the same “mind” and the “Intelligence” that we have. This concept where a single architecture and model of intelligence could be used to learn different seemingly even unrelated problems is called “General Artificial Intelligence”.

Until recently the Reinforcement Learning agents were handcrafted and tuned to perform individual and specific tasks. For example, we could have various scholars experimenting with innovative agents and mechanisms to get better in the game of “Backgammon”. Recently with AI gym and some other initiatives opening their platforms to Reinforcement Learning academician and enthusiast to work on standardized problems (in the form of exposed standard environments) and compare their results and enhancements for these problems with the community, there have been several papers and informal competitions where researchers and academicians try to propose innovative algorithms and other enhancements that could generate better scores/rewards in a specific environment of Reinforcement Learning. So essentially, from one evolution of agents to another, the Reinforcement Learning agents and algorithms that empower them keeps getting better in doing a particular task. These specific tasks may range from solving a particular environment of the “AI Gym” like playing “Backgammon” to balancing g “Cart-Pole” and others. But still, the concept of “General Artificial Intelligence” has remained evasive.

But things are changing now with the evolution of “Deep Reinforcement Learning”. As we discussed in an earlier chapter, “Deep Learning” has the capability of intelligently self-extracting important features from the data, without requiring human/SME involvement in handcrafting domain specific features for them. When we combine this ability with the self-acting capability of the Reinforcement Learning, we come closer to realizing the idea of “General Artificial Intelligence”.

8.2 An Introduction to “Google Deep Mind” and “AlphaGo”

Researchers at Google’s “Deep Mind” (“Deep Mind” was acquired by Google sometime back) developed this algorithm called as the Deep Q Network that we will be discussing in detail in this chapter. Researchers at Deep Mind combined the Q-Learning algorithm in Reinforcement Learning with the ideas in Deep Learning

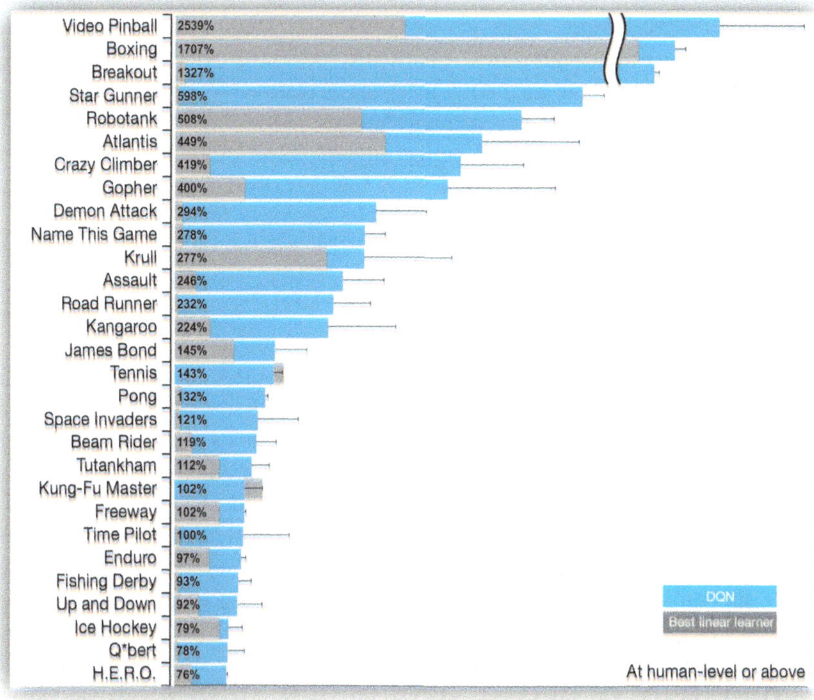

Fig. 8.1 Normalized performance of DQN versus human gamer (100*(DQN-score—random-play-score)/(human-score-random-play-score)) for games where DQN performed better than human gamer (*Ref* DQN-Nature-Paper)

to enable the concept of Deep Q Networks (DQN). A single DQN program could teach itself how to play 49 different games from the "Atari" titles ("Atari" used to be a very popular gaming console in the era of '80s and beyond. Atari had a lot of game titles with graphical interfaces.) and excel at most of them simultaneously, even defeating the best of human adversary's scores for most of these titles as shown in the Fig. 8.1.

Algorithms similar to the DQN also powered "Deep Mind"s' famous "AlphaGo" program. AlphaGo was the very first program that for the first time consistently and repeatedly defeated the best of human adversaries at the game of "Go". For the readers who are unfamiliar with the game of "Go", if they understand "Chess" then just for the sake of comparison, if they consider "Chess" as a game that challenges human intelligence, planning and strategizing capabilities to a significant level, then the game of "Go" is considered to take these challenges many notches higher. It is known that the number of possible moves in the game of "Go" is even more that the number of atoms in the entire universe, and hence it requires the best of human intelligence, thinking and planning capabilities to excel in this game.

With a Deep Reinforcement Learning agent, consistently defeating even the best of human adversaries in these games, and with many other similar Deep Reinforcement Learning algorithms consistently defeating their respective human adversaries in at least 49 other gaming instances as claimed in multiple comparative studies using standardized games/environments, we could assume that the advancements in the area of "Deep Reinforcement Learning" are leading us towards the concept of "General Artificial Intelligence" as described in the previous section.

8.3 The DQN Algorithm

The term "Deep" in the "Deep Q Networks" (DQN) refers to the use of "Deep" "Convolutional Neural Networks" (CNN) in the DQNs. Convolutional Neural Networks are deep learning architectures inspired by the way human's visual cortex area of the brain works to understand the images that the sensors (eyes) are receiving. We mentioned in Chap. 1, while discussing about state-formulations, that for image/visual inputs, the state could either be humanly abstracted or the agent could be made intelligent enough to make sense of these states. In the former case a separate human-defined algorithm to understand the objects in an image, their specific instances, and the position of each on the instance, is custom trained and then the agent is fed this simplified data as an input to form a simplified state for the agent to work on. In the latter case, we also discussed a way that we could enable our Reinforcement Learning agent itself to simplify the state of raw image pixels for it to draw intelligence from. We also discussed the role of CNN (Convolutional Neural Networks) briefly there.

CNNs contains layers of Convolutional Neurons, and within each layer there are different kernel (functions) that cover the image in different strides. A $3 \times N \times N$ dimensional input image (here $3 \times N \times N$ dimension input means an input image with 3 color channels, each of $N \times N$ pixels) when passed through a convolutional layer may produce multiple convolution maps of lower dimension as compared to input pixel size of $N \times N$ for each channel, but each resulting map use the same weight for the kernels. Since the weights for the kernels in a layer remains the same so only a single vector needs to be optimized hence for bringing out the key features in an image a CNN is more efficient for working on images than any a DNN (MLP based Deep Neural Network) counterpart delivering similar accuracies. But the output of a CNN is a multidimensional tensor, which is not effective for feeding into any subsequent classification or regression (value estimation) model. Therefore, the last convolutional layer of a CNN is connected to one or more flat layers (which are similar to the hidden layer in a DNN network) before it is fed into (mostly) a "SoftMax" activation layer for classification or (generally) a "Linear" activation layer for regression. The "SoftMax" activation layer produces the class-probabilities for each class for which classification is required and choosing the output class with the highest class-probability (argmax) determines the best action.

The DQN network contains the CNN network as described above. The specific DQN that we mentioned in the earlier section on the introduction to General Artificial Intelligence, that performed well on 49 Atari titles simultaneously, used an architecture having a CNN with 2 convolutional layers, followed by two fully connected layers, terminating into an 18 class "SoftMax" classification. These 18 classes represent the 18 actions possible from an Atari controller (Atari had a single 8-direction joystick, and just one button for all the games) that the game input could act on. These 18 classes (as used in the specific DQN by DeepMind for Atari) are Do-Nothing (i.e., don't do anything), then 8-classes representing the 8 directions of the joystick (Move-Straight-Up, Move-Diagonal-Right-UP, Move-Straight-Right, Move-Diagonal-Right-Down, Move-Straight-Down, Move-Diagonal-Left-Down, Move-Straight-Left, Move-Diagonal-Left-Up), Press-Button (alone without moving), then another 8 actions corresponding to simultaneously pressing the button and making one of the joystick-movement.

With every instance that the agent is required to act (such action instances may not exactly correspond with every step one to one as we will discuss later), the agent chooses one of the actions (note that one of the actions is Do-Nothing as well). Figure 8.2 shows the illustrative architecture of the Deep Learning model culminating into the required 18 action classes.

The motivation for this book enables the user to make their own real-life RL agent. Since the Atari based agent might not have the most suitable model for some of the other applications, we may have to change the CNN configurations and the structure of the output layer for the specific use cases and domain that we would be implementing it for.

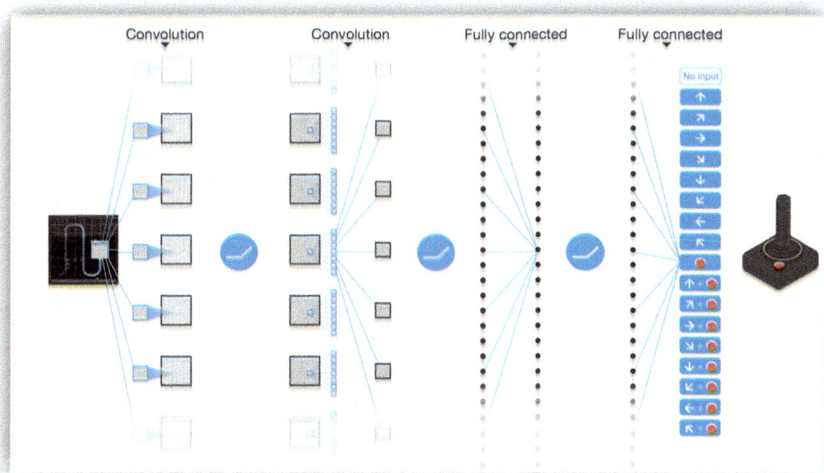

Fig. 8.2 DQN CNN schematic (*Ref* DQN-Nature-Paper)

Atari gives a 60 FPS video output. It means that every second the game generates and displays/sends 60 images as an input. This is the signal that we could use as an input to our agent as states. One drawback of using raw image pixels and working directly with all consecutive frames at such high frame rate to train a Q-Learning-Network is that the training of the Q-Learning-Network may not be very stable. Not only the training might take a lot of time to converge, but at times instead of converging the loss function may actually diverge or get stuck into a hunting loop. To overcome these challenges while working on high frame rate, high-dimension, correlated image data the DQN had to implement the following three enhancements to ensure descent convergence and practical applicability.

8.3.1 Experience Replay

It is important to understand the concept of "***Experience Trail***", before we discuss "***Experience Replay***" enhancement. In Chap. 4, while discussing Q-Learning, we referred to the quadruple of (state, action, reward, next-state) as an "***experience***" data instance to train the Q-Learning's Action-Value/Q function. In "***Experience Trail***", the first term "experience" is exactly the same experience instance, that is a tuple of (state, action, reward, next-state) or (s, a, r, s′) in abbreviated form. Now let us discuss the problem of convergence as we briefly touched upon in the earlier section in greater detail to understand why the "**trail**" of such experience instances is required.

While using graphical feed as input to our reinforcement learning agent we get numerous frames of raw pixels in quick succession. Also, since these frames are in sequence, there would be very high correlation amongst such consecutive input frames. The update that occurs to the Q function values during the training process is very sensitive to the number of times the algorithm encounters a particular experience instance. In the basic Q-Learning algorithm, the action-values/Q Function is updated in every step. Though we will understand in the later subsection that in DQN this shortcoming is also enhanced slightly for the same reason. Consecutively seeing similar experience instances very frequently, will result in the weights of the Q network updated in a very specific direction. Such biases in training may lead to the formation local "ravines" in the loss function's hyperparameter space. Such "ravines" are very difficult to maneuver by simple optimization algorithms and hence such biases from the ingestion of multiple similar experience instances slows down or hinders the optimization of the cost function. It may be difficult to optimize such a loss function under these challenges, and the training of such a Q network may warrant the use of very complex optimizers.

Therefore, in "Experience Trail" the "experience-tuples" are not directly used in the order that they are being generated from the source system (in our case the Atari processor) to train the agent. Instead, all the experience instance tuples as generated from the source system are collected in a memory-buffer (mostly having fixed size of memory). This memory-buffer is updated with new experience instances as they are received as a queue, i.e., in a first-in, first-out order. So as soon as the memory-buffer reaches its limit, the oldest experience instances are deleted to make way for the latest experience instances. From this pool/buffer of experience instances, the "experience-tuples" are picked randomly to train the agent. This process is known as "Experience Replay".

"Experience Replay" not only solves the problems arising from the use of *concurrent-sequence* of experiences for training the Q network as we discussed earlier but also limits the *similar-frames* problem as only a few frames from a concurrent sequence are likely to be picked in a random draw.

8.3.1.1 Prioritized Experience Replay

"***Prioritized Experience Replay***" is an enhancement to the Experience Replay mechanism used in the base/original DQN algorithm that outperformed humans in 49 of Atari games. A DQN with Prioritized Experience Replay was able to outperform the original DQN with "***uniform***" Experience Replay in 41 of the 49 games where the original DQN outperformed human gamers.

In the basic "Experience Replay" enhancement that we discussed earlier, we learnt that "***all***" the experience instances are stored in the experience train in the same order that they are received. Such buffered experience instances are "***randomly***" selected for training. As the name suggests, in Prioritized Experience Replay, we would like to use some sort of priority in this experience replay process.

There are two mode of prioritizing experience instances from the experience trail. The first mode to "prioritize" which input experience instances received from the source system are stored in the experience trail from where these could be picked at random for "***replay***". Alternatively, the second mode is to buffer all the experience instances as they are being generated from the source system and then to prioritize which specific experience instances are selected to be replayed from this unprioritized storage.

In the "Prioritized Experience Replay" enhancement we chose to prioritize using the second mode. Once we have determined the prioritization mode as that of prioritized replaying from an unprioritized experience trail (storage), the second decision aspect is to determine the specific criteria for prioritizing the experience instance for replay. For this, the "Prioritized Experience Replay" algorithm uses the Temporal Difference error "δ" as the criteria to prioritize specific experience instance for replay in subsequent iterations of the training. So, unlike the original ("uniform") Experience Replay method, where every experience instance ((s, a, r, s′) tuple) has a uniform probability to be selected for training, the Prioritized Experience Replay variant gives relatively higher priority to samples that produced a larger TD error "δ".

So, the probability of selection of a given experience tuple is given as

$$p_i = |\delta_i| + e \tag{8.1}$$

where e is an added constant to avoid zero probability for any available sample in the experience trail. One problem with the above formulation is that though such a prioritization is good when the training is in initial phases, later on when the agent has predominantly learnt from some specific experiences repeatedly, it develops biases towards such experience instances. This leads to over-fitting of the agent's model and associated nuances. To avoid this pitfall in the above equation is modified slightly and a stochastic formulation is applied to it to add some randomness and avoid a completely greedy solution. This is done as below

$$P_{(i)} = \frac{p_i^{\alpha}}{\sum_k p_k^{\alpha}} \tag{8.2}$$

In the equation above (Eq. 8.2), the process for determining the probability of sampling a particular experience instance could be controlled. We could have a sampling probability on a particular experience instance as one generated from a sampling process that ranges from a process that is purely random to a process that is purely greedy to anything in between. This control is defined is determined to be a parameter that is the ratio of the priority of transition as defined in the earlier equation, normalized over all transition priorities, each raised to the power "α". Here "α" is a constant that determines the greediness of the sampling process. α could be set to any value between 0 and 1. A process with $\alpha = 0$ denotes no prioritization and gives an effect of uniform sampling, leading to results similar to that of the original unprioritized Experience Replay algorithm. Conversely, a process with $\alpha = 1$, will be similar to the extreme prioritized experience replay for samples with large TD errors throughout the training and associated biases as we discussed earlier.

8.3.1.2 Skipping Frames

A further enhancement for the problem caused because of the bias due to training with frequent and multiple consecutive similar frames as discussed above is that we do not pick all 60 the frames generated per second for the purpose of training. In the DQN trained for "Atari" 4 consecutive frames were combined to make the data pertaining to one state. This also reduces computational cost, without losing much information. Assuming that the games are made for human reactable time between key events, there would be a lot of correlation in every frame if the feed is at 60 fps. The number 4 frames every 60 is not very hard. In practical application in one's own domain, this number could be adjusted depending upon the requirement of the specific use case and the input frequency and correlation amongst consecutive frames.

8.3.2 Additional Target Q Network

One major change that the Deep Q Networks made over that of the basic Q Learning algorithm, is that of the introduction of a new "Target-Q-Network". While discussing Q-Leaning in Chap. 4, we referred to the term "(r + γ $\max_{a'}(Q_{(s', a')})$" in the equation for the Q Function update (Eq. (4.7)) as the "***target***". Given below is the complete equation for reference.

$$Q_{(s,a)} = (1 - \alpha)Q_{(s,a)} + \alpha(r + \gamma \max_{a'} Q_{(s',a')}) \tag{4.7}$$

So essentially in this equation the Q Function Q (s, a) is being referred twice and each of this reference is for different purposes. The first reference, i.e., $(1 - \alpha)\boldsymbol{Q}_{(s,\,a)}$ is mainly to retrieve the present state-action value so as to update its value (use of Q as in: $\boldsymbol{Q}_{(s,\,a)} = (1 - \alpha)\,\boldsymbol{Q}_{(s,\,a)} + \cdots$), and the second is to get the "***target***" value for the *subsequent* Q value for the next state-action (i.e., Q as in: r + γ max $_{a'}(\boldsymbol{Q}_{(s',\,a')})$. Though in the basic Q Learning algorithms both these Q Functions/Networks (or Q-Tables in case of a tabular Q-Learning approach) were same, it may not necessarily be so always.

In DQN the "***target***" Q network is different from the one that is being continuously updated in every step. This is done to overcome the drawbacks related to using the same Q Network for both continuous updates and for referring the target values. These drawbacks are majorly because of two reasons. The first as we highlighted earlier in the section of basic DQN, i.e., related to issues related delayed/suboptimal convergence in case of too-frequent, and highly correlated data for training. It could be noted that if the targets for training are coming from the same network they are bound to be correlated. Another reason is that it is not a good idea to use the target values from the same function to correct its own update. This is because when we use the same function to update its own estimates then sometimes it may lead to "***unstable***" target function.

Thus, it is found that using two different Q networks for these two different purposes enhances the stability of the Q network. But if a target action-value is required for the training, and if this target value does not update at all after initialization (which as we learnt could even be all zeros in case of Q Learning as it is an off-policy algorithm), then the "active" (actively updated/estimated) network could not be updated effectively. Therefore, the "target" Q Network is synced and updated with the actively updated Q Network' once every "***c***" number of steps. For the "Atari" problem, the value of "c" was fixed to 1000 steps.

8.3.3 Clipping Rewards and Penalties

Although this is not a very significant change while considering training and deployment for a single application, when considered in perspective of developing a system for "General Artificial Intelligence" the mechanism for accumulating rewards and penalties needs to be balanced. Different games (and real-domain skills) may have a different scoring system. Some games may offer a relatively lower absolute score for even a very challenging task, and others may be too generous in giving absolute rewards (scores). For example, in a game like "Mario", it is easy to get score in the range of hundreds of thousands of points; whereas in a game like "Pong" the player gets just a single point for defending an entire game.

Since Reinforcement Learning and especially the idea of "General Artificial Intelligence" has spawned from the human mind's ability to learn different skills, let us analyze the constitution of our own body to understand this concept better. Human's and for that matter most of the animals learn different habits and stereotypes by a process called reinforcement, which is also the basis of Reinforcement Learning that we have modeled for the machines to become adept at different skills. Since Reinforcement Learning requires a reward to "reinforce" any behavior so our mind should also work on receiving some rewards to reinforce and learn any behavior. In humans, the sense of reward is achieved by the release of a chemical called "dopamine", which reinforces a particular behavior that acted as a trigger to this behavior. If you are curious why you get so addicted to your mobile and want to click on every notification, social media feeds and shopping apps to the point that they start controlling you instead of you controlling them, you can blame the dopamine response for the same. Similarly, the addictions to substances ranging from drugs to sugary foods are governed by the reinforcement caused by the release of dopamine which serves as the reward mechanism to make us reinforce certain behaviors.

Since the body's dopamine-producing capability is limited, so an automatic scaling and clipping effect is realized across different activities we do. When this dopamine response system is altered externally/chemically for example by consumption of drugs, it does lead to withdrawal from other activities and bring meaning to life, leading to an unstable behavior and outcome.

To achieve a similar reward/penalty scaling and clipping effects in the DQN as used in the "Atari" game, all the rewards across all games were fixed to $+1$ and all penalties to -1. Since rewards are key to reinforcement training and vary widely across applications, readers are encouraged to device their own scaling and clipping techniques for their respective use cases and domains.

8.4 Double DQN

In situations like the ones that warrant the application of Deep Reinforcement Learning, generally the state-space and state-size may be extremely large, and it may take a lot of time for the agent to learn sufficient information about the environment and ascertain which state/actions may lead to the most optimal instantaneous or total rewards. Under these conditions, the exploration opportunities may be overwhelmed (especially in the case of constant epsilon-based algorithms) and the agent may get stuck to exploiting the explored and estimated state-action combinations that have relatively higher values even if not the highest values possible but not yet explored. This may lead to the "*overestimation of Q Values*" for some of these combinations of state-actions leading to suboptimal training.

In the earlier section, we discussed about splitting the Q Network into two different Q Networks, one being the online/active and the other being the target Q Network whose values are used as a reference. We also discussed that the target Q network is not updated very frequently and instead is updated only after a certain number of steps. The above highlighted overestimation problem may become even more significant if the actions are taken on the basis of a Q network (Target Q-network) whose values are not even frequently updated (since these are updates from the active "*online*" Q Network after every thousands or so of steps).

We also discussed in the earlier section why it was important to split the Q Network into the active and the target Q Networks and the benefits of a dedicated target Q Network. So, we would like to continue using the "Target" Q Network as it offers better and more stable target values for the update. To combine the best of both worlds, the "***Double DQN***" algorithms propose to select the action on the basis of the "Online" Q Network but to use the values of the target state-action value corresponding to this particular state-action from the "Target" Q Network.

So, in Double DQN, in every step, the value of all action-value combinations for all possible actions in the given state is read from the "online" Q Network which is being updated continuously. Then an argmax is taken over all the state-action values of such possible actions, and whichever state-action combination value maximizes the value, that particular action is selected. But to update the "Online" Q Network the (target) corresponding value of such selected state-action combination is taken from the "target" Q Network (which is updated intermittently). Double DQN algorithm suggests and by doing so we could simultaneously overcome both the "overestimation" problem of Q Values while also avoiding the instability in the target values.

8.5 Dueling DQN

Until now the Deep Learning Models (here the term models refer to its usage as in supervised learning models as opposed to the MDP model) that we covered, were "Sequential" architectures (sequential architectures and sequential models may have different meaning in deep learning). In these models, all the neurons in any particular layer could be connected only to the neurons in just one layer before and one layer after their own layer. In other words, no branches or loops existed in these model architectures.

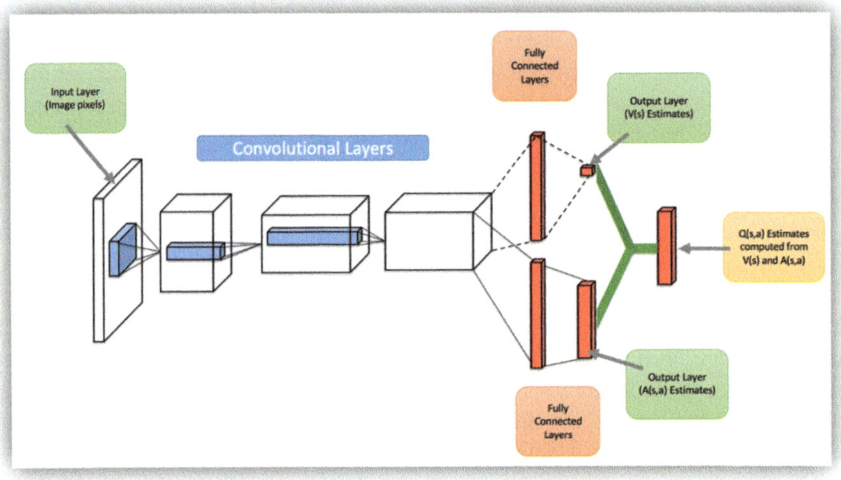

Fig. 8.3 Schematic—Dueling Q network

Though both DQN and Double DQN had two Q networks, but there was only one deep learning model and the other (target) network values was a periodic copy of the active (online) network's values. In Dueling DQN we have a non-sequential architecture of deep learning in which, after the convolutional layers, the model layers branches into two different streams (subnetworks), each having their own fully connected layer and output layers. The first of these two branches/networks are corresponding to that of the Value function which is used to "estimate" the value of a given state, and has a single node in its output layer. The second branch/network is called the "***Advantage***" network, and it computes the value of the "*advantage*" of taking a particular action over the base value of being in the current state (Fig. 8.3).

But the Q Function in Dueling DQN, still represents Q Function in any atypical Q Learning algorithm and thus the Dueling DQN algorithm should work in the same way conceptually as how the atypical Q Learning algorithm works by estimating the absolute action values or Q estimates. So somehow, we need to estimate the action-value/Q estimates as well. Remember action-value is the absolute value of taking a given action in a given state. So, if we could combine (add) the output of the state's base value (first network/branch) and the ***incremental*** "advantage" values of the actions from the second ("advantage") network/branch then we could essentially estimate the action-value or are Q Values as required in Q Learning. This could be represented mathematically as below

$$Q_{(s,a;\theta,\alpha,\beta)} = V_{(s;\theta,\beta)} + \left(A_{(s,a;\theta,\alpha)} - \max_{a' \in |A|} A_{(s,a';\theta,\alpha)}\right) \quad (8.3)$$

In the Eq. (8.3), above the terms Q, V, s, a, a′ have the same consistent meaning as we discussed earlier in this book. Additionally, the term "***A***" denotes the advantage value. "***θ***" represents the parameter vector of the convolutional layer which is common to both the "Value" network and the "Advantage" network. "***α***" represents the parameter vector of the "Advantage" network and "***β***" represents the parameter vector of the "State-Value" function. Since we have entered the domain of function approximators, therefore the values of any network are denoted with respect to the parameters of the "***estimating***" network to distinguish between the values/estimates of the same variable estimated from multiple different estimating functions.

The equation in simple terms mean that the Q value (the subscripts θ, α, β to the Q here indicates that the Q estimates here are as computed from the estimating model which has three series of parameters or is a function of θ, α, β) for a given state-action combination is equal to the value of that state or absolute utility of being in that state as estimated from the state-value (V) network (the subscripts θ, β of V in the equation denotes that the state values are coming from an estimation function that has parameters θ, β), plus the incremental value or the "advantage" (the subscripts θ, α of A in the equation denotes that the advantage is derived from an estimation function that has parameters θ, α) of taking that action in that state. The last part of the equation is to provide the necessary corrections to provide "***identifiability***".

Let us spend a moment to understand the "***identifiability***" part in greater details. The Eq. (8.3), from the simple explanation we discussed above which is also intuitive could have been as simple as below

$$Q_{(s,a;\theta,\alpha,\beta)} = V_{(s;\theta,\beta)} + A_{(s,a;\theta,\alpha)} \tag{8.4}$$

But the problem with this simple construct as in Eq. (8.4) above is that though we could get the value of Q (action values), provided the values of S and A are given, but the converse in not true. That is, we could not "*uniquely*" recover the values of S, A from a given value of Q. This is called "***unidentifiability***". The last part of the equation (in Eq. 8.1) solves this "***unidentifiability***" problem by providing "*forward-mapping*".

A better modification of Eq. (8.3) is provided below as Eq. (8.5). In Eq. (8.5) the last part as provided in the Eq. (8.3) is slightly modified. Though by subtracting a constant the values get slightly off-targeted, that does not affect the learning much as the value comparison is still intact. Moreover, the equation in this form adds to the stability of the optimization.

$$Q_{(s,a;\theta,\alpha,\beta)} = V_{(s;\theta,\beta)} + \left(A_{(s,a;\theta,\alpha)} - \frac{1}{|A|}\sum_{a} A_{(s,a;\theta,\alpha)}\right) \tag{8.5}$$

8.6 Summary

General Artificial Intelligence or the idea of a single algorithm or system learning and excelling at multiple seemingly different tasks simultaneously have been the ultimate goal of Artificial Intelligence. General AI is a step towards enabling machines and agents to reach human level intelligence of adapting to different scenarios by learning new skills.

The DQN paper by Deep Mind claims to making some progress in the creating a system that could learn the essential skills to the requirements of 47 different types of Atari games, even surpassing the best of the human adversaries' scores in many of these games.

Though DQN is very potent and could surpass human-level performance in many games as claimed by its success on standardized Atari environments, it has its own shortcomings. There are many enhancements that could be employed to overcome these shortcomings. The Double DQN and Dueling DQN, both use 2 different Q Networks instead of a single Q network as used in DQN and aims at overcoming the shortcomings of DQN though in slightly different manner.

The Dueling DQN also brings the concept of advantage or the incrementally higher utility of taking an action over the base state's absolute value. The concept of advantage will be explored further in some of the other algorithms we will cover in this book.

Chapter 9
Double DQN in Code

Coding the DDQN with Epsilon-Decay Behavior Policy

Abstract In this chapter, we will implement the Double DQN (DDQN) agent in code. As compared to a conventional DQN, the DDQN agent is more stable as it uses a dedicated target network which remains relatively stable. We also put into practice the concepts of MLP-DNN we learnt in Chap. 6 and have used Keras and TensorFlow for our deep learning models. We have also used the OpenAI gym for instantiating standardized environments to train and test out agents. We use the CartPole environment from the gym for training our model.

9.1 Project Structure and Dependencies

Like that of the Q Learning code covered in Chap. 5, we continue to use the same virtual environment (DRL) based on Python 3.6.5 and PyCharm IDE.

The additional requirements in this chapter are that of deep learning-based dependencies and OpenAI gym's environments (Fig. 9.1). For implementing deep learning models, we have used the Keras wrapper over TensorFlow backend. From gym we are using the "CartPole-v1" environment, but readers are encouraged to try other environments as well, and this is as simple as changing this name in the "environment" parameter.

The deep learning models are implemented in a very modular manner, and the network configuration of the implemented MLP-DNN architecture could change with respect to the number of hidden layers and the number of neurons in each hidden layer.

As compared to the Q Learning code covered in Chap. 5, here to isolate the concerns and make the code more modular, we have separated the Behavior Policy class in a separate module. Also, we have implemented an additional policy the "epsilon-decay" policy for selecting the actions. This policy is also implemented in the behavior policy class. Users are encouraged to also run the code with the previously implemented "epsilon-greedy" policy and compare the results and time.

Besides the behavior policy, we now have another module for the Experience Replay Buffer class. This is the base level class from which all the other

M. Sewak, *Deep Reinforcement Learning*,
https://doi.org/10.1007/978-981-13-8285-7_9

Fig. 9.1 Requirements.txt

requirements.txt

```
#runtime = Python3.6.5

numpy
matplotlib
tensorflow
keras
gym
```

implementations of different types of experiences replay memory buffers could be extended. In this code, we have implemented a Deque-based memory buffer which stores the experiences sequentially and has a fixed capacity. Whenever a new experience comes after the buffer is full, the oldest experience is deleted to make way for the new experience. The required number of experiences (batch-size) is retrieved for replay memory buffer randomly. Readers are encouraged to experiment with implementing other priority buffer types and compare the results.

Last, we have added two more custom exceptions to make the code easier to debug and experiment with for the readers. With these changes and enhancements, the project folder structure looks as in Fig. 9.2.

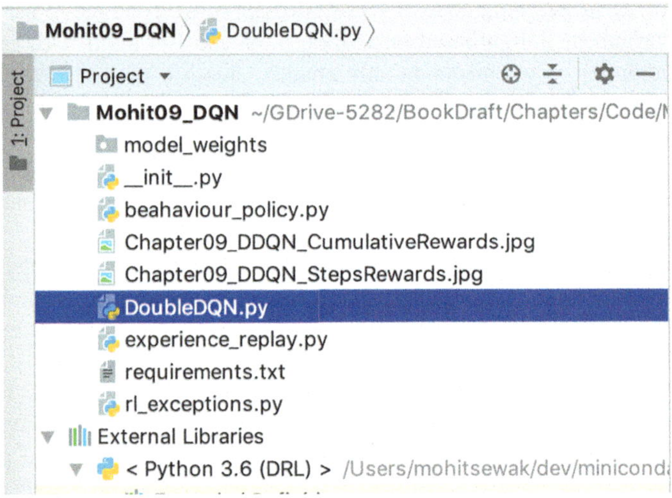

Fig. 9.2 Project structure for the DDQN project

9.2 Code for the Double DQN Agent (File: DoubleDQN.py)

```
""" DQN in Code - BehaviorPolicy

DQN Code as in the book Deep Reinforcement Learning, Chapter
9.

Runtime: Python 3.6.5
Dependencies: numpy, matplotlib, tensorflow (/ tensorflow-
gpu), keras
DocStrings: GoogleStyle

Author : Mohit Sewak (p20150023@goa-bits-pilani.ac.in)

"""

# make the general imports. Many of these libraries come
bundled in miniconda/ base-python and hence are excluded from
# requirements.txt
import logging
import numpy as np
from itertools import count
import matplotlib.pyplot as plt
import time
import os
# Make the imports from Keras for making Deep Learning model.
Keras is a wrapper to some of the popular deeplearning
# libraries like tensorflow, theano, mnist. One of these
needs to be installed for keras to work. We are using
# tensorflow as is indicated in requirements.txt
from keras.models import Sequential
from keras.layers import Dense
from keras.optimizers import Adam
from keras.losses import mean_squared_error
# We will require an environment for the agent to work. This
can be provided from an external code take instantiates
# the agent, and is not required here in that case. We can
use both a custom environment or one from OpenAI gym. A
# custom environment may require some changes in the
n_states, and n_action parameters to be compatible
import gym
# Last we import other cutom dependencies that we have coded
in external modules to make this code small, simple
# to understand, easy to maintain, and modular. For example
we use the epsilon_decay policy instead of epsilon_greedy
# in this code. So the policy and memory are separate modules
which can be enhanced, new ones implemented, and used
# as requirement as standard implementation for multiple
agents.
from experience_replay import SequentialDequeMemory
from beahaviour_policy import BehaviorPolicy
```

```
# Configure logging for the project
# Create file logger, to be used for deployment
# logging.basicConfig(filename="Chapter09_DDQN.log",
format='%(asctime)s %(message)s', filemode='w')
logging.basicConfig()
# Creating a stream logger for receiving inline logs
logger = logging.getLogger()
# Setting the logging threshold of logger to DEBUG
logger.setLevel(logging.DEBUG)


class DoubleDQN:
    """Double DQN Agent

        Class for training a Double DQN Learning agent on any
custom environment.

        Args:
            agent_name (str): The name of the agent. This
argument helps in continuing the training from the last auto
                            checkpoint. The system will check
if any agent's weight by the same name exists, if so then
                            the existing weights are saved
before resuming/ starting training.
            env (Object): An object instantiation of a OpenAI
gym compatible env class like the CartPole-v1 environment
            number_episodes (int): The maximum number of
episodes to be executed for training the agent
            discounting_factor (float): The discounting
factor (gamma) used to discount the future rewards to current
step
            learning_rate (float): The learning rate (alpha)
used to update the q values in each step
            behavior_policy (str): The behavior policy chosen
(as q learning is off policy). Example "epsilon-greedy"
            policy_parameters (dict): A dict with the
behavior policy parameters. The keys required for
epsilon_greedy is
                            just epsilon, and for
epsilon_decay additionally requires min_epsilon and
epsilon_decay_rate
            deep_learning_model_hidden_layer_configuration
(list): A list if integers corresponding to the number of
                        neurons in each hidden layer of the
MLP-DNN network for the model.
        Examples:
            agent = DoubleDQN()

    """

    def __init__(self, agent_name=None,
env=gym.make('CartPole-v1'), number_episodes = 500,
discounting_factor = 0.9,
                 learning_rate = 0.001, behavior_policy =
"epsilon_decay",
```

```
policy_parameters={"epsilon":1.0,"min_epsilon":0.01,"epsilon_
decay_rate":0.99},

deep_learning_model_hidden_layer_configuration=[32,16,8]):
        self.agent_name = "ddqa_"+str(time.strftime("%Y%m%d-
%H%M%S")) if agent_name is None else agent_name
        self.model_weights_dir = "model_weights"
        self.env = env
        self.n_states = env.observation_space.shape[0]
        self.n_actions = env.action_space.n
        self.n_episodes = number_episodes
        self.episodes_completed = 0
        self.gamma = discounting_factor
        self.alpha = learning_rate
        self.policy =
BehaviorPolicy(n_actions=self.n_actions,
policy_type=behavior_policy,

policy_parameters=policy_parameters).getPolicy()
        self.policyParameter = policy_parameters
        self.model_hidden_layer_configuration =
deep_learning_model_hidden_layer_configuration
        self.online_model =
self._build_sequential_dnn_model()
        self.target_model =
self._build_sequential_dnn_model()
        self.trainingStats_steps_in_each_episode = []
        self.trainingStats_rewards_in_each_episode = []
        self.trainingStats_discountedrewards_in_each_episode
= []
        self.memory =
SequentialDequeMemory(queue_capacity=2000)
        self.experience_replay_batch_size = 32

    def _build_sequential_dnn_model(self):
        """Internal helper function for building DNN model

            This function can make a custom MLP-DNN topology
based on the arguments provided during instantiation of
           the class.
           The MLP-DNN model starts with the input layer,
with as many nodes as the state cardinality,

            then add as many hidden layers with as many
neurons in each hidden layer as requested in the
instantiation
            parameter self.model_hidden_layer_configuration.
Then th output layer with as many layers as
            action space cardinality follows.
            The activation for input and hidden layers is
ReLU, and for output payer neurons is Linear.
            Optimizer used is ADAM, and Loss function used is
Mean Square Error (MSE)

        """
```

```
        model = Sequential()
        hidden_layers = self.model_hidden_layer_configuration
        model.add(Dense(hidden_layers[0],
input_dim=self.n_states, activation='relu'))
        for layer_size in hidden_layers[1:]:
            model.add(Dense(layer_size, activation='relu'))
        model.add(Dense(self.n_actions, activation='linear'))
        model.compile(loss=mean_squared_error,
optimizer=Adam(lr=self.alpha))
        return model

    def _sync_target_model_with_online_model(self):
        """Internal helper function to sync the target Q
network with the online Q network
        """

self.target_model.set_weights(self.online_model.get_weights()
)

    def _update_online_model(self,experience_tuple):
        """Internal helper function for updating the online Q
network
        """
        current_state, action, instantaneous_reward,
next_state, done_flag = experience_tuple
        action_target_values =
self.online_model.predict(current_state)
        action_values_for_state = action_target_values[0]
        if done_flag:
            action_values_for_state[action] =
instantaneous_reward
        else:
            action_values_for_next_state =
self.target_model.predict(next_state)[0]
            max_next_state_value =
np.max(action_values_for_next_state)

            target_action_value = instantaneous_reward +
self.gamma * max_next_state_value
            action_values_for_state[action] =
target_action_value
        action_target_values[0] = action_values_for_state
        logger.debug("Fitting online model with
Current_State: {}, Action_Values: {}".

format(current_state,action_target_values))
        self.online_model.fit(current_state,
action_target_values, epochs=1)

    def _reshape_state_for_model(self,state):
        """Internal helper function for shaping state to be
compatible with the DNN model
        """
        return np.reshape(state,[1,self.n_states])
```

```
    def train_agent(self):
        """Main function to train the agent

            The main function that needs to be called to
start the training of the agent after instantiating it.

            Returns:
                tuple: Tuple of 3 lists, 1st is the steps in
each episode, 2nd is the total un-discounted rewards in
                        each episode, and 3rd is the total
discounted rewards in each episode.

            Examples:
                training_statistics = agent.train_agent()

        """

        self.load_model_weights()
        for episode in range(self.n_episodes):
            logger.debug("-"*30)
            logger.debug("EPISODE
{}/{}".format(episode,self.n_episodes))
            logger.debug("-"*30)
            current_state =
self._reshape_state_for_model(self.env.reset())
            cumulative_reward = 0
            discounted_cumulative_reward = 0
            for n_step in count():
                all_action_value_for_current_state =
self.online_model.predict(current_state)[0]

                policy_defined_action =
self.policy(all_action_value_for_current_state)
                next_state, instantaneous_reward, done, _ =
self.env.step(policy_defined_action)
                next_state =
self._reshape_state_for_model(next_state)
                experience_tuple = (current_state,
policy_defined_action, instantaneous_reward, next_state,
done)
                self.memory.add_to_memory(experience_tuple)
                cumulative_reward += instantaneous_reward
                discounted_cumulative_reward =
instantaneous_reward + self.gamma *
discounted_cumulative_reward
                if done:

self.trainingStats_steps_in_each_episode.append(n_step)

self.trainingStats_rewards_in_each_episode.append(cumulative_
reward)
```

```
self.trainingStats_discountedrewards_in_each_episode.append(d
iscounted_cumulative_reward)

self._sync_target_model_with_online_model()
                    logger.debug("episode: {}/{}, reward: {},
discounted_reward: {}".format(n_step, self.n_episodes,

cumulative_reward, discounted_cumulative_reward))
                    break
                self.replay_experience_from_memory()
        if episode % 2 == 0: self.plot_training_statistics()
        if episode % 5 == 0: self.save_model_weights()
        return self.trainingStats_steps_in_each_episode,
self.trainingStats_rewards_in_each_episode, \

self.trainingStats_discountedrewards_in_each_episode

    def replay_experience_from_memory(self):
        """Replays the experience from memory buffer

             Replays the experience from the memory buffer.
The memory buffer is as selected during the class
             instantiation.

            Returns:
                bool: True if the replay happens, False if
the size of buffer is less than the batch size and hence
                        replay does not happens.
        """
        if self.memory.get_memory_size() <
self.experience_replay_batch_size:
            return False
        experience_mini_batch =
self.memory.get_random_batch_for_replay(batch_size=self.exper
ience_replay_batch_size)
        for experience_tuple in experience_mini_batch:
            self._update_online_model(experience_tuple)
        return True

    def save_model_weights(self, agent_name=None):
        """Save Model Weights

            Saves the model weights for both the target and
online Q network model from the directory given in class
            variable self.model_weights_dir (default =
model_weights) and adds .h5 extension.

            Args:
                agent_name (str): Name of the agent if need
to be forced a specific one other than the default unique one

            Returns:
                None

        """
```

```
        if agent_name is None:
            agent_name = self.agent_name
        model_file =
os.path.join(os.path.join(self.model_weights_dir,agent_name+"
.h5"))
        self.online_model.save_weights(model_file,
overwrite=True)

    def load_model_weights(self, agent_name=None):
        """Load Model Weights

            Loads the model weights for both the target and
online Q network model from the directory given in class
            variable self.model_weights_dir (default =
model_weights) and the one has .h5 extension.

            Args:
                agent_name (str): Name of the agent if need
to be forced a specific one other than the default unique one

            Returns:
                None
        """
        if agent_name is None:
            agent_name = self.agent_name
        model_file =
os.path.join(os.path.join(self.model_weights_dir, agent_name
+ ".h5"))
        if os.path.exists(model_file):
            self.online_model.load_weights(model_file)
            self.target_model.load_weights(model_file)

    def plot_training_statistics(self, training_statistics =
None):
        """Plot Training Statistics

            Function to plot training statistics of the Q
Learning agent's training. This function plots the dual axis
            plot, with the episode count on the x axis and
the steps and rewards in each episode on the y axis.

            Args:
                training_statistics (tuple): Tuple of list of
steps, list or rewards, list of cumulative rewards for
                                                each episode

            Returns:
                None

            Examples:
                agent.plot_statistics()

        """
```

```
        steps = self.trainingStats_steps_in_each_episode if
training_statistics is None else training_statistics[0]
        rewards = self.trainingStats_rewards_in_each_episode
if training_statistics is None else training_statistics[1]
        discounted_rewards =
self.trainingStats_discountedrewards_in_each_episode if
training_statistics is None \
            else training_statistics[2]
        episodes =
np.arange(len(self.trainingStats_steps_in_each_episode))
        fig, ax1 = plt.subplots()
        ax1.set_xlabel('Episodes (e)')
        ax1.set_ylabel('Steps To Episode Completion',
color="red")
        ax1.plot(episodes, steps, color="red")
        ax2 = ax1.twinx()
        ax2.set_ylabel('Reward in each Episode',
color="blue")
        ax2.plot(episodes, rewards, color="blue")
        fig.tight_layout()
        plt.show()
        fig, ax1 = plt.subplots()
        ax1.set_xlabel('Episodes (e)')
        ax1.set_ylabel('Steps To Episode Completion',
color="red")
        ax1.plot(episodes, steps, color="red")
        ax2 = ax1.twinx()
        ax2.set_ylabel('Discounted Reward in each Episode',
color="green")
        ax2.plot(episodes, discounted_rewards, color="green")
        fig.tight_layout()
        plt.show()


if __name__ == "__main__":
    """Main function

        A sample implementation of the above Double DQN agent
for testing purpose.
        This function is executed when this file is run from
the command prompt directly or by selection.

    """

    agent = DoubleDQN()
    training_statistics = agent.train_agent()
    agent.plot_training_statistics(training_statistics)
```

9.2.1 Code for the Behavior Policy Class (File: behavior_policy.py)

```
""" DQN in Code - BehaviorPolicy

DQN Code as in the book Deep Reinforcement Learning, Chapter
9.

Runtime: Python 3.6.5
Dependencies: numpy
DocStrings: GoogleStyle

Author : Mohit Sewak (p20150023@goa-bits-pilani.ac.in)
"""
# General imports
import logging
import numpy as np
# Import of custom exception classes implemented to make the
error more understandable
from rl_exceptions import PolicyDoesNotExistException,
InsufficientPolicyParameters, FunctionNotImplemented

# Configure logging for the project
# Create file logger, to be used for deployment
# logging.basicConfig(filename="Chapter09_BPolicy.log",
format='%(asctime)s %(message)s', filemode='w')
logging.basicConfig()
# Creating a stream logger for receiving inline logs
logger = logging.getLogger()
# Setting the logging threshold of logger to DEBUG
logger.setLevel(logging.DEBUG)

class BehaviorPolicy:
    """Behavior Policy Class
    Class for different behavior policies for use with an
Off-Policy Reinforcement Learning agent.

        Args:
            n_actions (int): the cardinality of the action
space
            policy_type (str): type of behavior policy to be
implemented.
                The current implementation contains only the
"epsilon_greedy" policy.
            policy_parameters (dict) : A dict of relevant
policy parameters for the requested policy.
                The epsilon-greedy policy as implemented
requires only the value of the "epsilon" as float.

        Returns:
            None

    """
```

```
    def __init__(self, n_actions, policy_type =
"epsilon_greedy", policy_parameters = {"epsilon":0.1}):
        self.policy = policy_type
        self.n_actions = n_actions
        self.policy_type = policy_type
        self.policy_parameters = policy_parameters
        if "epsilon" not in policy_parameters:
            raise InsufficientPolicyParameters("epsilon not
available")
        self.epsilon = self.policy_parameters["epsilon"]
        self.min_epsilon = None
        self.epsilon_decay_rate = None
        logger.debug("Policy Type {}, Parameters Received
{}".format(policy_type, policy_parameters))

    def getPolicy(self):
        """Get the requested behavior policy

        This function returns a function corresponding to the
requested behavior policy

            Args:
                None

            Returns:
                function: A function of the requested
behavior policy type.

            Raises:
                PolicyDoesNotExistException: When a policy
corresponding to the parameter policy_type is not
                                             implemented.
                InsufficientPolicyParameters: When a required
policy parameter is not available
                                             (or key spelled
incorrectly).

        """
        if self.policy_type == "epsilon_greedy":
            return self.return_epsilon_greedy_policy()
        elif self.policy_type == "epsilon_decay":
            self.epsilon = self.policy_parameters["epsilon"]
            if "min_epsilon" not in self.policy_parameters:
                raise
InsufficientPolicyParameters("EpsilonDecay policy also
requires the min_epsilon parameter")
            if "epsilon_decay_rate" not in
self.policy_parameters:
                raise
InsufficientPolicyParameters("EpsilonDecay policy also
requires the epsilon_decay_rate parameter")
            self.min_epsilon =
self.policy_parameters["min_epsilon"]
            self.epsilon_decay_rate =
self.policy_parameters["epsilon_decay_rate"]
            return self.return_epsilon_decay_policy()

        else:
            raise PolicyDoesNotExistException("The selected
policy does not exists! The implemented policies are "
                                             "epsilon-greedy
and epsilon-decay")

    def return_epsilon_decay_policy(self):
```

```
        """Epsilon-Decay Policy Implementation

            This is the implementation of the Epsilon-Decay
policy as returned by the getPolicy method when
            "epsilon-decay" policy type is selected.

            Returns:
                function: a function that could be directly
called for selecting the recommended action as per e-decay.

        """

        def
choose_action_by_epsilon_decay(values_of_all_possible_actions
):
            """Action selection by epsilon_decay policy

                This is the base function that is actually
invoked in each iteration to return the recommended action
                index as per the desired e_decay policy.

                Args:
                    values_of_all_possible_actions (array): A
float array of the action values from which the

recommended action has to be chosen

                Returns:
                    int: The index of the recommended action
as per the policy

            """
            logger.debug("Taking e-decay action for action
values"+str(values_of_all_possible_actions))
            prob_taking_best_action_only = 1 - self.epsilon
            prob_taking_any_random_action = self.epsilon /
self.n_actions
            action_probability_vector =
[prob_taking_any_random_action] * self.n_actions
            exploitation_action_index =
np.argmax(values_of_all_possible_actions)

action_probability_vector[exploitation_action_index] +=
prob_taking_best_action_only
            chosen_action =
np.random.choice(np.arange(self.n_actions),
p=action_probability_vector)
            if self.epsilon > self.min_epsilon:
                self.epsilon *= self.epsilon_decay_rate
            logger.debug("Decayed epsilon value after the
current iteration: {}".format(self.epsilon))
            return chosen_action
        return choose_action_by_epsilon_decay

    def return_epsilon_greedy_policy(self):
```

```
        """Epsilon-Greedy Policy Implementation

            This is the implementation of the Epsilon-Greedy
policy as returned by the getPolicy method when
            "epsilon-greedy" policy type is selected.

            Returns:
                function: a function that could be directly
called for selecting the recommended action as per e-greedy.

        """

        def
choose_action_by_epsilon_greedy(values_of_all_possible_action
s):
            """Action selection by epsilon-Greedy policy

                This is the base function that is actually
invoked in each iteration to return the recommended action
                index as per the desired e_decay policy.

                Args:
                    values_of_all_possible_actions (array): A
float array of the action values from which the

recommended action has to be chosen

                Returns:
                    int: The index of the recommended action
as per the policy

            """
            logger.debug("Taking e-greedy action for action
values"+str(values_of_all_possible_actions))
            prob_taking_best_action_only = 1 - self.epsilon
            prob_taking_any_random_action = self.epsilon /
self.n_actions

           action_probability_vector =
[prob_taking_any_random_action] * self.n_actions
            exploitation_action_index =
np.argmax(values_of_all_possible_actions)

action_probability_vector[exploitation_action_index] +=
prob_taking_best_action_only
            chosen_action =
np.random.choice(np.arange(self.n_actions),
p=action_probability_vector)
            return chosen_action
        return choose_action_by_epsilon_greedy


if __name__ == "__main__":
    raise FunctionNotImplemented("This class needs to be
imported and instantiated from a Reinforcement Learning"
                                 "agent class and does not
contain any invokable code in the main function")
```

9.2.2 Code for the Experience Replay Memory Class (File: experience_replay.py)

```
""" DQN in Code - ExperienceReplayMemory

DQN Code as in the book Deep Reinforcement Learning, Chapter
9.

Runtime: Python 3.6.5
DocStrings: GoogleStyle

Author : Mohit Sewak (p20150023@goa-bits-pilani.ac.in)

"""

# General Imports
import logging
import random
# Import for data structure for different types of memory
from collections import deque
# Import of custom exception classes implemented to make the
error more understandable
from rl_exceptions import FunctionNotImplemented
# Configure logging for the project
# Create file logger, to be used for deployment
# logging.basicConfig(filename="Chapter09_BPolicy.log",
format='%(asctime)s %(message)s', filemode='w')
logging.basicConfig()
# Creating a stream logger for receiving inline logs
logger = logging.getLogger()
# Setting the logging threshold of logger to DEBUG
logger.setLevel(logging.DEBUG)


class ExperienceReplayMemory:
    """Base class for all the extended versions for the
ExperienceReplayMemory class implementation
    """
    pass


class SequentialDequeMemory(ExperienceReplayMemory):
    """Extension of the ExperienceReplayMemory class with
deque based Sequential Memory

            Args:
                queue_capacity (int): The maximum capacity
(in terms of the number of  experience tuples) of the memory
                buffer.

    """
```

```
    def __init__(self, queue_capacity=2000):
        self.queue_capacity = 2000
        self.memory = deque(maxlen=self.queue_capacity)

    def add_to_memory(self,experience_tuple):
        """Add an experience tuple to the memory buffer

            Args:
                experience_tuple (tuple): A tuple of
experience for training. In case of Q learning this tuple
could be
                (S, A, R, S) with optional done_flag and in
case of SARSA it could have an additional action element.

        """
        self.memory.append(experience_tuple)

    def get_random_batch_for_replay(self, batch_size=64):
        """Get a random mini-batch for replay from the
Sequential memory buffer

            Args:
                batch_size (int): The size of the batch
required

            Returns:
                list: list of the required number of
experience tuples

        """
        return random.sample(self.memory,batch_size)

    def get_memory_size(self):
        """Get the size of the occupied buffer

            Returns:
                int: The number of the experience tuples
already in memory
        """
        return len(self.memory)


if __name__ == "__main__":
    raise FunctionNotImplemented("This class needs to be
imported and instantiated from a Reinforcement Learning"
                                "agent class and does not
contain any invokable code in the main function")
```

9.2.3 *Code for the Custom Exceptions Classes (File: rl_exceptions.py)*

```python
""" DQN in Code - Custom RL Exceptions

DQN Code as in the book Deep Reinforcement Learning, Chapter
9.

Runtime: Python 3.6.5
DocStrings: None

Author : Mohit Sewak (p20150023@goa-bits-pilani.ac.in)

"""


class PolicyDoesNotExistException(Exception):
    pass


class InsufficientPolicyParameters(Exception):
    pass


class FunctionNotImplemented(Exception):
    pass
```

9.3 Training Statistics Plots

See Figs. 9.3 and 9.4.

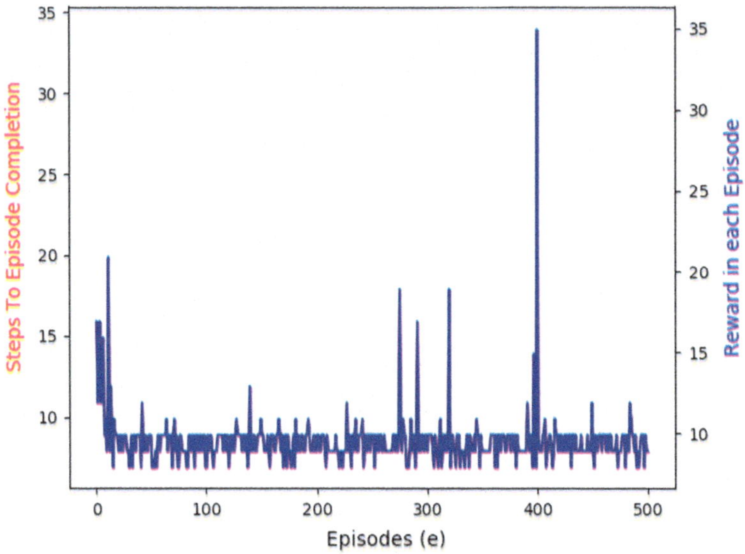

Fig. 9.3 Number of steps and total (un-discounted) rewards received in each episode

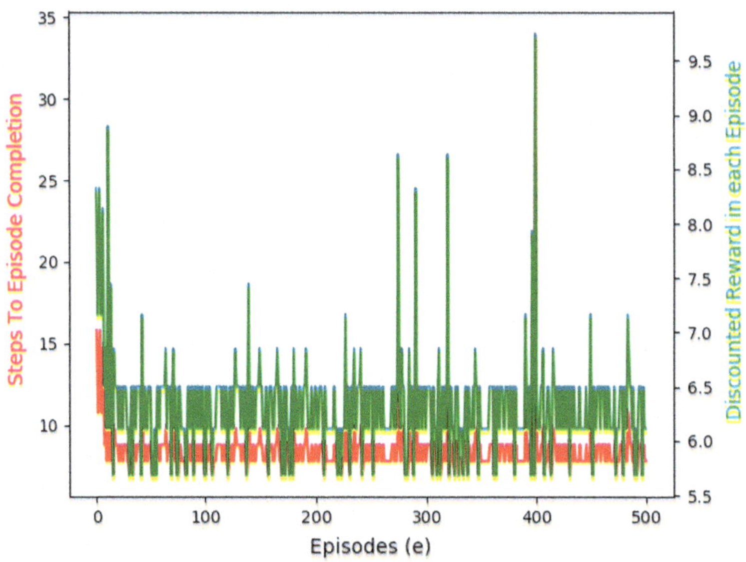

Fig. 9.4 Number of steps and total discounted rewards received in each episode

Chapter 10
Policy-Based Reinforcement Learning Approaches

Stochastic Policy Gradient and the REINFORCE Algorithm

Abstract In this chapter, we will cover the basics of the policy-based approaches especially the policy gradient-based approaches. We will understand why policy-based approaches are superior to that of value-based approaches under some circumstances and why they are also tough to implement. We will subsequently cover some simplifications that will help make policy-based approaches practical to implement and also cover the REINFORCE algorithm.

10.1 Introduction to Policy-Based Approaches and Policy Approximation

Until now in this book, we focused on estimating different types of values. Initially, we focused on state–value computation (as in classical DP), and then state–value estimation (as in TD Learning). Subsequently, we drew our focus toward action–value estimation (as in SARSA and Q Learning), and finally advantage (incremental value) estimation (as in Dueling DQN).

While discussing Q Learning, we also introduced the concept of value approximation. Since the value function in Q Learning and similar algorithms are modeled using function approximators (or machine learning models, as we otherwise refer to) therefore we called it value estimation process instead of value computation or determination process. Any such value estimation process, which is modeled using a value estimator and is not exact introduces some bias. Also note that we modeled the value as output of approximation ***functions*** (as in Q Learning, DQN, etc.) and started denoting the value (state–value or action-value) as a function of the parameter of these functions. In the case of deep learning-based function approximators (models), these parameters are the network weights which need to be optimized.

Maximizing the reinforcement learning reward, under such notations would have been equivalent to finding the set of weights which "***optimizes***" (as in mathematical optimization) these total rewards received. This is done by minimizing the

M. Sewak, *Deep Reinforcement Learning*,
https://doi.org/10.1007/978-981-13-8285-7_10

respective losses as an outcome of the training. Since in most of these occasions the approximation function was (purposely) differentiable, one of the best suited methods to optimize these functions proves to be computing the gradients of the expectancy of reward function (by differentiating them) and then moving in the direction of the gradient till a local "maximum is achieved so as to maximize the reward expectancy.

The nonclassical reinforcement learning system is often a combination of solutions to the underlying estimation problem and control problem. Optimization of the estimation model's loss function consummates the training of our function approximator which could later be deployed to estimate the "optimal" value of a state or action and serves to provide solution for the estimation subproblem. The estimations from such value estimation model "***combined with a specific policy***" (the policy provides solution to the control subproblem) help our agent take appropriate action. We also discovered the on-policy and off-policy methods, which would either have an inbuilt mechanism to strike a good balance between the exploration of new states/actions or exploiting the existing training or a different behavioral policy for that determines when to use the estimated values greedily and when to explore further. So essentially the value estimation/approximation process finally led to a single "action" being suggested corresponding to any given state that the agent is in. This action is either directly determined or greedily chosen (as in epsilon-greedy for instance) from the estimation process. So, the "policy" which directly resulted in the agent's action was not our focus throughout. Instead, the "value" of the state/state-action combination was the key focus until now, and this "value" form the basis of a *mostly deterministic* "policy".

Now just take a moment's pause and imagine why we were trying to estimate the value and approximate the ***value function*** (state–value or action-value function) when the whole intention was to take the best action. Remember we had a similar discussion earlier when we moved from state–value computation/estimation to action-value computation/estimation. Until then though we were still focusing on estimating the value but reasoned that since the ultimate goal is to determine the best action, therefore the action-value estimation-based approach could be a more direct means of achieving our goal than following the state–value estimation-based approaches. Using the same reasoning forward with respect to policy, we can argue that approximating the policy function could be a more direct means of achieving our goal than approximating the value function as we have been doing so far. So essentially, we would now like to parameterize the policy itself as below:

$$\pi_\theta(a|s) = \mathbb{P}[\partial|\sim\nRightarrow\theta] \tag{10.1}$$

This is the intuition behind most of the policy approximation-based approaches that we will discuss in this book. Policy gradient-based approaches are very popular under policy-based reinforcement learning paradigm. The policy gradient-based approaches under Policy Approximation would mostly try to leverage the property of differentiability (and hence computing gradient) of the (approximate) policy function to optimize it. Also, as in the case of value approximation, we would proceed with the focus on model-free (here the term model-free refers to the fact that we may not be in a position to mathematical model the MDP completely and hence have to rely on approximating it instead of knowing it) assumptions for policy approximations.

10.2 Broad Difference Between Value-Based and Policy-Based Approaches

The basic difference between the value-based and the policy-based approaches is that in the value-based approaches we learn a "value function" from which the "policy" is derived either explicitly or implicitly. Whereas in the policy-based approaches there is no need to learn or derive the value function, and we learn the "policy" directly. The value function is essentially nonexistent in policy-based approaches. Though there exist some variants of hybrid approaches as well, for now we will use this simple theme for the purpose of drawing intuitions for this chapter.

In "value-based" approaches, we derived the policy on the basis of the estimates generated by an optimal (well trained) value function. Although the value function was stochastic (that is it generates probabilistic estimate for selecting different actions in a particular state using a given value approximation model assuming no further updates to the model), the so implied policy in most of the implementation of value-based approaches has been mostly deterministic. This is because the policy in the case of value estimation approaches suggests a single action. This action could be either the best action suggested by the estimation function or any random action, but it lacks the suggested probability distribution for selecting across different actions.

Whereas in the case of "policy approximation" approaches, since the "policy" itself is parameterized, it is "stochastic" [refer to Eq. (10.1)]. This essentially means that for a given state, the policy may have varying probabilities of choosing different actions instead of choosing the "single" most optimal action. So, the "policy-based" approaches would essentially draw samples from this "stochastic policy" to refine their estimate of the policy parameter vector θ in a direction (as in the gradient) so as to optimize the policy which would subsequently enable the agent that follows such policy to accumulate maximum cumulative reward. Again, there are a dedicated series of models (like deterministic policy gradient and variants) which are exceptions to this principle. But for now, we will use this distinction to build our intuition further for the purpose of this chapter.

Since the value-based methods have "*deterministic*" or "non-stochastic" policy, it could select only one action. This has a similar effect of choosing one action with probability 1 and others with probability 0. Even in cases where the value difference between different actions is arbitrary, and hence also negligible or very small, such sort of deterministic (and hence absolute) action choice leads to discontinuous changes in the approximated function, leading to challenges with "***convergence-***

assurance" of algorithms following the value function approach. This shortcoming is not so much pronounced in the case of policy-based approaches as they could stochastically suggest multiple actions with appropriate probabilities.

In case if the importance of this distinction for practical application is not well realized, let us understand this with an example. Suppose during the initiation of a sport (say cricket) match the captain has to "choose" (takes action of choosing) between "heads" and "tails" in a toss (assumingly of an unbiased coin). If he wins the toss then he has to take decision pertaining to that match (say to bat or to ball first). Although the first decision (calling heads or tails) is supposed to be random and arbitrary, and only the second decision (match strategy of batting or balling first) is something that could influence the outcome of the match, using a deterministic policy will end up forcing the agent to learn and determine whether calling "heads" is better or calling "tails" is better in a toss given a particular state of the match conditions and team compositions. As the readers would have realized that here state (comprising of the match conditions and team compositions) will have no bearing on the call decision for the toss. By forcing "deterministic" proposal for actions/decision, we imply that there exists only "one" optimal action/decision, and restrict the stochastic recommendations across multiple actions/decisions choose one. A stochastic policy in this case could have recommended that with 50% probability we call "heads" and with the remaining 50% we call tails. If we force to train the approximation function under the assumption of existence of a "deterministic" policy, where the underlying optimal "policy" is actually "stochastic", such approximation function's training should obviously *not* converge. With reference to our example, convergence in training would have meant that we successfully trained a model that could clearly identify with a high degree of precision and recall that one action is better than all the other actions possible in a particular state as we proceed with the training. Since such observations are contrary to the ground truth, an attempt to train the model under such assumptions should fail to converge.

Another distinction between the value-based approaches and the policy-based approaches is that value-based approaches are suited mainly for scenarios with *small* and discrete action space. In case of ***large action space or continuous action space***. A continuous action space could be considered as a special case of large action space, with action space cardinality growing toward infinity. We have already hinted in the earlier chapters some intuition for the reasons behind this observation while discussing the algorithms in the value-based approaches, whereas other reasons could also be implicitly understood from our discussion on stochastic action probability in this section earlier.

Just to understand the reasons related to stochastic action probability which makes the policy-based approaches more suitable for applications with large and continuous action spaces as compared to value-based approaches let us take an example. Proceeding from our initial example from the cricket theme, let us assume that our agent needs to determine the optimal angle at which the batsmen should play a stroke on a particular delivery to ensure that the ball reaches the boundary. Each delivery from its start to the result that delivery is an episode in this example.

Assume the state here comprises two information. The first information is static for a given delivery/episode and is updated as the baller starts to ball. The other state information is dynamic which updates at a particular frequency, (say once every 1/100th s). The static information types are the ball condition (say age, roughness), pitch condition, field placements occupied or vacant (one hot encoded vector). Whereas the dynamic state comprises the ball velocity, ball direction, the swing/spin of the bowl, and the thrust generated by the swing of the bat, distance between the closest point of bat and ball. The desired decision output from the agent is the angle at which the bat should swing (for the given thrust and timing of the bat) to ensure a boundary. Assuming that the decision needs to be precise to a minute of an angle ($1^\circ = 60''$), the action space here if discrete could be considered as a vector of dimension $360 \times 60 = 21{,}600$ assuming the angle could be between [0°–360°]. Alternatively, the action space here ideally should not be a discrete action space but a continuous one in the range [0°–360°]. This is because there is little difference in the outcome between the bat swing between any two contiguous angles (precise up to a minute of an angle), say $45^\circ.0''$ and $45^\circ.1''$, but a discrete action space, especially in the case of value-based approaches have to select one of these angles and reject the another. From the explanation until now, it should be clear why some action criteria are better suited and more practical to be conceived as a continuous action space even when theoretically we could conceive them as a discrete action space with very high cardinality.

Continuing forward with the above example, let us assume that there is a fielder placed in an isolated area of the field where the field boundary is the shortest. Let the fielder's angle from the batting point is $45^\circ.0''$. Assuming the players reach to be similar, say $5^\circ 0''$, in both the clockwise and anticlockwise directions, we have equally high probability of scoring the boundary at angles $<45^\circ.0'' - 5^\circ 0''$ ($=40^\circ.0''$) and angles $>45^\circ.0'' + 5^\circ 0''$ ($=50^\circ.0''$). In the case of policy-based approaches where policy is stochastic, a similar probability distribution across these decision boundaries could reflect this phenomenon. But in the case of value-based approaches, even if the value of scoring the boundary may reflect a similar stochastic pattern across the discrete action spaces around these angles, but the deterministic action policy could only select one of the actions and has the reject the other. This distinction is very important for cases where the action suggestions of the agent have to feed into another intelligent system/agent/model that works on a large strategical decision process/prediction to which this agent's suggestions is one of the many inputs.

As the readers would have realized from the above example why the capability of taking actions in a continuous action space is so useful, and how the agents using policy-based approaches are naturally suited to provide more effective outcomes under these challenges. But the inherent capability of working well with large/continuous action space for the policy-based methods as compared to the value-based methods comes at a cost. For one, while "converging", the policy-based approaches could "converge" to a local "optimum", instead of a "global optima", and for another "evaluating" a policy has very high variance and could be highly inefficient for the policy-based approaches.

10.3 Problems with Calculating the Policy Gradient

From the discussion in the previous section, it should be evident that the policy-based approaches offer some valuable advantages over the value-based methods and are worth considering. In some scenarios learning the policy directly may be simpler or otherwise more effective. Also there may be instances where the action space is large or continuous. Under these situations the policy-based approaches may offer distinctive advantages beyond performance or accuracy considerations over value-based approaches.

Also, as we discussed in the previous section, in policy-based methods, we are interested in optimizing the policy approximator functions in order to maximize the rewards. Also, we learnt that to optimize the policy approximator we may need the gradient of the approximation function that represents this stochastic policy as moving in the direction of this gradient may help minimize the losses and hence optimize the policy. Alternatively, if the gradient is that of the reward function, we can move in the direction of the gradient to maximize the expectancy of the rewards.

But there exists a problem in implementing this theory in practice. To understand this problem let us understand mathematically what we are trying to do. Let us take a policy denoted by π. This policy π parameterized over the parameter vector θ. The value of this policy π could be defined as the expectancy of the (discounted) cumulative rewards following this policy. Similar to symbols V for denoting state–value and symbol Q denoting action value, we would use the symbol "J" to denote the value of the ***Performance*** of policy π. The policy value J could be mathematically defined as Eq. (10.2) below π.

$$J_{(\theta)} = \mathbb{E}\sum_{t \geq 0} [\gamma^t r_t | \pi_\theta] \tag{10.2}$$

Therefore, the most optimal parameter vector (θ^*) will maximize this expected reward value following this policy, such as

$$\theta^* = \underset{\theta}{\operatorname{argmax}}\, J_{(\theta)} \tag{10.3}$$

Now let us introduce a new term, "trajectory". We will use the symbol τ (called "tau") to denote "trajectory". The trajectory here refers to the sequence of states visited in an episode. In a stochastic policy, the next action and hence the subsequently visited state need not be deterministic. Hence even under a given stochastic policy, different sequences of states could be visited with varying probabilities. Any such sequence of visited states (by taking some action and receiving the corresponding instantaneous rewards) at different time steps in an episode is called a trajectory. The trajectory τ could be represented by $\tau = [(s_0, a_0, r_0); (s_1, a_1, r_1); \ldots; (s_t, a_t, r_t)]$.

The trajectory is influenced by the state-transition probabilities under a given policy. So, in terms of the trajectory, Eq. (10.2) for the policy value J could be rewritten as Eq. (10.4) below:

$$J_{(\theta)} = \mathop{\mathbb{E}}_{\tau} \sum \mathbb{P}(\tau \nRightarrow \theta) r_{(\tau)} \tag{10.4}$$

This equation simply says the performance value of a given stochastic policy could be expressed as the expectancy of reward in a particular trajectory under a policy, weighed by the probability of attaining that trajectory under that policy. Since Expectancy could be integrated, so we further represent the above expression of expectancy over the different trajectories using integration (so that we could demonstrate the differentiation step easily) as

$$J_{(\theta)} = \int_{\tau} r_{(\tau)} \mathbb{P}(\tau \nRightarrow \theta) \tau \tag{10.5}$$

To obtain the gradient of the above expression, the function J needs to be differentiated with respect to the parameters θ as below:

$$\Delta_{\theta} J_{(\theta)} = \int_{\tau} r_{(\tau)} \Delta_{\theta} \mathbb{P}(\tau \nRightarrow \theta) \tau \tag{10.6}$$

Equation (6) is difficult to solve because of mathematical "*intractability*". An *intractable* problem mathematics are the ones for which there exists no mathematical formulation to solve these problems efficiently. Equation (6) is intractable due to the fact that in the above equation we are trying to differentiate a function p (τ; θ) over the parameter (vector) θ when that function is itself conditioned (or depends) on the same parameter. So, in the exact mathematical solution, it is difficult to implement policy gradient method. Therefore, next, we will learn about a very important algorithm called "REINFORCE" and the associated mathematical simplification of the above equation to solve this problem.

10.4 The REINFORCE Algorithm

The REINFORCE algorithm was proposed by Ronald J. Williams. Ronald also gave some mathematical simplification to Eq. (10.6) above so as to implement it in the proposed algorithm. Under limiting conditions, the differential of part of Eq. (10.6) causing intractability could be rewritten as Eq. (10.7a, 10.7b) below:

$$\Delta_\theta \mathbb{P}(\tau \nRightarrow \theta)\tau = \mathbb{P}(\tau \nRightarrow \theta)\frac{\Delta_\theta \mathbb{P}(\tau \nRightarrow \theta)}{\mathbb{P}(\tau \nRightarrow \theta)} \tag{10.7a}$$

Or under limiting condition Eq. (10.7a) could be rewritten as Eq. (10.7b):

$$\Delta_\theta \mathbb{P}(\tau \nRightarrow \theta)\tau = \mathbb{P}(\tau \nRightarrow \theta)\Delta_\theta \log \mathbb{P}(\tau \nRightarrow \theta) \tag{10.7b}$$

Therefore, rewriting Eq. (10.6) under this limiting form we have Eq. (10.8) below:

$$\Delta_\theta J_{(\theta)} = \int_\tau (r_{(\tau)} \Delta_\theta \log \mathbb{P}(\tau \nRightarrow \theta))\mathbb{P}(\tau \nRightarrow \theta) d\tau \tag{10.8}$$

Rewriting Eq. (10.8) in Expectancy form, we get Eq. (10.9) as below:

$$\Delta_\theta J_\theta = \mathop{\mathbb{E}}_{\tau \sim \mathbb{P}(\tau \nRightarrow \theta)} [r_\tau \Delta_\theta \log \mathbb{P}(\tau \nRightarrow \theta)] \tag{10.9}$$

This is one part of the intended mathematical simplifications. In the above form, the method could be implemented using "Monte Carlo" sampling. In Monte Carlo sampling is we can simulate multiple experiments corresponding to a given policy and extract data from these experiments. REINFORCE method therefore could also be referred to as Monte Carlo approach to policy gradient or simply "***Monte Carlo Policy Gradient***". But there exists another practical (not necessarily mathematical) problem in implementing this yet. This is of knowing the $\mathbb{P}(\tau \nRightarrow \theta)$, that is the probability of different trajectories themselves under a given policy. Therefore, now even though we could solve this mathematically, but we have no efficient way to obtain the necessary trajectory probability in advance. This problem is also solved by slightly altering the mathematics of this equation as below:

$$\mathbb{P}(\tau \nRightarrow \theta) = \prod_{\approx \geq \nvdash} \mathbb{P}(\sim_{\approx + \nVdash} | \sim_\approx, \eth_\approx)\pi_\theta(\eth_\approx \; \eth \sqsupset \gtrapprox \ltimes \; \sim_\approx) \tag{10.10}$$

Since under Markov Decision Process (MDP), we assume that a given state once achieved is independent of previous happenings, so under this conditional independence assumption, we could essentially multiple the subsequent state-transition probabilities in a trajectory to obtain the overall trajectory probability as shown above in Eq. (10.10). Thus, the log p (τ; θ), could be rewritten as below:

$$\log \mathbb{P}(\tau \nRightarrow \theta) = \sum_{\approx \geq \nvdash} \log \mathbb{P}(\sim_{\approx + \nVdash} | \sim_\approx, \eth_\approx) + \log \pi_\theta(\eth_\approx | \sim_\approx) \tag{10.11}$$

Hence the differential of this formulation of log p (τ; θ) does not depend upon the trajectory probability distribution as earlier. It only depends on a series of state-transition probability as we were using earlier in some of the other algorithms.

This simplifies Eq. (10.11) further and removes the requirement to trajectory probability as can be seen below in Eq. (10.12).

$$\Delta_\theta \log \mathbb{P}(\tau \nRightarrow \theta) = \sum_{\approx \geq \nvdash} \Delta_\theta \log \pi_\theta(\eth_{\approx}|\sim_{\approx}) \tag{10.12}$$

Therefore, rewriting Eq. (10.9) for the gradient of policy value J to replace the trajectory probability distribution with the above form as in Eq. (10.12), we have Eq. (10.13) as below:

$$\Delta_\theta J_{(\theta)} \approx \sum_{t \geq 0} r_{(\tau)} \Delta_\theta \log \pi_\theta(a_t|s_t) \tag{10.13}$$

10.4.1 Shortcomings of the REINFORCE Algorithm

Even with the different mathematical simplifications and algorithmic enhancements, REINFORCE algorithm is not used in practice. This is because the gradient so obtained using the REINFORCE method has very ***high variance***.

One reason for such high variance is the form in which the rewards that are used in REINFORCE. In REINFORCE absolute rewards are used, and with each experiment of Monte Carlo, the rewards may vary a lot. This leads to a very high variance in the so obtained gradient. But nevertheless, the two mathematical enhancements that we discussed, are very important to know and understand as most of the policy gradient approaches use some part of REINFORCE algorithm especially the mathematical simplifications and develop further. Later we will discuss how some algorithms take these enhancements and slightly modify the computation to overcome this high variance problem.

Yet another reason for this high variance is the attribution of the reward to the specific state-action instances in the trajectory. Since REINFORCE in a sense averages out the rewards in a given trajectory, so if the rewards are due to some specific good state-action decisions only, and not because of most of the other state actions in the same trajectory/experiment, it becomes challenging to get the correct and specific attributions to those state actions alone. This effect further leads to high variance.

10.4.2 Pseudocode for the REINFORCE Algorithm

The above equations could be implemented in an iterative "Monte Carlo" like approach using the below pseudocode.

function **REINFORCE**
    Initialise θ arbitrarily
    for each episode $\{(s_1, a_1, r_2), \ldots, (s_{T-1}, a_{T-1}, r_T)\} \sim \pi_\theta$ **do**
        for $t = 1$ to $T - 1$ **do**
            $\theta \leftarrow \theta + \alpha \nabla_\theta \log \pi_\theta(s_t, a_t) v_t$
        end for
    end for
    return θ
end function

where v_t is the unbiased estimate sample of $Q_{\pi\theta}(s_t, a_t)$, and α is the step size.

10.5 Methods to Reduce Variance in the REINFORCE Algorithm

As we discovered in the earlier section on the shortcomings of the REINFORCE algorithm, the practicality of the REINFORCE algorithm is severely restricted because of the variance in the policy gradient. This high variance was mainly due to the fact that we were not able to deterministically and specifically identify which actions attributed to the reward in a given trajectory. This in turn meant that we were not able to positively move the gradient so that the subsequently updated policy could favor the best rewarding actions and restrict the gradient to discourage the actions which were not so rewarding. In this section, we will discuss some approaches that we could use to overcome this problem in the REINFORCE algorithm.

It should be pointed out that some of these approaches to reduce variance that we will be discussing next and their subsequent variants are common to most of policy gradient-based approaches and not just the REINFORCE algorithm. Hence, the techniques that will be discussed are also the basis of some of the other algorithms that fall under "policy-based approaches". So, we would carry forward some part of this discussion to later chapters when we would discuss those algorithms.

10.5.1 Cumulative Future Reward-Based Attribution

We discussed earlier that the gradient of the policy-estimation function (policy estimator) could be represented as Eq. 10.13

As we notice, in this form the attribution of reward (or penalties) that has been received in the past is also given to all the actions in the trajectory, even the actions that occur in the trajectory after receiving the specific instantaneous reward (future actions). That makes little sense.

For example, assume that in the grid-world example that we discussed earlier, one of the actions in a particular state made you lose 100 points (penalty) by moving to the ditch. Can this penalty be rightly attributed to an action in any other given state, say the last state just before you reached the "treasure-state" that led you to the receive the "treasure"? Obviously, such attribution does not seem correct.

Though we are not sure which specific future action could be attributed in which proportion to the subsequent future rewards, but we could at least say that any reward being realized before a particular action (in a particular state) could not be attributed to an action (as suggested by the policy) after realizing the reward. Therefore, we would slightly change Eq. (10.13) to restrict the attribution of only future cumulative rewards to any current actions or particular policy decision (action in a particular state). This could be expressed as Eq. (10.14) below:

$$\Delta_\theta J_{(\theta)} \approx \sum_{t \geq 0} \left(\sum_{t' \geq t} r_{(\tau)} \right) \Delta_\theta \log \pi_\theta(a_t | s_t) \tag{10.14}$$

10.5.2 Discounted Cumulative Future Rewards

As we discussed in the earlier section, changing the attribution from all rewards to all-future-rewards helps. We also discussed that we wanted to avoid equal attribution to all future actions (policy decisions). One way of doing this is by discounting the future rewards before attributing them to a given action. This ensures that the more recent actions/policy decisions get higher attribution for any upcoming rewards that the ones that occurred very early in the sequence. As we discussed earlier in this book, the intuition behind this is that more recent actions may better determine the realization of a reward, than something that has happened much earlier.

Modifying Eq. (10.14) to include the discounting parameter γ and raising it to the step/time difference between the action and the reward realization, we get Eq. (10.15) as below:

$$\Delta_\theta J_{(\theta)} \approx \sum_{t \geq 0} \left(\sum_{t' \geq t} \gamma^{t' - t} r_{(\tau)} \right) \Delta_\theta \log \pi_\theta(a_t | s_t) \tag{10.15}$$

10.5.3 REINFORCE with Baseline

In the present form as Eq. (10.15) stands, we have the ability to move aggressively in the direction the gradient that ensures higher rewards, and conservatively in the direction of the gradient that ensures less rewards. Continuing with the same theme of identifying and attributing the rewards/penalties to the correct actions, we need to start differentiating between better and worse rewards.

For illustration, let us take our grid-world example further. If from a particular state no matter where we move, we will get some positive reward, and the only thing that differs is either the quantum of reward or how delayed the response is (the delay or late rewards in turn will get reflected as the quantum of reward as well if discounting is used). We can end up moving in the direction of less favorable rewards as well (although slightly slow) along with moving in the direction of the more optimal rewards (although faster as compared to our movement in the direction of less rewarding actions). This is clearly counterproductive, as we intend to differentiate and identify the best action as lucidly and as soon as possible (from a training perspective). To ensure that we clearly identify the actions which we should have concentrated moving only toward the most optimal reward, even moving away from actions that lesser rewards even if these are positive rewards. This is because these actions have the opportunity cost associated with them. In the same step that we took a less rewarding action, we could have instead taken a more rewarding action. So, we need to now start differentiating across the actions with respect to their quantum of rewards as well.

So as to achieve this objective, we need to understand how much action is better or worse than a "***baseline***" scenario. This "baseline" could simply be a constant. But as such a constant baseline does not optimally serve the purpose to positively rewarding the better actions and negatively reward the not-so-good actions. Reflecting back to our discussion on "***advantage***" in the "Dueling DQN" algorithm, we had a similar discussion, and we discussed that the "advantage function" helps us identify the relative advantage of a given action in a particular state over the base value of the state. We were thus able to differentiate quantifiably across different actions permissible in a state. So, essentially, we used the Value of the state as the "***baseline***" (value) for any action permissible in that state. We would do a similar thing here and take a baseline reward value for a particular state and take a difference of the actual (future and discounted) rewards received with this baseline to assess the goodness, or in this case also worseness (in case if the difference is negative) with this baseline. This could be implemented as Eq. (10.16) below:

$$\Delta_{\theta} J_{(\theta)} \approx \sum_{t \geq 0} \left(\sum_{t^{\mathbb{P}\sqsupset>} \geq t} \gamma^{(t^{\mathbb{P}\sqsupset>} - t)} r_{(\tau)} - b_{(s_t)} \right) \Delta_{\theta} \log \pi_{\theta}(a_t | s_t) \tag{10.16}$$

10.6 Choosing a Baseline for the REINFORCE Algorithm

In the previous section, we identified that using a baseline reward value for each state may help distinguish a good action from a better one or a worse one, and hence also help in reducing the variance of the gradient of the REINFORCE method. We briefly also discussed the "advantage" function that we dealt in the "Dueling DQN" algorithm. But in a policy gradient-based REINFORCE we do not want to get into the state–value V(s) calculation (for now) and want a simpler baseline that can reflect some good indication of average (future, discounted) rewards from a particular state.

To achieve this one could come up with different types of baseline. Some of such baselines are presented in different research literature. One such "baeline" could be a constant moving average of the cumulative future discounted rewards received from all the trajectories which pass through this particular state. Since such rewards are computed in the REINFORCE algorithm itself, we do not need an external value computation function to enable this, and the resulting implementation could be simple and straightforward.

Yet another, more expressive baseline could be to take the actual advantage of a given action in a particular state, which is represented by the difference between the Q value of that action in that state and the state–value V of that state as [Q (s, a) − V (s)]. Also, since Q and V values already have a sense of reward inbuilt in them and a good treatment for differentiating across different types of future rewards and discounted rewards, we need not bother about including such factors separately. Therefore, Eq. (10.16) could be modified to replace the explicit reward and baseline as a composite reward with baseline using Q and V functions as Eq. (10.17) below:

$$\Delta_\theta J_{(\theta)} \approx \sum_{t\geq 0} \left(Q_{\pi_\theta,(s_t,a_t)} - V_{\pi_\theta,(s_t)}\right)\Delta_\theta \log \pi_\theta(a_t|s_t) \tag{10.17}$$

10.7 Summary

As opposed to value-based approaches, in which although the value estimates are stochastic, but the policy itself is deterministic, the policy-based approaches provides a mechanism to have a stochastic policy. Policy-based approaches are more direct as we are directly exploring the policy that takes action decisions instead of first estimating the values and then forming a policy based on such value estimates. Policy-based approaches also provide a better mechanism to work with scenarios having large action space and can also work with scenarios that require continuous action control.

But it is difficult to implement a policy-based approach, especially the policy gradient-based approaches. One reason for this is that the mathematics for finding the gradient of the policy value is intractable. With some simplifications and limiting assumptions, we were able to overcome this issue and implement in a Monte Carlo simulation-based algorithm called REINFORCE. But the resulting format of mathematical simplifications leads to a solution that has a lot of variance in gradient computation.

With some further assumptions and techniques leading to correct reward attribution for future rewards and reward baseline, we were able to bring down the variance in gradient computation in the REINFORCE algorithm. Such enhancements are not just limited to the REINFORCE algorithm but will go a long way forward in making other advanced policy-based approaches more practical to implement thereby opening the gates for more powerful reinforcement learning for real-life scenarios having large action space to work with and for scenarios requiring continuous actions control.

Chapter 11
Actor-Critic Models and the A3C

The Asynchronous Advantage Actor-Critic Model

Abstract In this chapter, we will take the idea of the policy-gradient-based REINFORCE with baseline algorithm further and combine that idea with the value-estimation ideas from the DQN, thus, bringing the best of both worlds together in the form of the Actor-Critic algorithm. We will further discuss the "advantage" baseline implementation of the model with deep learning-based approximators, and take the concept further to implement a parallel implementation of the deep learning-based advantage actor-critic algorithm in the synchronous (A2C) and the asynchronous (A3C) modes.

11.1 Introduction to Actor-Critic Methods

Until now, we have covered two different approaches in this book to solve the Reinforcement Learning problem, namely the value-estimation approach and the policy-gradient approach. The value-estimation approach had the advantage of being mathematically simple and easier to implement. It could even be implemented in an online approach. Some value-estimation approaches, especially the single-step approaches (as the ones based on TD (0)) could even be implemented in a truly online manner and are applicable even for continuous non-episodic tasks. The policy estimation approaches, on the other hand, were superior in terms of directly approximating the policy instead of indirectly estimating the values, and then determining the policy on the basis of the value. Also, policy estimation methods could be employed for tasks with large action-space cardinality and even for tasks requiring continuous action control (a limiting case with infinitely large action space).

The policy approximation approaches are difficult to implement because of their underlying intractable mathematics. With some simplifications, the REINFORCE algorithm provided a decent solution to implement policy-gradient approach using a Monte Carlo-like approach. Because of the inherent Monte Carlo-like

M. Sewak, *Deep Reinforcement Learning*,
https://doi.org/10.1007/978-981-13-8285-7_11

implementation, REINFORCE has issues in not being able to provide a true online solution and having a wide variance in the gradient approximation. REINFORCE with baseline provided a decent solution for the variability problem as discussed above. Of the different types of baselines, the state-value-based baseline is a straightforward one but we need to estimate the state-value externally somehow. Another way to get a good baseline that could reduce this variance is using the "advantage" estimates as the baseline.

With the use of "advantage" estimates as a baseline in the REINFORCE, the setup looks similar to that of the Dueling DQN that we discussed in Chap. 5. But apart from the concept of "advantage", there were not much of similarity between the Dueling DQN and the REINFORCE algorithm, as both are from a completely different family of algorithms and have different approaches and very different mathematics empowering them.

Introspecting carefully, we could see that the value-estimation and policy approximation-based approaches to a large extent complement one another. The weakness of one is nearly the strength of another. Therefore, combining the best of ideas from both the approaches may provide a very promising solution that combines their strengths. Also, we have learnt so far that the Q-Learning family of algorithms are the state-of-the-art methods in the value-estimation-based Reinforcement Learning, and REINFORCE with baseline is so far the only decent solution we have in the policy-gradient-based reinforcement learning approach. Combining these two approaches gives us the Actor-Critic method as shown in Fig. 11.1 ahead.

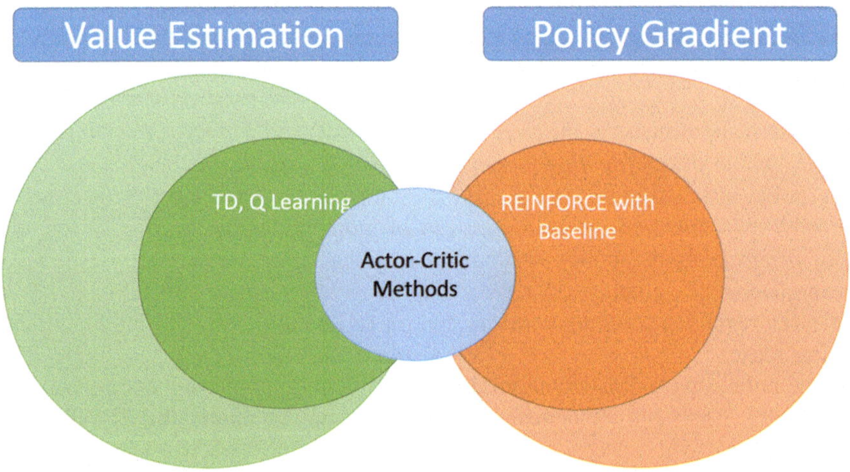

Fig. 11.1 Actor-critic methods inspiration

11.2 Conceptual Design of the Actor-Critic Method

At the very basic, as the name suggests, the actor-critic model consists of an actor and a critic. The role of the actor, again as the name suggests is to take an action. As we would have realized earlier that in the context of Reinforcement Learning, to take an action, we require a policy. So, the actor in the case of the actor-critic implements and uses a policy to take any action.

The critic, on the other hand, again as the name suggests, plays the role of a critic for the actor and provide feedback with respect to the goodness (or worseness) of the action taken by the actor when in a given state.

The actor and the critic work in tandem this way (Fig. 11.2). The actor plays an active role to engage with the environment to act upon it and change it. The resulting rewards are received by the critic, which updates and corrects its estimates and updates the actor with the corrected value of its estimates which helps the actor to update itself.

The environment subsequently changes as a result of the action taken by the actor and besides the instantaneous reward the environment also sends the new state reached as a result of the action taken. The new state is sent to both the actors, which uses it for taking the action and to the critic which uses it for evaluating its value estimates. This is shown in Fig. 11.3.

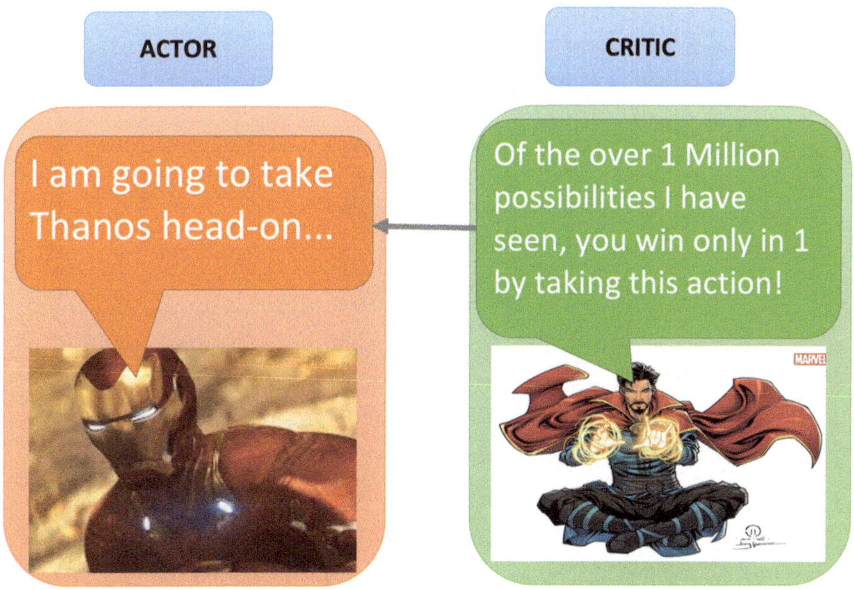

Fig. 11.2 Role of actor and critic

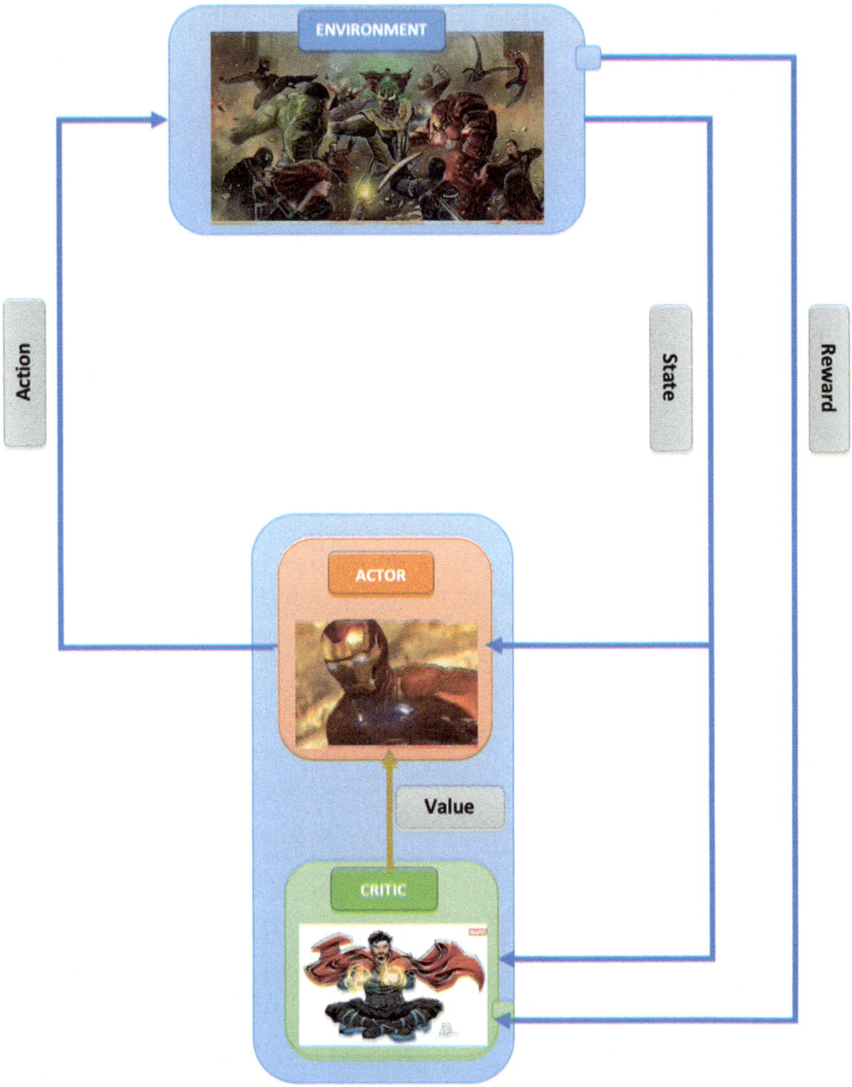

Fig. 11.3 Conceptual design of the actor-critic method

11.3 Architecture for the Actor-Critic Implementation

Let us dive deeper into the internal mechanics of the actor and the critic. To take any action in reinforcement learning, we require a policy. In the actor-critic model since the actor is taking the action, so this policy is needed to be with the actor. The actor, hence, has a (stochastic) policy which it uses to take an action in every step of

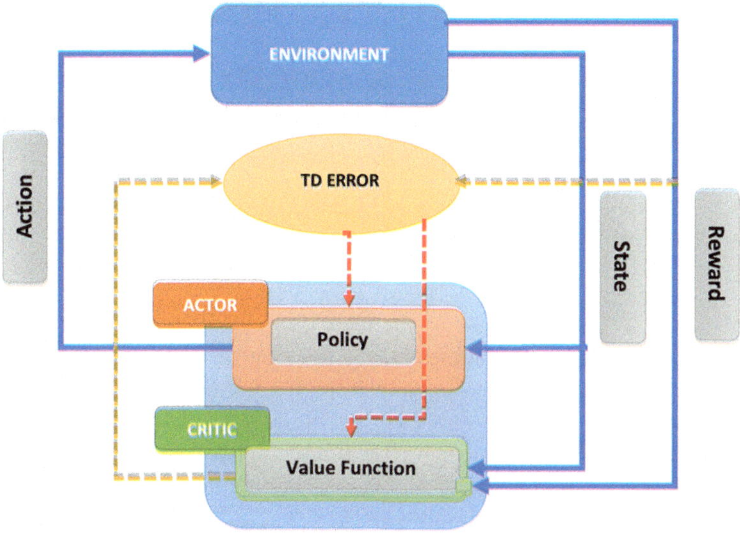

Fig. 11.4 High-level architecture for the implementation of actor-critic method

training, while also improving updating its policy (approximation) using the policy-gradient approach quite similar to what we have discussed in the last chapter. The actor's policy is updated continuously during training, and for updating this policy, it uses the (state) value estimates as received from the critic. The critic's value estimates serve as a baseline for the actor to update its policy using the policy-gradient approach (Fig. 11.4).

Though the "REINFOCE with baseline" algorithm also uses the estimates of state value as a baseline, but the state value as used in REINFORCE algorithm for baseline is not bootstrapped. That is, the value of the state does not update itself in each iteration as it does in the Q-Learning, and hence, it cannot be called a critic, because a "Critic" is essentially bootstrapped, and therefore for a critic, it is essential that the value estimates are updated in every iteration. The error between the subsequent state values estimates is computed using the instantaneous reward and discounted state value of subsequent state as shown below in Eq. (11.1). In this equation, γ is the discounting factor. The below Eq. (11.1) corresponds to one-step return updates, which is similar to TD (0) without the eligibility traces (or a special case of eligibility trace). If required, this equation could be expanded to an n-step update. In Eq. (11.1), V is the state-value estimator function parametrized by weight/parameter vector W. Since it's a bootstrapping approach as explained above, so with every step, the weight vector of the value estimator function also needs to change at every step. So, at the tth step, this parameter vector could be denoted as W_t. The value for any terminal state is set as 0.

$$\delta_t = R_t + \gamma V(S_{t+1}; W_t) - V(S_t; W_t) \tag{11.1}$$

Once the error at time t is estimated as in Eq. (11.1), in each bootstrapping step subsequently, the value estimator function of the critic is then updated. Since the value estimator function is parametrized by weight vector W, updating the weight vector W from W_t to W_{t+1} as in Eq. (11.2) in each iteration updates the value estimator function. In Eq. (11.2), α_w represents the learning rate for this value estimator function.

$$W_{t+1} = W_t + \alpha_w \delta_t \Delta_w V(S; W_t) \tag{11.2}$$

Similar to the update of value estimator function of the critic, the policy estimator function of the actor also updates in each iteration as shown in Eq. (11.3) below. In Eq. (11.3), π is the policy estimator function, which is parametrized over parameter vector θ. The parameter vector θ also updates in each iteration to θ_{t+1} from θ_t as shown in Eq. (11.3), and α_θ acts as a learning rate for the update of policy estimator function.

$$\theta_{t+1} = \theta_t + \alpha_\theta \delta_t \Delta_\theta \log \pi(A \mid S; \theta_t) \tag{11.3}$$

11.3.1 Actor-Critic Method and the (Dueling) DQN

In the chapter on Deep Q-Networks, we covered the Deep Learning approaches to action-value estimation and discussed how the Deep Learning-based estimators are superior to conventional machine learning based and other iterative estimators, especially in the case of applications have large state-spaces cardinality like the one using images and video feeds for input/observation.

In the case of Policy approximation, we use the stochastic policy-gradient approach like that of "REINFORCE with baseline" as we discussed in the chapter on policy-based approaches. But we would implement the estimator/approximator function of this as an online Deep Learning model, which could update the policy in a true online manner instead of the Monte Carlo simulation-like approach of the REINFORCE. The Convolutional Neural Network-based models would be ideal for this, especially as in many of the real-life cases, we might be processing images/video feeds as input states.

The "REINFORCE with baseline" algorithm required a baseline so we would need some mechanism to have such a baseline here as well, we could use the State-Value estimates for this. Also, as we have discussed earlier in this chapter, since we want a critic whose value updates/bootstrap with every iteration and not just any simple baseline, we could use an online Deep Learning Network for the (State) Value-estimation piece as well. Similar to the Deep Learning model of the policy estimator, the Deep Learning model of the Value estimator also needs to be

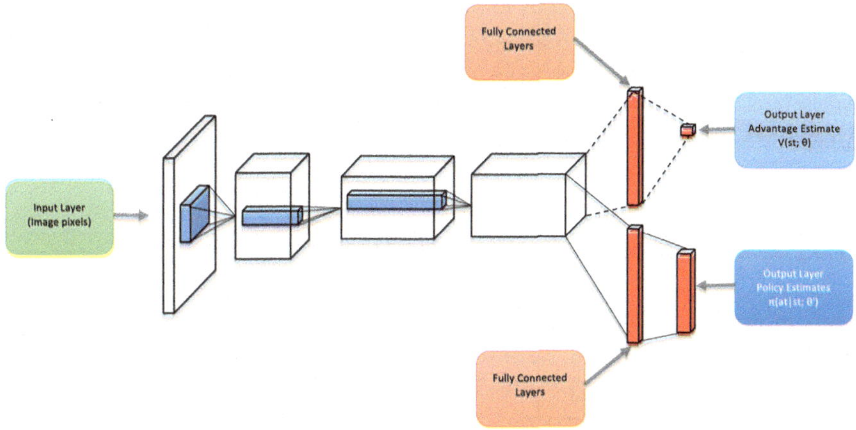

Fig. 11.5 Illustrative CNN-based implementation of actor-critic with state-value-based critic

updated in every iteration to provide the online bootstrapping effect that would make it a true critic (Fig. 11.5).

Since we require two Deep Learning-based function approximators here, one for the policy estimation (the actor) and another for the value estimation (the critic), and since both the approximators would require the common state inputs, so by sharing the deep learning network's architecture to as much extent possible between these two network requirements, we can notonly make the computations more efficient, but also ensure that the underlying processing of the input state and hence, the interpretation of the received state is common for both the actor and the critic, hence can ensure better coordination between them.

This idea is very similar to the one in the Dueling DQN networks that we discussed in the chapter on Deep Q-Learning. We also discovered in that chapter that the Dueling DQN owing to this unique architecture is more powerful than the simple DQN and could surpass its performance on standardized tests. With the similar implementation as earlier with Dueling DQN, we would share the Convolution Layers in the architecture between both the networks of the actor and critic approximators and have dedicated fully connected layers for both of them that leads to their respective output layers.

The actor needs to output a stochastic policy. So, for discrete action space, the actor-network needs to end in a SoftMax activation layer with as many numbers of neurons as the cardinality of the action space, with each neuron's output representing the probability of taking that action. The output of the actor-network represents the probability of goodness of each action for a given state and ranges between [0, 1], where the sum of probabilities across all possible actions is 1.

The critic network needs to output the value estimates for the input state/observation as received from the environment such that it could be used as a bootstrapped baseline for the policy estimator. Since this estimate is a single real value, which is also a continuous linear output, therefore, the critic network ends in a single node with "Linear Activation" to represent this value. While using Deep Learning, it is always good to scale the values. So, in the actual implementation in some cases, this value may not be the absolute state value but some scaled representation of the same.

11.3.2 Advantage Actor-Critic Model Architecture

While discussing the enhancements for the REINFORCE algorithm in the chapter on policy-based approaches, we discussed that one of the desirable enhancements would be to use "advantage" estimates instead of other baselines like a constant baseline value as baseline, or a moving average or even the absolute state value. We also discussed that how by using the "advantage" as a baseline the variance in the gradients of the agent/actor's approximation function could be reduced, thereby making it learn faster.

Also, in the chapter on Dueling DQN, we saw that instead of computing the Action-Value, these algorithms find it more optimal to naturally estimate the "advantage" instead. We merge these ideas, here, the make the critic generate a bootstrapped "advantage" estimate instead of the state-value estimate. Since the "advantage" estimates generated by the critic is bootstrapped, it still is considered a true critic and it also updates its approximation function in every iteration. The subsequent "advantage" estimate from the critic is fed into the actor, which uses it as a baseline (Fig. 11.6).

With REINFORCE, since it was already difficult to implement the algorithm, and since the "advantage" estimates required a separate computation so many a times "advantage" is not used to trade in for simplicity in the case of REINFORCE

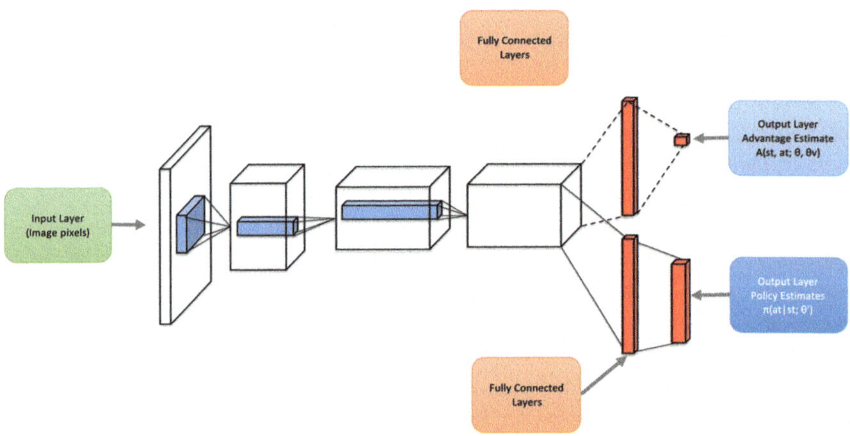

Fig. 11.6 Illustrative CNN-based implementation of "advantage" actor-critic

algorithm's implementation. But in the case of Actor-Critic, especially the Deep Learning-based implementations of Actor-Critic, since the implementation complexity is not very different from that of the state-based baseline implementation in a similar deep learning-based approach, the "advantage" based implementation is preferred in the case of Actor-Critic and many of the works in the literature uses this variant.

11.4 Asynchronous Advantage Actor-Critic Implementation (A3C)

In the case of Q-Learning, when we enhanced the underlying mechanism of function approximators and replaced them with the powerful Deep Learning models-based approximators like the Convolution Neural Networks, we got a model that surpassed all known models' performance, and even human adversaries' performance at many tasks. Now when we combine the best of value/ advantage-estimation approaches, the best of policy approximation-based approaches and the best of Deep Learning enhancements then though it is sure to tick all the right boxes in the performance area, but the only drawback of this system that could be envisaged is that the efficiency of such algorithmic implementations over complex input states would be found lagging.

But fortunately, Deep Learning could be massively parallelized over Graphical Processing Units (GPUs). This is exactly how even the Advantage-based Actor-Critic algorithms with Deep Learning models are implemented, but still, it requires a lot of time to train for each iteration of the agent sequentially. Another problem of this sequential single-agent approach is what we have already discussed in the chapter on DQN, which is that related to frequent correlated sequential input states that could lead to instability and bias-related issues, finally leading to convergence-related problems for the approximator. We also discussed some of the workarounds like using experience replays from a prioritized memory buffer to solve this problem. But with the size of network at hand, we would require a very large memory buffer for an effective training in the case of sizeable actor-critic implementations.

A better approach as suggested by the team at DeepMind is the use of Asynchronous agents for the Actor-Critic Advantage (A3C) design (Fig. 11.7). In this approach, instead of a single-agent learning in sequence, multiple agents are spawned simultaneously and they all train in parallel (across multiple GPU cores) across different instances of the environment.

There exists a global centralized network parameter server to store the parameters for both the actors and the critics. Any new agent that spawns, copies the current values of the parameters from the global networks parameter server and updates their copy of the parameters while training with their instance of the environment independently. After some fixed steps, or reaching the terminal state,

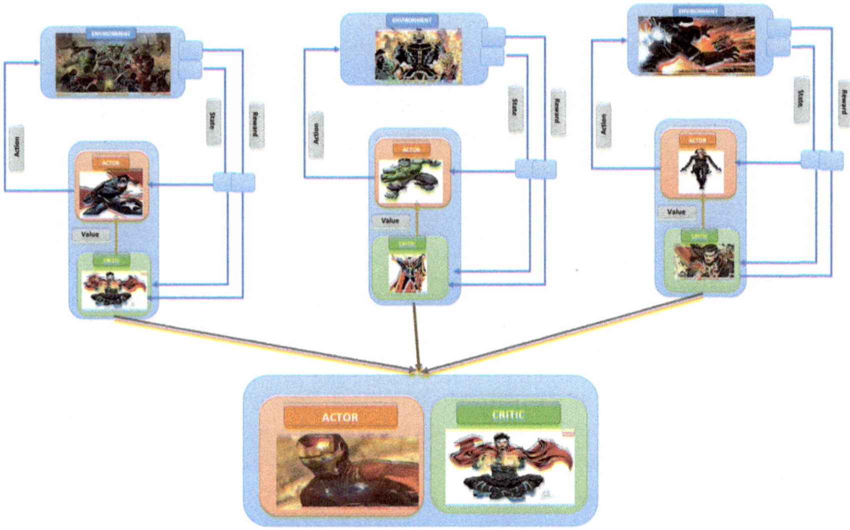

Fig. 11.7 High-level idea of the A3C

the agents would merge their updates with the global parameters as in the centralized parameter server, then copy the now updated global network parameters, and resume interacting with their respective instance of the environment.

Since each agent has their own copy of the environment, essentially each agent is working on different and uncorrelated states (from different instances of the same environment class), and hence, the subsequent global updates are uncorrelated. This brings the stability in the training and obviates the need for provisioning very large memory for experience replays for each agent individually.

The Asynchronous Advantage Actor-Critic (A3C) model implementation could be considered as the state of the art in Deep Reinforcement Learning. The Asynchronous Advantage Actor-Critic Model did not only play as well or better than the DQN in the Atari 2600 games and many more, but it could achieve the DQN level performance in half the time that DQN took, and that too while training on CPUs instead of GPUs. Of the different asynchronous parallel implementation of the algorithms like SARSA (0), Q-Learning (n-step), and the Actor-Critic (A3C), the A3C was found to have delivered the best results.

11.5 (Synchronous) Advantage Actor-Critic Implementation (A2C)

The Asynchronous Advantage Actor-Critic (A3C) is the parallel implementation of the (nonparallel) Actor-Critic advantage architecture that we covered earlier. A3C implementation works very well and has demonstrated its effectiveness on the

Atari2600 and other standardized reinforcement learning challenges. But there is one drawback in A3C, that is that since different parallel agents are asynchronously and independently syncing with the global network parameters in the centralized parameter server, all the agents are for some duration working with an outdated copy of the network parameters. Also, since the last sync of any particular agent with the global network parameters, some other agents could have updated the network parameters, then when this agent comes back to update the global network parameter again, it updates the global parameters which are based on its initial synced copy of parameters, which is outdated by this time. Because of this, the training is not very stable and the convergence may not be very smooth.

To avoid this phenomenon, a synchronous variant of the parallel implementation of the Advantage Actor-Critic (A2C) is also proposed (Fig. 11.8). But this proposal has been only in the form of some blogs with not many standardized comparisons of the performance results available for this proposal's implementation in a standard research literature.

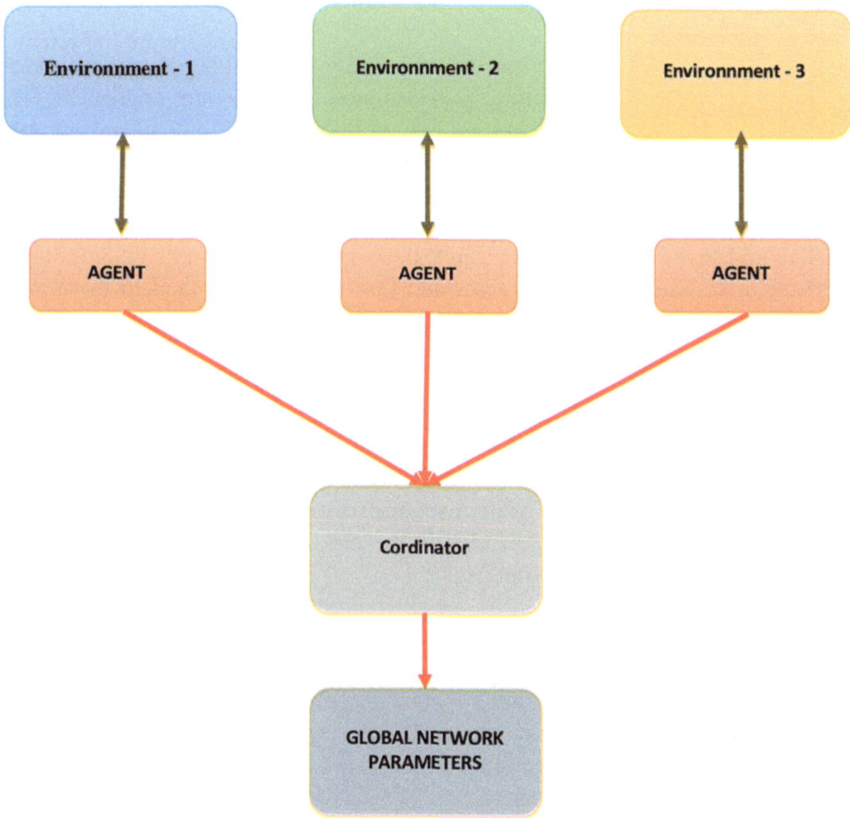

Fig. 11.8 High-level idea of the (Synchronous) A2C

In the Synchronized parallel A2C, instead of all agents syncing with the global network parameter as in the centralized parameter server asynchronously, they are all made to update in a synchronous way. As all the agents work synchronously and make the updates at the same time, they all need not update the global network individually and directly.

The synchronous parallel A2C works much like a mini-batch gradient update, and since the number of steps is same across each agent, a simple average of the updates of all agents' gradients updates could be computed and the global network parameters updated with this computed average gradient updates.

This work of coordinating across all the independent agents is done by a system called the "coordinator". Since all the agents are similar and updates synchronously after the same number of steps so in practical implementation, different agents need not be spawned and the same agent with different instantiations of the environment class could give the intended effect.

11.6 Summary

The policy-based approaches, especially the Policy-Gradient-based approaches are very promising but at the same time also not very easy to implement. The Value-estimation-based approaches are easy to implement but not as good as their policy-gradient counterparts. Combining the two gives us the Actor-Critic algorithm, which brings the best of both worlds for reinforcement learning implementations. As opposed to the "REINFORCE with baseline" algorithm, the baseline updates in Actor-Critic are bootstrapped and hence works like a critic.

In the actor-critic model, the actor and the critic work in tandem to form an agent. The actor actively engages with the environment to manipulate it. The critic provides the baseline estimates for the agent's update, and in turn, receives the next state from the environment to update itself similar to that in an online value-estimation method. The actor-critic thus requires two function approximators, one for the value estimator of the critic and another for the policy approximator of the actor. These two model networks could ideally be deep learning-based models as well, and in that case, they could also share a substantial part of their network (like CNN layers) architecture, especially the part of the model architecture that extracts features from the incoming state.

Multiple agents of the actor-critic model could even work in parallel to interact with their individual instances of the environment thereby not only making the training faster but also removing a lot of bias and obviating large memory requirements. The parallel approach could be implemented in both synchronous and asynchronous manners. The Asynchronous Advantage Actor-Critic (A3C) implementation has been quite successful in surpassing many best scores of previous models across the Atari2600 games.

Chapter 12
A3C in Code

Coding the Asynchronous Advantage Actor-Critic Agent

Abstract In this chapter, we will cover the Asynchronous Advantage Actor-Critic Model. We use the TensorFlow's own implementation of the Keras for this. We define the actor-critic model using the Sub-Classing and eager execution functionality of Keras. Both the master and worker agents use this model. The asynchronous workers are implemented as different threads, syncing with the master after every few steps or completion of their respective episodes.

12.1 Project Structure and Dependencies

Like that of the Q-Learning code covered in Chap. 9, we continue to use the same virtual environment (DRL) based on Python 3.6.5, and PyCharm IDE.

The additional requirements in this chapter are that of deep learning-based dependencies and OpenAI Gym's environments. For implementing Deep Learning models, we have used the Keras wrapper from the TensorFlow implementation (v 1.12.0) as shown in Fig. 12.1. From Gym, we are using the "CartPole-v0" environment, but the readers are encouraged to try other environments as well, and this is as simple as changing this name in the "environment" parameter.

The code is largely inspired from the A3C implementation provided in TensorFlow's official GitHub repository (link in references). The code has been further enhanced with respect to the model architecture, and rewritten to make its structure compatible with the flow of code used so far in this book and to enhance the lucidity and intuitiveness of the code.

The code has an Actor-Critic Model class, which defines the common approximator model for both the master and the workers in an A3C. The worker works on a copy of the model and their own instance of the environment to compute the gradient updates required, and then update the gradient of the master model with the computed updates, followed by copying the master's parameters.

The Model class is defined using the Sub-Classing feature of the tf.pyhton.keras. Model class. This is an advanced feature, which makes the implementation of complex models, the ones that require a shared network, shared inputs, or residual

M. Sewak, *Deep Reinforcement Learning*,
https://doi.org/10.1007/978-981-13-8285-7_12

Fig. 12.1 Requirements.txt

```
requirements.txt

# runtime = Python3.6.5

tensorflow
numpy
gym
matplotlib
```

connections, simpler. We use a shared network architecture in which both the policy and the value approximator functions share a major part of the implemented DNN network and then diverge to have their own layers. The model also uses TensorFlow's "eager execution" feature which makes it easier to build and debug the model in a functional programming manner, and also in case of our implementation where the model needs to be pre-built for instantiation. Another way to achieve a similar feat (although will require some more code) is using the Keras' Functional API. Readers are encouraged to go through the links in references for both the Functional API and the Model Sub-Classing and experiment with different implementations.

The code further, has a Master class and Worker class. The Master class is the entry point to the A3C implementation. The Master instantiate a copy of the Actor-Critic Model to retain its trainable weight such that the workers have a global copy of the weights/network parameters to update and to sync with. The Master class invokes as many workers as the number of CPU threads (in the case of modern CPUs, each CPU core can have multiple threads) on the local machine. Each of the workers instantiates a local copy of the Actor-Critic Model and the environment.

In our implementation of the model, we have two hidden layers for the DNN which are shared between the policy and the value networks. From the last shared hidden layer, both the policy and value networks diverge into their dedicated layers. Both the policy and the value network have a dedicated hidden layer of their own, followed by their respective value layers. As covered in Chap. 11 about the architecture of these models, the policy network ends in a SoftMax layer (or alternatively a "Dense" logit layer over which SoftMax function is applied as in this code) with as many neurons as the cardinality of the action space that provides the class probabilities to enable a Stochastic policy (the actions are samples based on their action probabilities as predicted by this layer). The Value network ends in a single neuron layer, providing the value estimate.

The workers keep playing with their copy of the environment and keep updating their local copy of the model, until they either complete an episode or reach the maximum number of steps for a forced sync with the master. During the synchronization process, the workers compute their model's required gradient update, and then updates the global model's network parameters as they stand then with this update. Following this update, the worker copies the updated state (model trainable weights) from the global model to their local copy of the model and resumes playing with their copy of the environment.

Worker class is implemented as an instance of the "threading.Thread" class. The threaded implementation of the worker allows to directly share the memory space across different workers making it very easy to share the global variables required for interaction without going through slightly more complex ways of achieving a similar effect in a multiprocessor environment. But the multi-threaded implementation may not be as efficient or scalable as a true multiprocessing implementation. Python has a Global Interpreter Lock (GIL) because of which true multiprocessing is not possible directly in Python and may require external library/software support to do so. An easier way to achieve this is through multiprocessing task queues using software packages that support distributed task queues. The multiprocessing library within python may also provide a decent, though not so scalable option. Readers are encouraged to experiment with different mechanisms of the worker class' asynchronous implementation and the related mechanism for sharing variable, and coordination between the worker and the master.

Lastly, we also have a custom implementation of the Memory class. This time we use a very simple list with memory instead of a Deque. The custom exception class has no changes from what we covered in Chap. 9.

The final structure of the project with all these code and model files is as shown in Fig. 12.2.

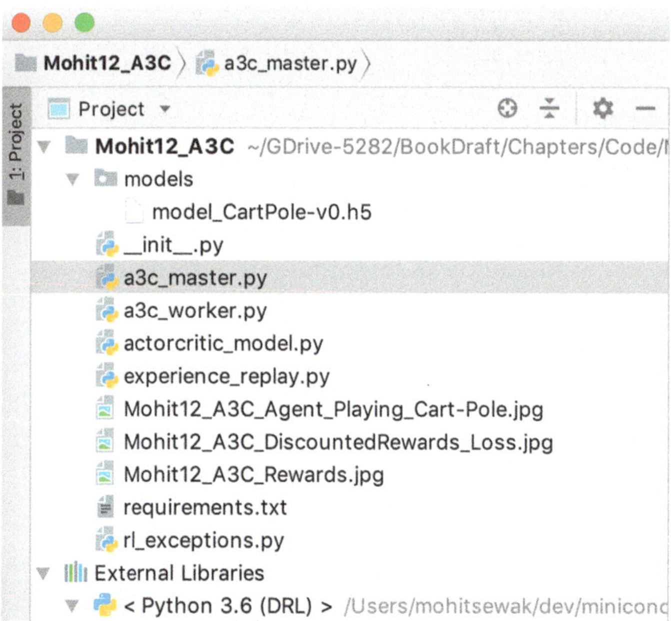

Fig. 12.2 Project structure for the DDQN project

12.2 Code (A3C_Master—File: a3c_master.py)

```
""" A3C in Code - Centralized/ Gobal Network Parameter
Server/ Controller

A3C Code as in the book Deep Reinforcement Learning, Chapter
12.

Runtime: Python 3.6.5
Dependencies: numpy, matplotlib, tensorflow (/ tensorflow-
gpu), gym
DocStrings: GoogleStyle

Author : Mohit Sewak (p20150023@goa-bits-pilani.ac.in)
Inspired from: A3C implementation on TensorFLow official
github repository (Tensorflow/models/research)

"""

import logging
# making general imports
import multiprocessing
import os
import numpy as np
# making deep learning and env related imports
import tensorflow as tf
import gym
import matplotlib.pyplot as plt
# making imports of custom modules
from experience_replay import SimpleListBasedMemory
from actorcritic_model import ActorCriticModel
from a3c_worker import A3C_Worker
# Configuring logging and Creating logger, setting the log to
streaming, and level as DEBUG
logging.basicConfig()
logger = logging.getLogger()
logger.setLevel(logging.DEBUG)


class A3C_Master():
    """A3C Master

        Centralized Master class of A3C used for hosting the
global network parameters and spawning the agents.

        Args:
            env_name (str): Name of a valid gym environment
            model_dir (str): Directory for saving the model
```

```
during training, and loading the same while playing
            learning_rate (float): The learning rate (alpha)
for the optimizer

        Examples:
            agent = A3C_Master()
            agent.train()
            agent.play()

    """

    def __init__(self, env_name='CartPole-v0',
model_dir="models", learning_rate=0.001):
        self.env_name = env_name
        self.model_dir = model_dir
        self.alpha = learning_rate
        if not os.path.exists(model_dir):
            os.makedirs(model_dir)
        self.env = gym.make(self.env_name)
        self.state_size = self.env.observation_space.shape[0]
        self.action_size = self.env.action_space.n
        self.optimizer = tf.train.AdamOptimizer(self.alpha,
use_locking=True)
        logger.debug("StateSize:{},
ActionSize:{}".format(self.state_size, self.action_size))
        self.master_model =
ActorCriticModel(self.action_size)  # global network

self.master_model(tf.convert_to_tensor(np.random.random((1,
self.state_size)), dtype=tf.float32))

    def train(self):
        """Train the A3C agent
            Main function to train the A3C agent after
instantiation.

            This method uses the number of processor cores to
spawns as many Workers. The workers are spawned as
            multiple parallel threads instead of multiple
parallel processes. Being a threaded execution, the workers
            share memory and hence can write directly into
the shared global variables.

            A more optimal, completely asynchronous
implementation could be to spawn the workers as different
processes
            using a task queue or multiprocessing. In case if
this is adopted, then the shared variables need to made
            accessible in the distributed environment.
```

```
        """
        a3c_workers = [A3C_Worker(self.master_model,
self.optimizer, i, self.env_name, self.model_dir)
                       for i in
range(multiprocessing.cpu_count())]
        for i, worker in enumerate(a3c_workers):
            logger.info("Starting worker {}".format(i))
            worker.start()
        [worker.join() for worker in a3c_workers]
        self.plot_training_statistics()

    def play(self):
        """Play the environment using a trained agent

            This function opens a (graphical) window that
will play a trained agent. The function will try to retrieve
            the model saved in the model_dir with filename
formatted to contain the associated env_name.
            If the model is not found, then the function will
first call the train function to start the training.
        """
        env = self.env.unwrapped
        state = env.reset()
        model = self.master_model
        model_path = os.path.join(self.model_dir,
'model_{}.h5'.format(self.env_name))
        if not os.path.exists(model_path):
            logger.info('A3CMaster: No model found at {},
starting fresh training before playing!'.format(model_path))
            self.train()
        logger.info('A3CMaster: Playing env, Loading model
from: {}'.format(model_path))
        model.load_weights(model_path)
        done = False
        step_counter = 0
        reward_sum = 0
        try:
            while not done:
                env.render(mode='rgb_array')
                policy, value =
model(tf.convert_to_tensor(state[None, :], dtype=tf.float32))
                policy = tf.nn.softmax(policy)
                action = np.argmax(policy)
                state, reward, done, _ = env.step(action)
                reward_sum += reward
                logger.info("{}. Reward: {}, action:
{}".format(step_counter, reward_sum, action))
                step_counter += 1

        except KeyboardInterrupt:
            print("Received Keyboard Interrupt. Shutting
down.")
```

```
        finally:
            env.close()

    def plot_training_statistics(self,
training_statistics=None):
        """Plot training statistics

        This function plot the training statistics like the
steps, rewards, discounted_rewards, and loss in each
        of the training episode.

        """
        training_statistics =
A3C_Worker.global_shared_training_stats if
training_statistics is None \
            else training_statistics
        all_episodes = []
        all_steps = []
        all_rewards = []
        all_discounted_rewards = []
        all_losses = []
        for stats in training_statistics:
            worker, episode, steps, reward,
discounted_rewards, loss = stats
            all_episodes.append(episode)
            all_steps.append(steps)
            all_rewards.append(reward)
            all_discounted_rewards.append(discounted_rewards)
            all_losses.append(loss)
        self._make_double_axis_plot(all_episodes, all_steps,
all_rewards)

self._make_double_axis_plot(all_episodes,all_discounted_rewar
ds,all_losses, label_y1="Discounted Reward",
                                    label_y2="Loss",
color_y1="cyan", color_y2="black")

    @staticmethod
    def _make_double_axis_plot(data_x, data_y1, data_y2,
x_label='Episodes (e)', label_y1='Steps To Episode
Completion',
                               label_y2='Reward in each
Episode', color_y1="red", color_y2="blue"):
        """Internal helper function for plotting dual axis
plots
        """
        fig, ax1 = plt.subplots()
        ax1.set_xlabel(x_label)
        ax1.set_ylabel(label_y1, color=color_y1)
        ax1.plot(data_x, data_y1, color=color_y1)
        ax2 = ax1.twinx()
```

```
            ax2.set_ylabel(label_y2, color=color_y2)
            ax2.plot(data_x, data_y2, color=color_y2)
            fig.tight_layout()
            plt.show()


    if __name__ == "__main__":
        """Main function for testing the A3C Master code's
    implementation
        """
        agent = A3C_Master()
        agent.train()
        agent.play()
```

12.2.1 A3C_Worker (File: a3c_worker.py)

```
""" A3C in Code - A3C Worker

A3C Code as in the book Deep Reinforcement Learning, Chapter
12.

Runtime: Python 3.6.5
Dependencies: numpy, matplotlib, tensorflow (/ tensorflow-
gpu), gym
DocStrings: GoogleStyle

Author : Mohit Sewak (p20150023@goa-bits-pilani.ac.in)

"""
import logging
# making general imports
import threading
import os
import numpy as np
# making deep learning and env related imports
import tensorflow as tf
import gym
# making imports of custom modules
from experience_replay import SimpleListBasedMemory
from actorcritic_model import ActorCriticModel
# Configuring logging and Creating logger, setting the log to
streaming, and level as DEBUG
logging.basicConfig()
logger = logging.getLogger()
logger.setLevel(logging.DEBUG)


class A3C_Worker(threading.Thread):
    """A3C Worker Class
```

```
        A3C Worker implemented as a thread (extends
threading.Thread). The function computes the gradient of the
policy
        and value networks' updates and then update the
global network parameters of a similar policy and value
        networks after every some steps or after completion
of a worker's episode.

    """
    global_constant_max_episodes_across_all_workers = 10000
    global_constant_total_steps_before_sync_for_any_workers =
10
    global_shared_best_episode_score = 0
    global_shared_total_episodes_across_all_workers = 0
    global_shared_semaphore = threading.Lock()
    global_shared_training_stats = []
    global_shared_episode_reward = 0

    def __init__(self, central_a3c_model, optimizer,
worker_id, env_name, model_dir, discounting_factor=0.99):
        """Initialize the A3C worker instance

            Args:
                central_a3c_model (ActorCriticModel): An
instance of the ActorCriticModel or similar model shared by
the
                                                       A3C
master
                optimizer (tf.train.Optimizer): An instance
of the Optimizer object as used in the A3C_Master to update
                                                       its
network parameters.
                worker_id (int): An integer representing the
id of the instantiated worker.
                model_dir (str): dir for saving the model.
Should be the same location from where the A3C_Master will
                                                       retrieve
the trained model for playing.
                discounting_factor (float): Value of gamma,
the discounting factor for future rewards.
        """
        super(A3C_Worker, self).__init__()
        self.central_a3c_model = central_a3c_model
        self.optimizer = optimizer
        self.worker_id = worker_id
        self.env_name = env_name
        self.env = gym.make(env_name).unwrapped
        self.n_states = self.env.observation_space.shape[0]
        self.n_actions = self.env.action_space.n
```

```
        self.gamma = discounting_factor
        self.worker_model = ActorCriticModel(self.n_actions)
        self.memory = SimpleListBasedMemory()
        self.model_dir = model_dir
        self.this_episode_loss = 0
        self.this_episode_steps = 0
        self.this_episode_reward = 0
        self.this_episode_discountedreward = 0
        self.total_steps = 0
        self.steps_since_last_sync = 0
        logger.debug("Instantiating env for worker id:
{}".format(self.worker_id))
    def run(self):
        """Thread's run function

            This is the default function that is executed
when a the start() function of a class instance that extends
            threading.Thread class is called
            This function has the majority of the logic for
the worker's functioning.

        """
        logger.debug("Starting execution of thread for worker
id: {}".format(self.worker_id))
        while
A3C_Worker.global_shared_total_episodes_across_all_workers <
A3C_Worker.global_constant_max_episodes_across_all_workers:

A3C_Worker.global_shared_total_episodes_across_all_workers +=
1
            logger.info("Starting episode {}/{} using worker
{}".format(

A3C_Worker.global_shared_total_episodes_across_all_workers,

A3C_Worker.global_constant_max_episodes_across_all_workers,
self.worker_id))
            done = False
            current_state = self._reset_episode_stats()
            while not done:
                self._increment_all_steps()
                policy_logits, values =
self.worker_model(tf.convert_to_tensor(np.random.random((1,
self.n_states)), dtype=tf.float32))
                stochastic_action_probabilities =
tf.nn.softmax(policy_logits)
                stochastic_policy_driven_action =
np.random.choice(self.n_actions,
p=stochastic_action_probabilities.numpy()[0])
```

```
                    action = stochastic_policy_driven_action
                    new_state, reward, done, _ =
self.env.step(action)
                    if done:
                        reward = -1
                    self.this_episode_reward += reward
                    self.memory.store(current_state, action,
reward)

                    if self.steps_since_last_sync >=
A3C_Worker.global_constant_total_steps_before_sync_for_any_wo
rkers or done:

self._sync_worker_gradient_updates_with_global_model(done,
new_state)
                    if done:

A3C_Worker.global_shared_training_stats.append((self.worker_i
d,
A3C_Worker.global_shared_total_episodes_across_all_workers,
                        self.this_episode_steps,
self.this_episode_reward, self.this_episode_discountedreward,
self.this_episode_loss))
                        if self.this_episode_reward >
A3C_Worker.global_shared_best_episode_score:
                            self._update_best_model()

    def _update_best_model(self):
        """Rewrite the saved model with a beteer performing
one

            This function rewrites the existing model (if
any) saved in the model_dir, if any worker thread happens
            to obtain a better score in any of the episodes
than the laste best score for an episode by any of the
            workers.

        """
        A3C_Worker.global_shared_best_episode_score =
self.this_episode_reward
        with A3C_Worker.global_shared_semaphore:
            logger.info("Saving best model - worker:{},
episode:{}, episode-steps:{}, "
                        "episode-reward: {}, episode-
discounted-reward:{}, episode-loss:{}".
                        format(self.worker_id,

A3C_Worker.global_shared_total_episodes_across_all_workers,
                               self.this_episode_steps,
self.this_episode_reward,
```

```
self.this_episode_discountedreward, self.this_episode_loss))

self.central_a3c_model.save_weights(os.path.join(self.model_d
ir, 'model_{}.h5'.format(self.env_name)))

    def _reset_episode_stats(self):
        """Internal helper function to reset the episodal
statistics
        """
        self.this_episode_steps = 0
        self.this_episode_loss = 0
        self.this_episode_reward = 0
        self.this_episode_discountedreward = 0
        self.memory.clear()
        return self.env.reset()

    def _increment_all_steps(self):
        """Internal helper function to increment the step
counts in a workers execution.
        """
        self.total_steps += 1
        self.steps_since_last_sync += 1
        self.this_episode_steps += 1

    def _sync_worker_gradient_updates_with_global_model(self,
done, new_state):
        """Internal helper function to sync the gradient
updates of the worker with the master

            This function is called whenever either an
episodes ends or a pecified number of steps have elapsed
since
            a particular worker synced with the master.
            In this process the losses for the policy and
values are computed and the loss function is differentiated
            to fund the gradient. The so obtained gradient is
used to update the weights of the master (global network)
            model parameters. Then the worker copies the
updated weights of the master and resumes training.

        """
        with tf.GradientTape() as tape:
            total_loss = self._compute_loss(done, new_state)
        self.this_episode_loss += total_loss
        # Calculate local gradients
        grads = tape.gradient(total_loss,
self.worker_model.trainable_weights)
        # Push local gradients to global model
        self.optimizer.apply_gradients(zip(grads,
self.central_a3c_model.trainable_weights))
```

```
        # Update local model with new weights

self.worker_model.set_weights(self.central_a3c_model.get_weig
hts())
        self.memory.clear()
        self.steps_since_last_sync = 0

    def _compute_loss(self, done, new_state):
        """Function to compute the loss

            This method compute the loss as required by the
_sync_worker_gradient_updates_with_global_model

            method to compute the gradients

        """
        if done:
          reward_sum = 0.  # terminal
        else:
          reward_sum =
self.worker_model(tf.convert_to_tensor(new_state[None,
:],dtype=tf.float32))[-1].numpy()[0]
        # Get discounted rewards
        discounted_rewards = []
        for reward in self.memory.rewards[::-1]:  # reverse
buffer r
            reward_sum = reward + self.gamma * reward_sum
            discounted_rewards.append(reward_sum)
        discounted_rewards.reverse()

self.this_episode_discountedreward=np.float(discounted_reward
s[0])
        # logger.info("Reward episode:{},step:{} =
{}".format(A3C_Worker.global_shared_total_episodes_across_all
_workers, self.this_episode_steps, self.memory.rewards[::-
1]))
        # logger.info("Discounted-Reward episode:{},step:{} =
{}".format(A3C_Worker.global_shared_total_episodes_across_all
_workers, self.this_episode_steps, discounted_rewards))
        logits, values =
self.worker_model(tf.convert_to_tensor(np.vstack(self.memory.
states), dtype=tf.float32))
        # Get our advantages
        advantage =
tf.convert_to_tensor(np.array(discounted_rewards)[:, None],
dtype=tf.float32) - values
        # Value loss
        value_loss = advantage ** 2
        # Calculate our policy loss
```

```
        policy = tf.nn.softmax(logits)
        entropy =
tf.nn.softmax_cross_entropy_with_logits_v2(labels=policy,
logits=logits)
        policy_loss =
tf.nn.sparse_softmax_cross_entropy_with_logits(labels=self.me
mory.actions, logits=logits)
        policy_loss *= tf.stop_gradient(advantage)
        policy_loss -= 0.01 * entropy
        total_loss = tf.reduce_mean((0.5 * value_loss +
policy_loss))
        return total_loss
if __name__ == "__main__":
    raise NotImplementedError("This class needs to be
imported and instantiated from a Reinforcement Learning "
                              "agent class and does not
contain any invokable code in the main function")
```

12.2.2 Actor-Critic (TensorFlow) Model (File: actorcritic_model.py)

```
""" A3C in Code - The Deep Learning Model for the
Approximators

A3C Code as in the book Deep Reinforcement Learning, Chapter
12.

Runtime: Python 3.6.5
Dependencies: numpy, matplotlib, tensorflow (/ tensorflow-
gpu), gym
DocStrings: GoogleStyle

Author : Mohit Sewak (p20150023@goa-bits-pilani.ac.in)

"""

# Making common imports
import logging
# Making tensorflow and keras(tensorflow instance of keras)
imports for subclassing the model and define architecture.
import tensorflow as tf
from tensorflow.python import keras
from tensorflow.python.keras import layers
# Configuring logging and Creating logger, setting the log to
streaming, and level as DEBUG
logging.basicConfig()
logger = logging.getLogger()
```

```
logger.setLevel(logging.DEBUG)

# Enabling eager execution for tensorflow
tf.enable_eager_execution()


class ActorCriticModel(keras.Model):
    """A3C Model

        This class is for the policy and value approximator
model for the A3C
        Both the master and the all the workers use
individual instances of the same model class.

        This variant of the model class extends the
keras.model and use tf.Model Sub-Classing feature.

        In a sub-class(ed) model, advanced features like
shared network, shared inputs and residual networks could
        be easily implemented. The network layers need to
defined in the __init__() method, and then their connection

        as required in the forward pass needs to be defined
in the call or __call__ method.

        TensorFlow eager execution needs to be enabled for
this to work as desired.

        Arguments:
            n_action (int): Cardinality of the action_space
            common_network_size (list): Defines the number of
neurons in different hidden layers of the common/
                                shared layers
            policy_network_size (int): Number of neurons in
the hidden layer specific to the policy_network
            value_network_size (int): Number of neurons in
the hidden layer specific to the value_network

    """
    def __init__(self, n_actions,
common_network_size=[128,64], policy_network_size=32,
value_network_size=32):
        super(ActorCriticModel, self).__init__()
        logger.info("Defining tf model with layers
configuration as: {}, {}, {}".format(common_network_size,

policy_network_size, value_network_size))
        self.action_size = n_actions
        self.common_hidden_1 =
layers.Dense(common_network_size[0], activation='relu')
        self.common_hidden_2 =
layers.Dense(common_network_size[1], activation='relu')
        self.policy_hidden =
layers.Dense(policy_network_size, activation='relu')
        self.values_hidden = layers.Dense(value_network_size,
activation='relu')
```

```
        self.policy_logits = layers.Dense(n_actions)
        self.values = layers.Dense(1)

    def call(self, inputs):
        """Forward pass for the actorcritic model

            The call function is the wrapper on Python's
__call__ magic function that is called when a class object is
            directly called without a specific method name.

            The Sub-Classing use this method to implement the
forward pass logic.

        """
        # Forward pass
            common = self.common_hidden_1(inputs)
            common = self.common_hidden_2(common)
            policy_network = self.policy_hidden(common)
            logits = self.policy_logits(policy_network)
            value_network = self.values_hidden(common)
            values = self.values(value_network)
            return logits, values


if __name__ == "__main__":
    raise NotImplementedError("This class needs to be
imported and instantiated from an A3C master/ worker "
                              "agent class and does not
contain any invokable code in the main function")
```

12.2.3 *SimpleListBasedMemory (File: experience_replay.py)*

```
""" A3C in Code - ExperienceReplayMemory

A3C Code as in the book Deep Reinforcement Learning, Chapter
12.

Runtime: Python 3.6.5
DocStrings: GoogleStyle

Author : Mohit Sewak (p20150023@goa-bits-pilani.ac.in)

"""
```

```
# General Imports
import logging
import random
# Import for data structure for different types of memory
from collections import deque

# Configure logging for the project
# Create file logger, to be used for deployment
# logging.basicConfig(filename="Chapter09_BPolicy.log",
format='%(asctime)s %(message)s', filemode='w')
logging.basicConfig()
# Creating a stream logger for receiving inline logs
logger = logging.getLogger()
# Setting the logging threshold of logger to DEBUG
logger.setLevel(logging.DEBUG)

class ExperienceReplayMemory:
    """Base class for all the extended versions for the
ExperienceReplayMemory class implementation
    """
    pass


class SimpleListBasedMemory(ExperienceReplayMemory):
    """Simple Memory Implementation for A3C Workers

    """
    def __init__(self):
        self.states = []
        self.actions = []
        self.rewards = []

    def store(self, state, action, reward):
        """Stores the state, action and reward for the A3C
        """
        self.states.append(state)
        self.actions.append(action)
        self.rewards.append(reward)

    def clear(self):
        """Resets the memory
        """
        self.__init__()


class SequentialDequeMemory(ExperienceReplayMemory):
    """Extension of the ExperienceReplayMemory class with
deque based Sequential Memory

            Args:
                queue_capacity (int): The maximum capacity
(in terms of the number of  experience tuples) of the memory
                buffer.

    """
```

```
    def __init__(self, queue_capacity=2000):
        self.queue_capacity = 2000
        self.memory = deque(maxlen=self.queue_capacity)

    def add_to_memory(self,experience_tuple):
        """Add an experience tuple to the memory buffer

            Args:

                experience_tuple (tuple): A tuple of
experience for training. In case of Q learning this tuple
could be
                (S, A, R, S) with optional done_flag and in
case of SARSA it could have an additional action element.

        """
        self.memory.append(experience_tuple)

    def get_random_batch_for_replay(self, batch_size=64):
        """Get a random mini-batch for replay from the
Sequential memory buffer

            Args:
                batch_size (int): The size of the batch
required
            Returns:
                list: list of the required number of
experience tuples

        """
        return random.sample(self.memory,batch_size)

    def get_memory_size(self):
        """Get the size of the occupied buffer

            Returns:
                int: The number of the experience tuples
already in memory
        """
        return len(self.memory)


if __name__ == "__main__":
    raise NotImplementedError("This class needs to be
imported and instantiated from a Reinforcement Learning "
                              "agent class and does not
contain any invokable code in the main function")
```

12.2.4 Custom Exceptions (rl_exceptions.py)

```
""" A3C in Code - Custom RL Exceptions

A3C Code as in the book Deep Reinforcement Learning, Chapter
12.

Runtime: Python 3.6.5
DocStrings: None

Author : Mohit Sewak (p20150023@goa-bits-pilani.ac.in)

"""


class PolicyDoesNotExistException(Exception):
    pass


class InsufficientPolicyParameters(Exception):
    pass
```

12.3 Training Statistics Plots

See Figs. 12.3 and 12.4.

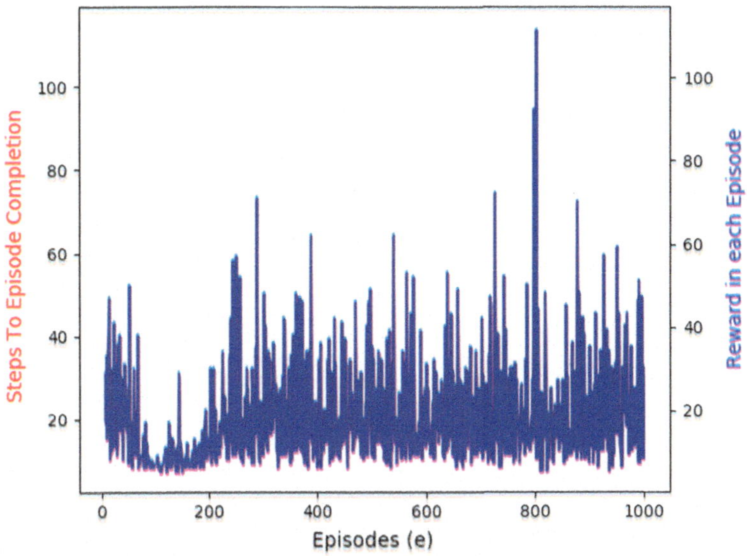

Fig. 12.3 Un-discounted reward in each global episode

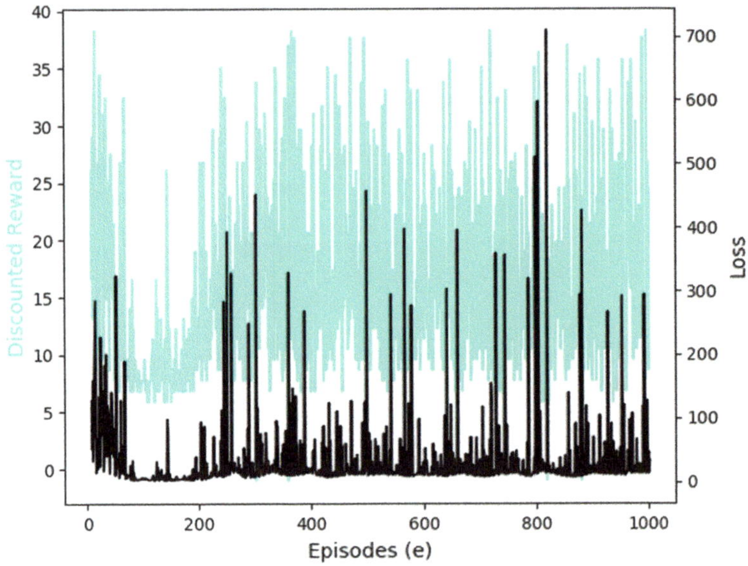

Fig. 12.4 Discounted reward and loss in each global episode

Chapter 13
Deterministic Policy Gradient and the DDPG

Deterministic-Policy-Gradient-Based Approaches

Abstract In this chapter, we will cover the Deterministic Policy-Gradient algorithm (DPG), with the underlying Deterministic Policy-Gradient Theorems that empower the underlying mathematics. We would also cover the Deep Deterministic Policy-Gradient (DDPG) algorithm, which is a combination of the DQN and the DPG and brings the deep learning enhancement to the DPG algorithm. This chapter leads us to a more practical and modern approach for empowering reinforcement learning agents for continuous-action control.

13.1 Deterministic Policy Gradient (DPG)

In the earlier chapters on Policy-Based Approaches and Actor-Critic Models, the algorithms that we have covered typically comes under the Stochastic Policy-Gradient approaches for Reinforcement Learning. In fact, both the classes of algorithms that we have studied so far in the Policy-Based approaches, namely the REINFORCE and its variants and the Actor-Critic model and its variants, all comes under the family of "On-Policy" "Stochastic Policy Gradient" methods for Reinforcement Learning. These algorithms are on-policy, that is the behavior policy is in-built in the action policy of the model, and this policy takes care of the exploration requirements as well in the model. Also, these models have a stochastic action policy. Unlike a deterministic action policy of any "Value Estimation" algorithms like the one in typical Q-Learning algorithm, in which the action policy only provides recommendation of a single (best) action for the current state as the policy's outputs, the "On-Policy" "Stochastic Policy Gradient" models could provide the action-probability function over all possible in a given state as their output. The action in such stochastic on-policy algorithms could be taken directly on the basis of the probabilistic sampling from the set of output probabilities for each action. So, this has the exploration in-built, as even the less optimal actions have a nonzero probability of being chosen based on the model's standardized output

M. Sewak, *Deep Reinforcement Learning*,
https://doi.org/10.1007/978-981-13-8285-7_13

probabilities for such actions. The estimation/target policy in the case of Q-Learning was stochastic though, but the action policy was deterministic.

We also have algorithms in the Stochastic Policy-Gradient-based approaches that adopt the "Off-Policy" mechanism, and comes under the family called the "Off-Policy" "Policy Gradient" algorithms. In the earlier case where the action policy is stochastic in itself, there are ample opportunities for exploration in-built inside the action policy, but in the case of more complex problems, the in-built exploration capabilities of these models may be overwhelmed and an external behavior policy that ensures optimal exploration could help. Even from a training data perspective, in the case of Off-Policy (Stochastic) Policy-Gradient-based algorithms, we do not require the complete trajectory of a sequence of events for training, and the training could use the past episodes randomly. Also, being from the off-policy family of algorithms, these algorithms have a dedicated external behavior policy and hence the exploration could be made better than that in their On-Policy counterparts. Sometimes additional noise could be added in the On-Policy Stochastic Gradient algorithms to ensure better exploration, even comparable to an off-policy mechanism and also to prevent the training updates getting stuck in the local optimum due to lack of adequate exploration.

In the Stochastic Gradient-based approaches, mostly, we have been using the gradient of our Performance Function (J) and by moving in the direction of this gradient we could maximize the Performance Function (J). We also discussed the issue of mathematical intractability in computing this stochastic gradient. This intractability was alleviated by some simplification under limiting conditions as proposed in the (Stochastic) Policy-Gradient Theorem. Until recently it was believed that a Deterministic Gradient is not possible when using a model, and the only approaches possible under the Policy-Gradient-based approaches had to be Stochastic Gradient Policy-based approaches with the applicable limiting conditions for any practically implementable solution. But recently some good work has been published in the area of the Deterministic Policy-Gradient-based approaches which are, in turn, is powered by the Deterministic Policy-Gradient Theorem. The Deterministic Policy-Gradient Theorem, in turn, provides the required simplifications for the underlying mathematics to enable a practically implementable algorithm with this approach.

The Deterministic Policy Gradient though has a different approach and mathematical derivation, it can be proved that the Deterministic Policy Gradient itself is a limiting case of the Stochastic Policy Gradient. This is also intuitive as a Deterministic Policy is a limiting condition of a Stochastic policy under the conditions that the resulting probability distribution function has nonzero probability only one action in the permissible action space. In the case of the Policy Gradient, the Deterministic Policy Gradient could be shown as a limiting condition of the Stochastic Policy Gradient under the limiting condition that the variance of the underlying policy becomes zero.

The Deterministic Policy-Gradient algorithms that we will be discussing in this chapter are both based on the Actor-Critic class of models, and comes in both the On-Policy and Off-Policy variants. Since the action policy is deterministic in nature

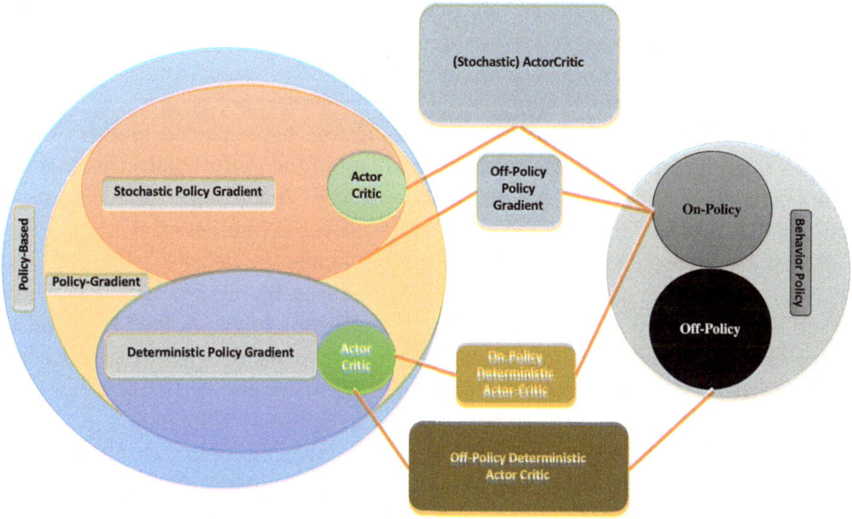

Fig. 13.1 Hierarchy of policy-based approaches

in these algorithms, the on-policy variant of these model does not provide enough exploration opportunities and hence external variations/noise have to be added in the policy implementation to allow for greater exploration. Hence, there are not many popular models or their variants in the On-Policy Deterministic Policy-Gradient class of models, and most of the promising variants come from the Off-Policy Deterministic Policy-Gradient-based approaches. This fact is also evident from the size of the boxes representing these algorithm classes in Fig. 13.1 earlier.

13.1.1 Advantages of Deterministic Policy Gradient Over Stochastic Policy Gradient

The Deterministic Policy Gradient is a more recent advent than its Stochastic Policy-Gradient counterpart and was published very recently. We have also discussed that both from the output perspective and the from a mathematical proof perspective, the Deterministic Policy Gradient could be considered as an extreme limiting case of Stochastic Policy Gradient. Instead of offering the complete Action-Probability function for all permissible actions in a given state, the Deterministic Policy-Gradient algorithm just suggests a single action. We also discussed in the chapter on Policy-Gradient Approaches taking appropriate examples that such form of deterministic output might not be ideal in certain conditions and not suitable for a certain application. Then, the question remains that why so much of recent effort has gone into the Deterministic Policy-Gradient class of algorithms and what advantages do they bring as compared to the Stochastic Policy-Gradient class of algorithms. We will try to understand some of the reasons for this below.

The first reason for this is simplicity. The deterministic policy gradient follows a simple model-free form and happens to actually be the expected gradient of the action-value (Q) function. Remember the gradient of the Performance function was challenging to find. Also remember that we have derived the gradient of the action-value function easily earlier in the case of value-estimation methods.

The second reason is efficiency. The gain in efficiency is because of two reasons. One is that because of its simplicity itself, that is a by-product of the previous reason. Being the expected gradient of the action-value function, the Deterministic Policy Gradient could be estimated much more efficiently than the usual stochastic policy gradient. Another reason for the efficiency is because of the fact that since the algorithm output is deterministic hence the integration of the policy gradient is not required over all the state–action pair combinations, but only over all the states. This considerably reduces the computation complexity. This efficiency also converts to performance and it could be demonstrated that because of these factors the deterministic policy gradient significantly has a better performance as compared to their stochastic counterparts especially in problems with high-dimensional action spaces.

The third reason is that there are some unique cases in which the Stochastic Policy Gradient is not possible, but Deterministic Policy Gradient is still applicable. Some use cases, especially in the area of Robotics, provides a differentiable control policy, but has no functionality to inject noise. As we have discussed earlier, the Stochastic Policy Gradient, especially in the On-Policy settings which is also the predominant class of algorithms under the Stochastic Policy Gradient, requires an injection of noise for optimal exploration over complex problems. Under these conditions, an Off-Policy Deterministic Policy Gradient may be the best algorithm choice under Policy Gradient.

13.1.2 Deterministic Policy Gradient Theorem

The deterministic policy-gradient theorem provides a particular simplification for finding the deterministic policy gradient under some mathematical conditions. A deterministic policy could be expressed as (13.1a) below. Here, μ is a policy parametrized by θ such that it maps the states in the state set S to the actions in the action set A.

$$\mu_\theta : S \rightarrow A \tag{13.1a}$$

The state transition probability and the discounted state distribution could be denoted as (13.1b) and (13.1c) below.

$$p(s \rightarrow s', t, \mu) \tag{13.1b}$$

$$\rho_\mu(s) \tag{13.1c}$$

Given these notations, the Performance Value (J) under the deterministic policy μ could be expressed as the expectancy of all discounted rewards under the policy as expressed in Eq. (13.2) below.

$$J(\mu_\theta) = \mathbb{E}[r_1^\gamma|\mu] \tag{13.2}$$

The Performance Value could be expanded in terms of the notations (13.1a, 13.1b, 13.1c) above as Eq. (13.3a) below. This essentially means that the Expectancy of cumulative discounted rewards as in Eq. (13.2) above is the weighted product of the probability of reaching a particular state under a given policy and the reward accumulated from that under the given policy parameterized under the given parameter summed over all states possible. The Performance Value as in Eq. (13.3a) could be further expressed in terms of the expectancy as Eq. (13.3b) below.

$$J(\mu_\theta) = \int_S \rho_\mu(s) r(s, \mu_\theta(s)) ds \tag{13.3a}$$

$$J(\mu_\theta) = \mathbb{E}_{s \sim \rho_\mu}[r(s, \mu_\theta(s))] \tag{13.3b}$$

The deterministic policy-gradient Theorem 1 states that if the conditions as in (Theorem 1 conditions) are satisfied and the deterministic policy gradient exists, then the gradient of the Performance Value function could be expressed as Eq. (13.4a) below. Equation (13.4a) is in integral form as Eq. (13.3a) and Eq. (13.3b) is in expectation form as Eq. (13.3b).

$$\Delta_\theta \mu_\theta(s), \Delta_a Q_\mu(s, a) \text{ exists.} \qquad \text{(Theorem 1 Condition)}$$

$$\Delta_\theta J(\mu_\theta) = \int_S \rho_\mu(s) \Delta_\theta \mu_\theta(s) \Delta_a Q_\mu(s, a; \theta)|_{a=\mu_\theta(s)} ds \tag{13.4a}$$

$$\Delta_\theta J(\mu_\theta) = \mathbb{E}[\Delta_\theta \mu_\theta(s) \Delta_a Q_\mu(s, a; \theta)|_{a=\mu_\theta(s)} \tag{13.4b}$$

The deterministic policy-gradient Theorem 2 states that under certain limiting condition, when the variance of the stochastic policy gradient tends to zero then under these limiting conditions the stochastic policy gradient is equivalent to the deterministic policy gradient.

13.1.3 Off-Policy Deterministic Policy-Gradient-Based Actor-Critic

In off-policy deterministic policy gradient, the behavior uses an external policy. That is a policy $\pi(s, a)$ is used to draw the trajectories to train a deterministic action policy $\mu_\theta(s)$. Note that since μ is a deterministic policy, so it just requires a state as input to provide a single action recommendation, also μ is parametrized over parameter vector θ. The true action-value function over the target policy $\mu_\theta(s)$ could be given as $Q_\mu(s, a)$. But like as in the stochastic actor-critic case, since this true action value is non-differentiable we will use an approximation function to approximate this action value. The action value is parametrized over the policy w instead, such that $Q_w(s, a) \approx Q_w(s, a)$.

The rest of the computation is similar to that of Stochastic Deterministic Policy, except for the fact that the gradient of the deterministic policy is the gradient of the action-value function as shown in the series of equations below. We compute the error between the target and actual values as in Eq. (13.5). This is atypical to how it is computed in Q-Learning.

$$\delta_t = r_t + \gamma Q_w(s_{t+1}, \mu_\theta(s_t, a_t)) - Q_w(s_t) \tag{13.5}$$

Then, we update the target policy parameter w with this error, by moving in the direction of the gradient of the target function Q_w at time step t, using the learning rate α_w as shown in Eq. (13.6) below.

$$w_{t+1} = w_t + \alpha_w \delta_t \Delta_w Q_w(s_t, a_t) \tag{13.6}$$

Then, we update the deterministic action policy parameter θ. This uses the chain rule similar to that we used in the stochastic policy-gradient parameter's update. The partial differential of the deterministic action policy with respect to the policy parameter is the product of the partial differential of the target function with respect to the action and the action policy with respect to its parameter. The update in the action policy parameter θ is, thus, done by moving in the direction of this gradient using a learning rate as α_θ as shown in Eq. (13.7) below.

$$\theta_{t+1} = \theta_t + \alpha_\theta \Delta_\theta \mu_\theta(s_t) \Delta_a Q_w(s_t, a_t)|_{a=\mu_\theta(s)} \tag{13.7}$$

13.2 Deep Deterministic Policy Gradient (DDPG)

The Deterministic Policy Gradient (DPG) as covered in earlier section uses Q-Learning for value estimation, which in turn use a linear model as a function approximator. Though the experiments conducted in the original DQN paper use only linear function approximators, it is possible to replace this linear function approximator with a deep learning model. This is where the Deep Deterministic Policy Gradient (DDPG) comes into the picture.

The Deep Deterministic Policy Gradient is a model-free, off-policy, actor-critic, model-free algorithm based on the deterministic policy-gradient theorem and could operate over continuous-action spaces. Essentially, DDPG aims to combine the actor-critic model implementation of DPG for continuous-action control and implement DQN for policy estimation and policy update. The DDPG paper ("Continuous Control with Deep Reinforcement Learning" paper as in references section) claims that this algorithm consistently outperforms the DPG algorithm on more than 20 tasks with continuous-action control requirements, and requires less data samples for training on discreet action problems as compared to that required by the Deep Q Networks (algorithm). All these 20 different tasks were performed without retraining or reconfiguring the network. That is, the network configuration and its weight was unchanged before making it switch from task to another. As the readers could recall, which discussing the topic on "General Artificial Intelligence" we discussed how the human brain at any instance remembers/knows multiple skills, and does not has to forget one skill completely to learn another one. So, these types of performances could be considered taking us closer to realizing the idea of General AI for continuous-action domains, and for action domains with very large action space.

Ideally, we could have simply replaced the linear function approximator as used in DPG with a deep learning neural network. So, for example, we could have directly replaced the linear approximator with a Multi-Layer Perceptron based Deep Neural Network (MLP-DNN) in the case of a sensor domain input or a Convolutional Neural Network (CNN) (followed by some Fully Connected (FC) layers) for situations where we need to work on video feeds input and both of these models ending in a SoftMax activated layer (for discreet action control) or a Linearly activated layer (for continuous-action control). But as we would have realized owing to the discussions as in the chapter on DQN, this is not going to work out in the case of Reinforcement Learning training. We learnt some enhancements to enable deep learning-based approximators in the chapter on DQN. In the case of DDPG, some of these enhancements are used as-is and some modified to better suit the implementation with actor-critic. DDPG also use some more recent advancements in the field of deep learning besides the one we discussed in the context of the DQN. These modifications are discussed in the next sub-section.

13.2.1 Deep Learning Implementation-Related Modifications in DDPG

There are essentially three modifications that the Deep Deterministic Policy Gradient (DDPG) adopts over the originally proposed linear approximator function based Deterministic Policy Gradient (DPG) to have a DQN like deep learning-based function approximators.

First, most of the Reinforcement Learning training methods working under the model-free assumptions assume that the training samples are independent (that is the samples are not correlated) and are identically distributed (that is the samples have a fair representation of the different unique phenomena in the underlying process). As we had discussed in the chapter on DQN, this assumption is severely violated in the case when the inputs observations are drawn from the games' (like Atari2600 games) consecutive video frames. We discussed the approach to overcome this by using "***experience replays***" from a "***memory buffer***" (a fixed size memory cache). The incomings frames are stored in these "memory buffers" as experience tuples, i.e., tuples of (s_t, a_t, r_t, s_{t+1}, <done>). In this mechanism, the states could be either a direct frame of image pixels or some relevant abstraction of the video frames with other relevant data concatenated to represent an observation state. Subsequently, training happens from the (experience) samples drawn from this buffer randomly or as per a sampling policy (with some noise). We had also discussed some advanced variants of this mechanism in the form of different types of prioritized experience replays/buffers. The DDPG algorithm uses the basic variant of this memory buffer as discussed in the earlier chapter.

Second, we learnt in the DQN chapter that if we have the same network (of action-value function approximation) which is being updated continuously (Online Network), also being used as a target network for computing the error (which itself goes in the update of the online network), then this will make the network updates very unstable. In the chapter on DQN, we learnt the two approaches to overcome this problem. One approach is as followed by the Double DQN algorithm, that is of having two different Q-Networks, one that works as (an offline) target network and hence should be relatively stable, and the other that is being updated continuously (online network). The target network copies the weight from the active online network after some defined steps to avoid being completely out of sync leading to irrelevance of target estimates. The other solution was an even advanced one of having a shared deep learning architecture, thus having some common layers in the neural network model, and then splitting the deep learning layer architecture after the convolutional layers into dedicated dense layers for the two different models, one computing the state value, and the other computing the advantage. The output from these two splits is later combined to get the action-value Q-function approximation. The first approach of using a relatively stable second target network is what we draw inspiration from in the case of DDPG. But since we need to implement it with Actor-Critic, which as we learnt in the earlier two chapters requires more of an online setting for the value estimation, we would require to adopt an approach to make an online implementation mechanism possible for this relatively stable (offline) target network. To achieve this in DDPG, we use a mechanism called "***soft updates***". In using soft updates, we do have a target network which is offline. Instead, the target network is also continuously updated and they try to continuously albeit very slowly track the active (online) action-value network. The "soft updates" are done by updating the target network parameter similar to that in the case of an exponential series as shown in the Eq. (13.8) below.

$$\theta_{t+1} = \tau\theta_t + (1 - \tau)\theta_{t+1} \tag{13.8}$$

In the above equation, τ is constant in the range (0, 1), such that $\tau \ll 1$.

To understand the third enhancement, let us take a note of this achievement. As we discussed earlier, the DDPG claimed to perform well on 20 different types of continuous-action tasks without requiring any reconfiguration of the network or retraining of the weights. The challenge to achieve a similar accomplishment has been one of the endeavors for Deep Learning as well even out of Deep Reinforcement Learning. To understand why it is difficult to achieve, let us take the same example we used in an earlier chapter. In that example, the agent is trying to learn different games, and each game had their own scoring criteria and scoring scales, thus making it very difficult for the agent to compare the rewards from one game to another and hence simultaneously learn the skills required in all these games. To overcome this problem, the rewards across all these games were scaled and clipped to ± 1. But this only takes care of solving the problem at the reward's end, but there are many more problems that need to be catered in the case of deep learning model and architecture. One such issue that arises in case of deep learning models while dealing with inputs from multiple distributions is called "***covariate shifts***". Most of the modern Deep Learning activation functions are nonlinear, and most of them are also not zero-symmetric mirror functions. This leads to the changes in underlying distributions of the features between each layer in a deep learning network, until the nonlinearities saturate, thus making it very difficult to train a deep network. This phenomenon is called "(Internal) Covariate Shift". Traditionally, this has been dealt with by adopting a very low learning rate or one that does not increase very rapidly (in case of adaptive learning rates-based optimizers), and by carefully selecting the initialization function/values for each layer. Needless to say, such approaches will not only considerably slow the training speed, but also requires expert/SME care to set the initialization values. Around the same year that DDPG was worked on an approach of "***Batch Normalization***" was proposed. Batch Normalizing means normalizing (having unit mean and variance) each dimension of input to any layer across all samples in a minibatch as a part of the network architecture (that is having additional normalizing layers in the network architecture in addition to the regular CNN and DNN layers). Besides Interval Covariate Shifts, Batch normalization also (to some extent) solves the overfitting problem and can complement or supplement the dropout mechanism in deep learning for providing a similar regularization effect. The DDPG as a third enhancement uses additional Batch Normalization in their deep learning architecture to overcome the problem of internal covariate shifts.

Last, although not a major enhancement but a slight diversion from the regular DPG implementation is the choice of noise function used in the behavior policy to ensure optimal exploration. The behavior policy for an off-policy policy-gradient-based mechanism is given as Eq. (13.9) below.

$$\mu_b(s_t) = \mu_a(s_t|\theta_t) + \mathcal{N} \tag{13.9}$$

In the above Eq. (13.9), $\mu_b(s_t)$ is the action recommended by the behavior policy for a state—s at time—t, which is an outcome of the action recommended by the action policy μ_a, which is parametrized by parameter vector θ at time t, for the state —s at time—t, and some noise, from a noise function N.

The added noise N is an important component of the behavior policy and helps in providing exploration effect. If N tends to 0, then the behavior policy will mimic the action policy with only exploitation and no exploration. The above expression is common to most off-policy policy-gradient approaches, even the DPG. What changes between the DPG and the DDPG is the choice for noise function. N should be chosen as per the environment and the underlying training requirements. As we have discussed this earlier, the more uncertain and complex the environment is and the more demanding the approximation function models are, the more exploration is required and hence greater should be the added noise as generated from the noise function. We have also discussed that as training progress, we may require lesser exploration to ensure fast convergence without losing out on initial exploration. This could be done only if we have an adaptive exploration rate that encourages higher exploration in the beginning and subsequently allows the exploration to taper as a function of either the time (steps), or the error rate of the estimation function or other suitable variables. The DDPG algorithm uses a noise function, which provides varying level of noise as the training proceeds. The noise function used thus generate temporally correlated exploration for exploration efficiency in physical control problems with inertia.

13.2.2 DDPG Algorithm Pseudo-Code

The DDPG algorithms with its modifications and enhancements to implement deep learning function approximators is given in Fig. 13.2.

Algorithm 1 DDPG algorithm

Randomly initialize critic network $Q(s,a|\theta^Q)$ and actor $\mu(s|\theta^\mu)$ with weights θ^Q and θ^μ.
Initialize target network Q' and μ' with weights $\theta^{Q'} \leftarrow \theta^Q$, $\theta^{\mu'} \leftarrow \theta^\mu$
Initialize replay buffer R
for episode = 1, M **do**
  Initialize a random process $\mathcal{N}$ for action exploration
  Receive initial observation state s_1
  for t = 1, T **do**
    Select action $a_t = \mu(s_t|\theta^\mu) + \mathcal{N}_t$ according to the current policy and exploration noise
    Execute action a_t and observe reward r_t and observe new state s_{t+1}
    Store transition (s_t, a_t, r_t, s_{t+1}) in R
    Sample a random minibatch of N transitions (s_i, a_i, r_i, s_{i+1}) from R
    Set $y_i = r_i + \gamma Q'(s_{i+1}, \mu'(s_{i+1}|\theta^{\mu'})|\theta^{Q'})$
    Update critic by minimizing the loss: $L = \frac{1}{N}\sum_i (y_i - Q(s_i, a_i|\theta^Q))^2$
    Update the actor policy using the sampled policy gradient:

$$\nabla_{\theta^\mu} J \approx \frac{1}{N} \sum_i \nabla_a Q(s,a|\theta^Q)|_{s=s_i, a=\mu(s_i)} \nabla_{\theta^\mu} \mu(s|\theta^\mu)|_{s_i}$$

    Update the target networks:

$$\theta^{Q'} \leftarrow \tau\theta^Q + (1-\tau)\theta^{Q'}$$
$$\theta^{\mu'} \leftarrow \tau\theta^\mu + (1-\tau)\theta^{\mu'}$$

  end for
end for

Fig. 13.2 DDPG algorithm (*Source* DDPG paper)

13.3 Summary

Many domains essentially mandate a continuous-action control for effective and efficient implementation of an agent. Though a continuous-action control problem may be broken down to discreet action control one by careful selection of the number and position of breakpoints in action control range, but such an approach is not only not suitable for all the domains, but may often lead to astronomically high computational loads. With the proliferation of numerous sensors and/or images as inputs using which an agent may have to take an action, especially a continuous action, algorithms like DDPG and DPG algorithm and the underlying Deterministic Policy-Gradient theorem provides an effective and modern approach to build and train such agents.

The Deterministic Policy Gradient was earlier assumed to have not existed in a model-free assumption. But recently not only it has been established, but interestingly found to be simpler to compute and implement than its Stochastic counterpart. Owing to the underlying simplicity, it is also efficient to compute as compared to the respective Stochastic Policy Gradient wherever it exists, and many a times is the only feasible option. The first Deterministic Gradient Theorem provides the required mathematical simplification comparable to that of the (Stochastic) Policy-Gradient Theorem applicable for Stochastic Policy Gradient and the second theorem shows that the Deterministic Gradient is actually a limiting case of the Stochastic Gradient under the limiting condition that the variance of the underlying action policy tends to zero.

The Deep Deterministic Policy-Gradient (DDPG) algorithm provides the essential modifications required to replace the linear function approximator as used in the DPG with a deep learning-based approximator. Since directly replacing the linear approximator with a deep learning model may make it unstable, so DDPG takes clues from DQN and provides certain essential enhancements like using experience replay, doing soft updates to the target network and incorporating batch normalization in the network architecture. This led to the DDPG performing well in over 20 different tasks requiring continuous-action control using the same network configuration and weights across all these tasks.

Chapter 14
DDPG in Code

Coding the DDPG Using High-Level Wrapper Libraries

Abstract In this chapter, we will code the Deep Deterministic Policy Gradient algorithm and apply it for continuous action control tasks as in the Gym's Mountain Car Continuous environment. We use the Keras-RL high-reinforcement learning wrapper library for a simplified and succinct implementation.

14.1 High-Level Wrapper Libraries for Reinforcement Learning

Until now in this book, we have been coding most of the algorithms in a low-level coding platform. First, we started with pure Python and NumPy-based implementations, then we used the TensorFlow, and its wrapper library Keras. None of these is a dedicated special-purpose Reinforcement Learning library, but instead, a general-purpose platform for either any program, and mathematical computation, or any deep learning operation. In this chapter, we will do things in a slightly different manner. We will use a high-level special-purpose Reinforcement Learning wrapper over these lower lever libraries and wrappers. We use Keras-RL (link as in Chap. 7's references) library, that we have introduced in Chap. 7 earlier on implementation resources. Readers are encouraged to explore further high-level reinforcement learning wrapper libraries and experiment coding in them as well. Some such libraries we have covered in an earlier chapter on Implementation Resources.

We are using a special-purpose reinforcement learning high-level wrapper library instead of coding directly in low-level platforms like TensorFlow in this chapter for multiple reasons. First, is that we have so far only introduced the implementation resources in Chap. 7, but have not used the same for coding purpose. Second, in real-life scenarios, often the key challenge would be to convert your actual application domain into a reinforcement learning scenario, and to aid that process you will require a quick prototyping mechanism for testing different agents, and hence we wanted to give our readers a taste of that. Third, is that we have utilized a low-level

M. Sewak, *Deep Reinforcement Learning*,
https://doi.org/10.1007/978-981-13-8285-7_14

programming approach until now as it helps to intuitively understand the concepts and also relate to the theory, mathematics and the research developments that we covered in the last chapter. But since DDPG is very similar to Actor-Critic from a coding difficulty perspective, we did not want to repeat a low-level implementation and instead wanted to take this opportunity for demonstrating some more practical approaches. Fourth, it makes the code really succinct (as is evident by the length of this code as compared to that of the A3C in Chap. 12), allowing us to focus on application instead.

14.2 The Mountain Car Continuous (Gym) Environment

In the chapter, we implement the Deep Deterministic Policy Gradient algorithm for the continuous action control tasks. Since this is the first time that in this book are using continuous action control so we can no longer use our custom "Grid World" or Gym's "Cart Pole" environment as both of these presents a discreet action control scenario. We, therefore, use the Gym's "Mountain Car Continuous" environment where the challenge is to drive a car up a steep hill to make it touch a flag.

To make the challenge interesting, the car does not have an engine powerful enough to drive up that steep hill starting from a stationary position. Therefore, we have to take it uphill in a reverse direction to give it enough momentum to drive up the hill ahead of it while coming downhill. The contiguous action control required is that for the throttle to the car. A negative value takes the car and a positive value takes it in front. The absolute throttle amount indicates the engine power. The reward for reaching the goal is +100, and the penalty is the squared sum of actions from start to goal.

14.3 Project Structure and Dependencies

We use the same "DRL" Python 3.6.5 environment as we have been using earlier in this book. Besides the general dependencies like the Gym, NumPy, and Keras, we would require the "keras-rl" (Fig. 14.1) library which could be installed from "pip" package manager ("pip install keras-rl"). Keras-RL is itself dependent on Keras.

Since this is a very simplistic, and a highly abstracted implementation, most of the details are hidden under the "keras-rl" library itself, and we have a rather very succinct code that we have implemented in a single file named ddpg_contiuous_action.py. The file contains the DDPG which have methods to make very modular deep learning models for the actor and critic using the Keras deep learning wrapper for TensorFlow. The actor ends in a linearly activate layer having as many

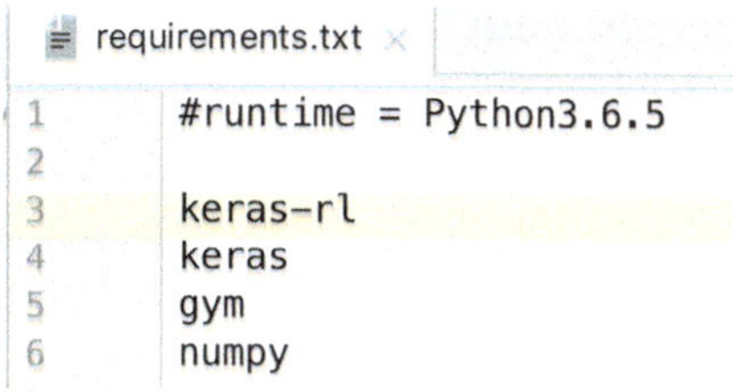

Fig. 14.1 Project dependencies

neurons as the number of actions, and the critic has just a single linearly activated neuron to output the baseline value. The number of hidden layers in both the actor and critic, and the number of neurons in each of these hidden layers could be customized the agent tested with different such configurations. Rest of all codes is very simple and directly calls the wrapper's underlying implementation of DDPG. The project structure is as shown in Fig. 14.2.

The train function when called, see if the actor, critic, and the agent model exist, else it creates a fresh instance of each. If they exist, then the method tries to locate any existing model weights to resume training from there, else starts fresh training. During training and testing, by keeping the visualize flag as True, a popup with the agent actually playing the environment live as shown in Fig. 14.3, next appears.

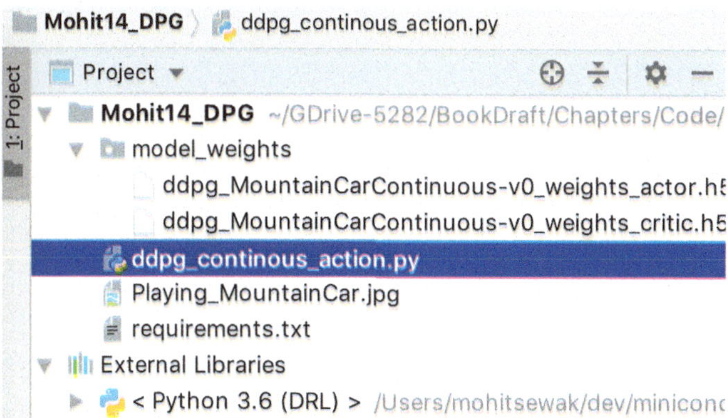

Fig. 14.2 Project structure for the DDPG project

14.4 Code (File: ddpg_continout_action.py)

```
""" DDPG HighLevel implementation in Code

DDPG Code as in the book Deep Reinforcement Learning, Chapter
13.

Runtime: Python 3.6.5
Dependencies: keras, keras-rl, gym
DocStrings: GoogleStyle

Author : Mohit Sewak (p20150023@goa-bits-pilani.ac.in)
Inspired from: DDPG example implementation on Keras-RL github
repository (keras-rl/keras-rl/blob/master/examples)
"""
# make general imports
import numpy as np
import os, logging
# Make keras specific imports
from keras.models import Sequential, Model
from keras.layers import Dense, Activation, Flatten, Input,
Concatenate
from keras.optimizers import Adam
# Make reinforcement learning specific imports
import gym
from rl.agents import DDPGAgent
from rl.memory import SequentialMemory
from rl.random import OrnsteinUhlenbeckProcess
# Configuring logging and setting logger to stream logs at
DEBUG level
logging.basicConfig()
logger = logging.getLogger()
logger.setLevel(logging.DEBUG)


class DDPG:
    """Deep Deterministic Policy Gradient Class

        This is an implementation of DDPG for continuous
control tasks made using the high level keras-rl library.

        Args:
            env_name (str): Name of the gym environment
            weights_dir (str): Dir for storing model weights
(for both actors and critic as separate files)
            actor_layers (list(int)): A list of int
representing neurons in each subsequent the hidden layer in
actor
            critic_layers (list(int)): A list of int
representing neurons in each subsequent the hidden layer in
actor
            n_episodes (int): Maximum training eprisodes
            visualize (bool): Whether a popup window with the
environment view is required
    """
```

```
    def __init__(self,env_name = 'MountainCarContinuous-v0',
weights_dir = "model_weights",
                 actor_layers = [64,64,32], critic_layers =
[128,128,64], n_episodes=200, visualize=True):
        self.env_name=env_name
        self.env = gym.make(env_name)
        np.random.seed(123)
        self.env.seed(123)
        self.actor_layers = actor_layers
        self.critic_layers = critic_layers
        self.n_episodes = n_episodes
        self.visualize=visualize
        self.n_actions = self.env.action_space.shape[0]
        self.n_states = self.env.observation_space.shape
        self.weights_file =
os.path.join(weights_dir,'ddpg_{}_weights.h5f'.format(self.en
v_name))
        self.actor = None
        self.critic = None
        self.agent = None
        self.action_input = None

    def _make_actor(self):
        """Internal helper function to create an actor custom
model
        """
        self.actor = Sequential()
        self.actor.add(Flatten(input_shape=(1,) +
self.n_states))
        for size in self.actor_layers:
            self.actor.add(Dense(size,activation='relu'))

self.actor.add(Dense(self.n_actions,activation='linear'))
        self.actor.summary()

    def _make_critic(self):
        """Internal helper function to create an actor custom
model
        """
        action_input = Input(shape=(self.n_actions,),
name='action_input')
        observation_input = Input(shape=(1,) + self.n_states,
name='observation_input')
        flattened_observation = Flatten()(observation_input)
        input_layer = Concatenate()([action_input,
flattened_observation])
        hidden_layers = Dense(self.critic_layers[0],
activation='relu')(input_layer)
        for size in self.critic_layers[1:]:
            hidden_layers = Dense(size,
activation='relu')(hidden_layers)
        output_layer = Dense(1,
activation='linear')(hidden_layers)
        self.critic = Model(inputs=[action_input,
observation_input], outputs=output_layer)
        self.critic.summary()
        self.action_input = action_input

    def _make_agent(self):
        """Internal helper function to create an actor-critic
custom agent model
        """
```

```
        if self.actor is None:
            self._make_actor()
        if self.critic is None:
            self._make_critic()
        memory = SequentialMemory(limit=100000,
window_length=1)
        random_process =
OrnsteinUhlenbeckProcess(size=self.n_actions, theta=.15,
mu=0., sigma=.3)
        self.agent = DDPGAgent(nb_actions=self.n_actions,
actor=self.actor, critic=self.critic,

critic_action_input=self.action_input, memory=memory,
                               nb_steps_warmup_critic=100,
nb_steps_warmup_actor=100,
                               random_process=random_process,
gamma=.99, target_model_update=1e-3)
        self.agent.compile(Adam(lr=.001, clipnorm=1.),
metrics=['mae'])

    def _load_or_make_agent(self):
        """Internal helper function to load an agent model,
creates a new if no model weights exists
        """
        if self.agent is None:
            self._make_agent()
        if os.path.exists(self.weights_file):
            logger.info("Found existing weights for the model
for this environment. Loading...")
            self.agent.load_weights(self.weights_file)
    def train(self):
        """Train the DDPG agent
        """
        self._load_or_make_agent()
        self.agent.fit(self.env, nb_steps=50000,
visualize=self.visualize, verbose=1,
nb_max_episode_steps=self.n_episodes)
        self.agent.save_weights(self.weights_file,
overwrite=True)

    def test(self, nb_episodes=5):
        """Test the DDPG agent
        """
        logger.info("Testing the agents with {}
episodes...".format(nb_episodes))
        self.agent.test(self.env, nb_episodes=nb_episodes,
visualize=self.visualize, nb_max_episode_steps=200)


if __name__ == "__main__":
    """Main function for testing the A3C Master code's
implementation
    """
    agent = DDPG()
    agent.train()
    agent.test()
```

14.5 Agent Playing the "MountainCarContinous-v0" Environment

See Fig. 14.3.

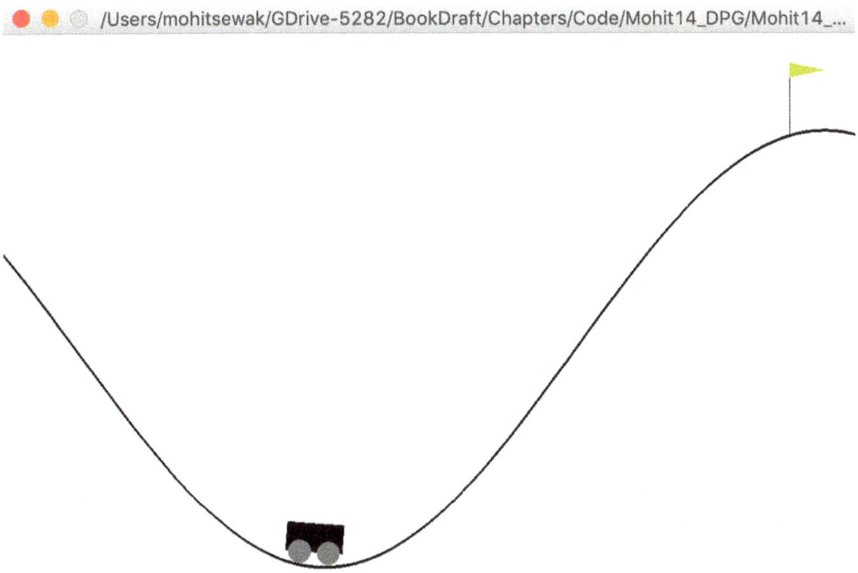

Fig. 14.3 DDPG playing the continuous mountain cart environment

Bibliography

1. Sutton, R.S., Barto, A.G.: Introduction to Reinforcement Learning. MIT Press (1998)
2. Bellman, R.: A Markovian decision process. Indiana Univ. Math. J. **6**(4), 679–684 (1957)
3. Markov Decision Process, wikipedia.org. https://en.wikipedia.org/wiki/Markov_decision_process. Accessed Aug 2018
4. Markov Chain, wikipedia.org. https://en.wikipedia.org/wiki/Markov_chain. Accessed Aug 2018
5. Markov Property, wikipedia.org. https://en.wikipedia.org/wiki/Markov_property. Accessed Aug 2018
6. Solving MDPs with dynamic programming, towardsdatascience.com. https://towardsdatascience.com/reinforcement-learning-demystified-solving-mdps-with-dynamic-programming-b52c8093c919. Accessed Aug 2018
7. Dynamic Programming in Python for reinforcement learning, medium.com. https://medium.com/harder-choices/dynamic-programming-in-python-reinforcement-learning-bb288d95288f. Accessed Aug 2018
8. Understanding RL—The Bellman Equation, joshgreaves.com. https://joshgreaves.com/reinforcement-learning/understanding-rl-the-bellman-equations/. Accessed Aug 2018
9. Reinforcement Learning in Finance, Coursera. https://coursera.org/lecture/reinforcement-learning-in-finance. Accessed Aug 2018
10. Deep Reinforcement Learning Demystified, medium.com. https://medium.com/@m.alzantot/deep-reinforcement-learning-demysitifed-episode-2-policy-iteration-value-iteration-and-q-978f9e89ddaa. Accessed Aug 2018
11. Brockman, G., Cheung, V., Pettersson, L., Schneider, J., Schulman, J., Tang, J., Zaremba, W.: OpenAI Gym (2016). https://arxiv.org/abs/1606.01540
12. Docs—Open AI Gym. https://gym.openai.com/docs/. Accessed Aug 2018
13. Keras-RL, GitHub Repository Keras-RL. https://github.com/keras-rl. Accessed Aug 2018
14. Shani, G.: A Survey of Model-Based and Model-Free Methods for Resolving Perceptual Aliasing. Ben-Gurion University (2004)
15. Temporal Difference Learning, Wikipedia. https://en.wikipedia.org/wiki/Temporal_difference_learning. Accessed Aug 2018
16. Sutton, R.: Learning to predict by the methods of temporal differences. Mach. Learn. **3**(1), 9–44 (1988)
17. Eligibility Traces, incompleteideas.net. http://www.incompleteideas.net/book/ebook/node72.html. Accessed Aug 2018
18. SARSA, Wikipedia. https://en.wikipedia.org/wiki/State%E2%80%93action%E2%80%93reward%E2%80%93state%E2%80%93action. Accessed Aug 2018

M. Sewak, *Deep Reinforcement Learning*,
https://doi.org/10.1007/978-981-13-8285-7

19. Diving deep into reinforcement learning, freecodecamp.org. https://medium.freecodecamp.org/diving-deeper-into-reinforcement-learning-with-q-learning-c18d0db58efe. Accessed Aug 2018
20. Tokic, M.: Adaptive epsilon-greedy exploration in reinforcement learning based on value differences. In: KI 2010: Advances in Artificial Intelligence, pp. 203–210. Springer, Berlin (2010)
21. Imaddabbura, Bandit Algorithms, github.io. https://imaddabbura.github.io/blog/data%20science/2018/03/31/epsilon-Greedy-Algorithm.html. Accessed Aug 2018
22. Sewak, M., Rezaul Karim, Md., Pujari, P.: Practical Convolutional Neural Networks: Implement Advanced Deep Learning Models Using Python. Packt Publishing (2018). ISBN: 1788392302, 9781788392303.
23. Sewak, M., Sahay, S.K., Rathore, H.: An overview of deep learning architecture of deep neural networks and autoencoders. In: International Conference on Intelligent Computing, 25–27 Oct 2018. Amrita University, Proceedings in Journal of Computational and Theoretical Nanoscience (2018)
24. Sewak, M., Sahay, S.K., Rathore, H.: Comparison of deep learning and the classical machine learning algorithm for the malware detection. In: 19th IEEE/ACIS International Conference on Software Engineering, Artificial Intelligence, Networking and Parallel/Distributed Computing, SNPD (2018)
25. Sewak, M., Sahay, S.K., Rathore, H.: An investigation of a deep learning-based malware detection system. In: Proceedings of the 13th International Conference on Availability, Reliability and Security, ARES 2018, pp. 26:1–26:5 (2018)
26. "OpenAI Universe", GitHub Repository. https://github.com/openai/universe
27. "OpenAI Retro", GitHub Repository. https://github.com/openai/retro
28. Brockman, G., Cheung, V., Pettersson, L., Schneider, J., Schulman, J., Tang, J., Zaremba, W.: Openai gym (2016)
29. "DeepMind Lab". https://deepmind.com/blog/open-sourcing-deepmind-lab/
30. "DeepMind Control Suite", GitHub Repository. https://github.com/deepmind/dm_control
31. Johnson, M., Hofmann, K., Hutton, T., Bignell, D.: The Malmo platform for artificial intelligence experimentation. In: Kambhampati, S. (ed.) Proceedings 25th International Joint Conference on Artificial Intelligence, pp. 42–46. AAAI Press, Palo Alto, California USA (2016). https://github.com/Microsoft/malmo
32. Duan, Y., Chen, X., Houthooft, R., Schulman, J., Abbeel, P.: Benchmarking deep reinforcement learning for continuous control. In: Proceedings of the 33rd International Conference on Machine Learning (ICML) (2016)
33. "DeepMind's TRFL", GitHub Repository. https://github.com/deepmind/trfl
34. "OpenAI Baselines", GitHub Repository. https://github.com/openai/baselines
35. Plappert, M.: "Keras-RL", GitHub Repository (2016). https://keras-rl.https://github.com/keras-rl/keras-rl
36. Caspi, I., Leibovich, G., Novik, G., Endrawis, S.: Reinforcement learning coach (2017). https://doi.org/10.5281/zenodo.1134899
37. Liang, E., Liaw, R., Nishihara, R., Moritz, P., Fox, R., Goldberg, K., Gonzalez, J.E., Jordan, M.I., Stoica, I.: RLlib: abstractions for distributed reinforcement learning. In: International Conference on Machine Learning (ICML) (2018)
38. DQN, deepmind.com. https://deepmind.com/research/dqn/. Accessed Aug 2018
39. AlphaGo, deepmind.com. https://deepmind.com/research/alphago/. Accessed Aug 2018
40. Mnih, V., Kavukcuoglu, K., Silver, D., Graves, A., Antonoglou, I., Wierstra, D., Riedmiller, M.A.: Playing Atari with Deep Reinforcement Learning (2013). https://arxiv.org/abs/1312.5602
41. Mnih, V., Kavukcuoglu, K., Silver, D., Rusu, A.A., Veness, J., Bellemare, M.G., Graves, A., Riedmiller, M., Fidjeland, A.K., Ostrovski, G., Petersen, S., Beattie, C., Sadik, A., Antonoglou, I., King, H., Kumaran, D., Wierstra, D., Legg, S., Hassabis, D.: Human-level control through deep reinforcement learning. Nature **518** (2015). 10.1038/nature14236

42. Schaul, T., Quan, J., Antonoglou, I., Silver, D.: Prioritized Experience Replay (2015). https://arxiv.org/abs/1511.05952
43. Lin, L.-J.: Reinforcement learning for robots using neural networks. Carnegie Mellon University, Ph.D. Thesis Lin:1992: RLR:168871 (1992)
44. Seno, T.: Welcome to deep reinforcement learning, towardsdatascience.com. https://towardsdatascience.com/welcome-to-deep-reinforcement-learning-part-1-dqn-c3cab4d41b6b. Accessed Aug 2018
45. Juliani, A.: Simple reinforcement learning with tensorflow, medium.com. https://medium.com/@awjuliani/simple-reinforcement-learning-with-tensorflow-part-4-deep-q-networks-and-beyond-8438a3e2b8df. Accessed Aug 2018
46. van Hasselt, H., Guez, A., Silver, D.: Deep Reinforcement Learning with Double Q-Learning (2015). https://arxiv.org/abs/1509.06461
47. Wang, Z., de Freitas, N., Lanctot, M.: Dueling Network Architectures for Deep Reinforcement Learning (2015). https://arxiv.org/abs/1511.06581
48. Sutton, R.S., McAllester, D., Singh, S., Mansour, Y.: Policy gradient methods for reinforcement learning with function approximation. In: Proceedings of the 12th International Conference on Neural Information Processing Systems, NIPS'99, pp. 1057–1063 (1999)
49. Silver, D., Lever, G., Heess, N., Degris, T., Wierstra, D., Riedmiller, M.: Deterministic policy gradient algorithms. In: Proceedings of the 31st International Conference on Machine Learning, pp. 387–395 (2014)
50. Silver, D.: Lecture 7—Policy Gradient, University College London. http://www0.cs.ucl.ac.uk/staff/d.silver/web/Teaching_files/pg.pdf. Accessed Aug 2018
51. Li, F.-F., Johnson, J., Yeung, S.: Lecture 14, CS231—Stanford. http://cs231n.stanford.edu/slides/2017/cs231n_2017_lecture14.pdf. Accessed Aug 2018
52. Williams, R.J.: A class of gradient-estimating algorithms for reinforcement learning in neural networks. In: Proceedings of the IEEE First International Conference on Neural Networks, San Diego, CA (1987)
53. Williams, R.J.: Simple statistical gradient-following algorithms for connectionist reinforcement learning. Mach. Learn. **8**(3), 229–256 (1992)
54. Mnih, V., Badia, A.P., Mirza, M., Graves, A., Lillicrap, T.P., Harley, T., Silver, D., Kavukcuoglu, K.: Asynchronous methods for deep reinforcement learning (2016). https://arxiv.org/abs/1602.01783
55. Degris, T., Pilarski, P.M., Sutton, R.S.: Model-free reinforcement learning with continuous action in practice. In: 2012 American Control Conference (ACC), pp. 2177–2182 (2012)
56. Bhatnagar, S., Sutton, R.S., Ghavamzadeh, M., Lee, M.: Natural actor-critic algorithms. Automatica **45**(11), 2471–2482 (2009)
57. Sutton, R.S., Barto, A.G.: Reinforcement learning—an introduction. In: Adaptive Computation and Machine Learning. MIT Press (1998)
58. Wu, Y., Mansimov, E., Liao, S., Radford,.A., Schulman, J.: Openai baselines: Acktr a2c (2017). https://blog.openai.com/baselines-acktr-a2c
59. Konda, V.R., Tsitsiklis, J.N.: On actor-critic algorithms. SIAMJ. Control Optim. **42**(4), 1143–1166 (2003)
60. Abadi, M., et al.: Model Sub-classing, TensorFlow Guide: High Level API—Keras (2019). https://www.tensorflow.org/guide/keras#model_subclassing
61. Abadi, M., et al.: Functional API, TensorFlow Guide: High Level API—Keras (2019). https://www.tensorflow.org/guide/keras#model_subclassing
62. Abadi, M., et al.: Gradient Tapes, TensorFlow Tutorial: Automatic Differentiation and Gradient Tapes (2019). https://www.tensorflow.org/tutorials/eager/automatic_differentiation
63. Abadi, M., et al.: apply_gradient(), TensorFlow API Docs: tf.train.Optimizer Class (2019). https://www.tensorflow.org/api_docs/python/tf/train/Optimizer

64. Yuan, R.: Deep reinforcement learning: playing CartPole through asynchronous advantage actor critic (A3C) with tf.keras and eager execution, Medium.com (2018). https://medium.com/tensorflow/deep-reinforcement-learning-playing-cartpole-through-asynchronous-advantage-actor-critic-a3c-7eab2eea5296
65. Daoust, M.: A3C Blog Post, GitHub repository: TensorFlow/Models/Research (2018). https://github.com/tensorflow/models/tree/master/research/a3c_blogpost
66. Silver, D., Lever, G., Heess, N., Degris, T., Wierstra, D., Riedmiller, M.: Deterministic policy gradient algorithms. In: Proceedings of the 31st International Conference on Machine Learning, Proceedings of Machine Learning Research, vol. 32, pp. 387–395, Beijing, China, 22–24 Jun 2014
67. Lillicrap, T.P., Hunt, J.J., Pritzel, A., Heess, N., Erez, T., Tassa, Y., Silver, D., Wierstra, D.: Continuous control with deep reinforcement learning (2015). https://arxiv.org/abs/1509.02971
68. Ioffe, S., Szegedy, C.: Batch normalization: accelerating deep network training by reducing internal covariate shift (2015). https://arxiv.org/abs/1502.03167
69. Weng, L.: Policy Gradient Algorithms (2018). https://lilianweng.github.io/lil-log/2018/04/08/policy-gradient-algorithms.html#off-policy-policy-gradient. Accessed Jan 2019

Index

M. Sewak, *Deep Reinforcement Learning*,
https://doi.org/10.1007/978-981-13-8285-7

Printed by Printforce, the Netherlands